A
PRINCELY
PURSUIT

A PRINCELY PURSUIT

THE MALCOLM D. GUTTER COLLECTION OF EARLY MEISSEN PORCELAIN

MARIA L. SANTANGELO

IN ASSOCIATION WITH
MALCOLM D. GUTTER

AND WITH CONTRIBUTIONS BY
SEBASTIAN KUHN &
COLLEEN O'SHEA

Fine Arts Museums of San Francisco • Legion of Honor
HIRMER

CONTENTS

MAX HOLLEIN
DIRECTOR AND CEO
FINE ARTS MUSEUMS OF SAN FRANCISCO

FOREWORD

The discovery of porcelain in Europe is a romantic story that is filled with great intrigue, as well as a scientific one of chemistry and countless secretive experiments. Precious cargos of Asian porcelain arrived in Europe via the Dutch East India Company in the late seventeenth and early eighteenth centuries, whetting the insatiable desire for porcelain among the West and particularly for Augustus II, "the Strong," elector of Saxony and king of Poland. Europeans at the time referred to porcelain as "white gold" and it was received with profound wonderment. To this end, Augustus the Strong dedicated incredible financial and personal resources toward uncovering its elusive formula to produce true porcelain. The Meissen manufactory was established in 1710 by Augustus II, and it became the fountainhead for the production of porcelain in Europe. The king amassed a tremendous repository of Meissen and Asian porcelains for his own personal collection and pieces were also distributed by the Saxon court to the royalty and elite of Europe. More than three hundred years later, Meissen is still recognized for its luxurious porcelain.

Malcolm D. Gutter has cultivated his porcelain collection over the course of more than four decades, focusing on early Meissen examples, particularly those from the royal collection that Augustus II commissioned for the Japanisches Palais, his pleasure palace in Dresden. The king avidly collected those pieces imported from China and Japan in addition to the objects produced at Meissen. *A Princely Pursuit* reproduces thirty-one documented Meissen and Asian works from his royal collection. The Gutter collection exemplifies the significant range of early Meissen wares, including many examples of early red stoneware (*Böttgersteinzeug*) and numerous pieces created under Johann Gregorius Höroldt's direction—arguably the most innovative period of decoration at the manufactory. Through tremendous grit and research, Malcolm formed his holdings primarily on a professor's salary. This is no small feat when we consider the wealthy collectors and porcelain dealers with whom he competes to this day. To capture Malcolm's own voice, this volume includes numerous "collector's stories" describing his determined—and sometimes painstaking—hunt for Meissen porcelain and the legendary figures he has met and worked with along the way.

We are immensely grateful of Maria L. Santangelo, former associate curator at the Fine Arts Museums of San Francisco, who expertly guided all aspects of this project for our institution, from stewarding Malcolm's generous gift to procuring the wonderful scholarship and documentation contained in this catalogue. Over the years of her steadfast work, Maria has been supported by many colleagues here at the Museums, including John E. Buchanan, Jr., and Colin B. Bailey, former directors; Julian Cox, former founding curator of photography and chief curator; and Martin Chapman, curator in charge of European decorative arts and sculpture. And we are, of course, forever indebted to Malcolm D. Gutter, who has entrusted his beautiful works of art—or "babies" as he refers to them—to our Museums, where they will serve as a legacy of his fine connoisseurship and his tenacious passion. It is our tremendous pleasure to share his unparalleled collection with our audiences here in San Francisco, a place that Malcolm has called home for nearly sixty years, and a place where lovers of porcelain will surely travel to see Malcolm's visionary holdings on display at the Legion of Honor.

MAX HOLLEIN
DIRECTOR AND CEO
FINE ARTS MUSEUMS OF SAN FRANCISCO

ACKNOWLEDGMENTS

The Malcolm D. Gutter Collection of porcelain works at the Fine Arts Museums of San Francisco, along with this companion catalogue, has been realized because of the incredible passion, tremendous sensitivity, and deep generosity of its collector and our friend, Malcolm D. Gutter. His exceptional gift to the Museums has been shepherded by Maria L. Santangelo, former associate curator. Maria has been supported in this endeavor by various past and present colleagues here, among them Colin B. Bailey and John E. Buchanan, Jr., former directors; Julian Cox, former founding curator of photography and chief curator; and Martin Chapman, curator in charge of European decorative arts and sculpture. Our conservators also offered indelible support of these efforts, including Lesley Bone, former head of objects conservation; Jane Williams, head of objects conservation; Jena Hirschbein, assistant objects conservator; and Colleen O'Shea, Mellon Fellow in objects conservation, who also contributed technical texts to this volume.

The original display of the Gutter collection at the Legion of Honor was the result of dedicated work from persons across departments at the Museums. We specifically recognize Krista Brugnara, director of exhibitions, and Hilary Magowan, exhibitions manager; and Deanna Griffin, director of registration and collections management, and Doug DeFors and Julian Drake, registrars.

This important and beautiful catalogue was thoughtfully overseen by Leslie Dutcher, director of publications, and it was expertly and unflappably managed and edited by Jane Hyun, editor. Additional editorial support was provided by Danica Michels Hodge, managing editor; Victoria Gannon, editor; Trina Enriquez, associate editor; and Adrienn Mendonça-Jones, editorial assistant. Abigail Dansiger, librarian, assisted with the research. The fresh photography contained in his book was made possible by Sue Grinols, director of photo services, and Randy Dodson, head photographer. Diana K. Murphy, digital production coordinator, helped with the image rights and reproductions. We thank Bob Aufuldish of Aufuldish & Warinner for his delightful design, which draws from so many details in the works contained in the Gutter Collection. And we are grateful to our colleagues at Hirmer Publishers, including Elisabeth Rochau-Shalem, senior editor, for the distribution of this book

in the trade. This catalogue is published with the assistance of the Andrew W. Mellon Foundation Endowment for Publications.

Our Board of Trustees, led by Diane B. Wilsey, makes all of our valuable projects possible. Furthermore, we acknowledge many individuals and their staffs who work dedicatedly behind the scenes to realize our many programs, including Megan Bourne, chief of staff; Ed Prohaska, chief financial officer, and Jason Seifer, director of finance; Melissa E. Buron, director of the art division; Sheila Pressley, director of education; Patty Lacson, director of facilities; Tricia Robson, director of digital strategy; and Skot Jonz, manager of board relations. We thank Amanda Riley, director of development, and Linda Butler, director of marketing, communications, and visitor experience. We also extend our gratitude to Stuart Hata, director of retail operations, and Tim Niedert, book and media manager.

Outside of our Museums, we graciously acknowledge Sebastian Kuhn, departmental director of European ceramics at Bonhams, London, for sharing his insightful text for our catalogue and reading over our scholarship. Numerous other porcelain colleagues fostered this publication, including London-based porcelain dealers Errol and Henriette Manners, who were always ready sources of support. Further encouragement came from porcelain specialists Jody Wilke at Christie's, New York, and Leticia Roberts, formerly at Sotheby's, New York. Ulrich Pietsch, former director of the Porzellansammlung, Dresden, and their new director, Julia Weber, were also supportive over the years of research and writing required for this publication. The great Meissen collector Henry Arnhold also generously shared his time, collection, and expertise. Similarly, porcelain dealer Michele Beiny and collector Giles Ellwood provided much kind encouragement. Conservation scientists Aniko Bezur and Francesca Casadio offered guidance on the analysis of Meissen enamels. Questions about Chinese and Japanese ceramics were vetted through Amelia Chau, adjunct curator at the Crocker Art Museum, Sacramento, and Bonhams's consultant; and Laurie Barnes, curator at the Norton Museum of Art, West Palm Beach, Florida.

SEBASTIAN KUHN

A LEGACY OF COLLECTING: THE TASTE FOR EIGHTEENTH-CENTURY MEISSEN PORCELAIN IN THE UNITED STATES

Early eighteenth-century Meissen porcelain was produced first and foremost for an elite court culture. In our own age of mass production, the material is so abundant that it is difficult to imagine that it once was considered so rare and precious that it could be an appropriate gift among royalty, and that even apparently utilitarian objects, such as cups and saucers, were intended solely for display. One of the aims of modern collectors has always been to try to cast off the spectacles of their age and to so rediscover the wonder that Meissen porcelain evoked in the first half of the eighteenth century. Moreover, collectors such as Malcolm Gutter collect stories in addition to the objects themselves. The provenance of an object can, at the very least, be a guarantee of age and authenticity, and—in the case of porcelain made for the palaces of Augustus the Strong, for example—an indication of quality and importance. The subsequent collecting history also inspires and influences collectors. Perceptions evolve and values fluctuate with the ebb and flow of taste, advances in art historical knowledge, and even the availability of the objects themselves. These narratives about Meissen collecting, and how some of the best collections of the modern era were formed in the United States, are reflected in Gutter's collection.

The first and greatest collector of Meissen porcelain was of course the factory's founder, Augustus II or the Strong (1670–1733), elector of Saxony and king of Poland. His famous *Porzellankrankheit* (porcelain sickness) shaped the stylistic and technical development of Meissen porcelain during the 1720s and early 1730s, in that he sought to furnish an entire palace with the precious material. The many thousands of pieces made for his "Japanese Palace" were intended for display rather than use: a unique example of princely representation that was designed to underscore his political ambitions.

This use of porcelain for display continued after his death, although his son Augustus III (1696–1763) did not share his level of personal enthusiasm. Rather, its rarity and beauty ensured that it remained a means by which the Saxon/Polish court dazzled and flattered both its friends and its enemies. Augustus III's chief minister, count Heinrich von Brühl (1700–1763), became the greatest customer of the Meissen manufactory. He was often required to represent the elector and so ordered

Detail of coffee cup and saucer, ca. 1740–1750, painting possibly attributed to Christian Freidrich Herold (cat. no. 69/pl. 52)

11

vast quantities of its porcelain—most famously, the Swan service (see cat. nos. 108 and 110 and pls. 73–74)—for his own use.[1] He also used Meissen porcelain liberally for diplomatic gifts to cultivate influence, reward service, and cement dynastic ties.[2]

Meissen porcelain retained this cachet until the third quarter of the eighteenth century, when the establishment in quick succession of numerous other porcelain factories across Europe and the effects of the Seven Years' War led to a decline in its status. The new abundance of porcelain also accelerated its shift toward becoming a material of use rather than purely display, albeit still among an elite. Although little evidence of how porcelain was displayed in the eighteenth century has survived, there was a change in taste around this time from the Baroque idea of a single porcelain room or cabinet to the more sparing use of porcelain distributed on furniture among many rooms. The earliest collections including Meissen porcelain were often entailed by their royal and aristocratic owners, which meant that they were preserved within families and, over time, were treated as closed, historic collections.

While there is some evidence of collecting interest in early Meissen porcelain toward the end of the eighteenth century, it is probable that this remained something of a minority antiquarian interest.[3] The development of taste from the Rococo to Neoclassicism in the second half of the eighteenth century ensured that it would remain so.[4] The "rediscovery" of early Meissen porcelain began in a modest way as early as the 1820s, when English dealers began to order porcelain in eighteenth-century taste from the Meissen manufactory (known as "old French taste," Louis XV and Louis XVI style continued to be favored by English connoisseurs). The prevailing European Empire fashion was perhaps least felt in England, where the Rococo taste—particularly in porcelain—was popular from the 1820s and remained so throughout the nineteenth century. The English dealers' preference appears to have been mainly for larger decorative pieces after models in Rococo style of the late 1740s onward, though there is some evidence that vases were also decorated with earlier chinoiserie and European landscape scenes of the 1730s and early 1740s.[5] This historical-revival taste gradually spread from England back to the Continent, though it is difficult to gauge whether the eventual buyers regarded their porcelain simply as decoration or with more of a connoisseur's eye.

For much of the nineteenth century, there was—with a few exceptions—little interest among antiquarian collectors for early Meissen porcelain. Art historians and collectors were, on the whole, more interested in the Gothic and Renaissance periods, and it was only in the last quarter of the nineteenth century that the modern era of Meissen collecting began in earnest. The first art historical articles on Meissen porcelain appeared in the 1880s and—thanks to several distinguished museum curators—there followed numerous exhibitions and publications in subsequent decades, all of which helped inspire and inform collectors. The dispersal of historic collections on the art market, and the now-scholarly auction catalogues often written by leading museum specialists, also stimulated interest. The first decades of the twentieth century were a "golden age" of collecting, when eighteenth-century Meissen porcelain was accorded an unparalleled level of scholarly importance by leading art historians. The rediscovery of porcelain as an expression of eighteenth-century court culture and of its role in eighteenth-century interiors made it fashionable among numerous wealthy and cultivated collectors in the highest levels of society and, for a time, it ranked in importance as a collecting area alongside the fine arts.

FIG. 1 Reverse view of fragments of a bottle-gourd vase, ca. 1726–1730, painting attributed to Johann Ehrenfried Stadler (cat. no. 77/pl. 54)

With more knowledge came greater connoisseurship and specialization among collectors. Whereas earlier collections had often included a broad spectrum of the decorative arts, some collectors now had the knowledge and means to focus their interest. Among the finest collectors to focus on early Meissen porcelain during the prewar period were, in Dresden, Gustav (1852–1926) and Charlotte (1857–1934) von Klemperer and Heinrich (1885–1935) and Lisa (1890–1972) Arnhold, and, in Berlin—one of the leading art markets and centers of collecting in Europe—Wolfgang von Dallwitz (1863–1928), Erich von Goldschmidt-Rothschild (1894–1987), and Franz (1881–1950) and Margarete (1878–?) Oppenheimer, who concentrated only on chinoiserie decoration and figures but assembled a collection of unparalleled quality.[6] The sales in 1919 and 1920 of porcelain from the historic collection of Augustus the Strong were attended by many of the major German museum directors of the day, the most important collectors, as well as dealers from Germany and across Europe, focusing attention on the early period of Meissen as never before.[7]

This era is all the more poignant for the abruptness and violence with which it ended. The eponymous fictional collector of Meissen porcelain in Bruce Chatwin's novel *Utz* (1989) observes the tragic irony that "wars, pogroms, and revolutions . . . offer excellent opportunities for the collector." The increasing persecution of Jews in Germany resulted in the forced sale or confiscation of numerous art collections and caused those who could to flee the country. The war also ensured the destruction of numerous collections, including the Dallwitz collection—probably the best collection of early Meissen in private hands—in its entirety, as well as most of the Klemperer collection (see fig. 1) and many others, and led to a sudden and dramatic shift of collecting gravity from Europe to the United States.

The outbreak of the Second World War was crucial in establishing the taste for eighteenth-century Meissen porcelain in the United States, which—for a time—experienced its own golden age of collecting. Despite the alarm that had been expressed already before World War I by distinguished German art historians, such as Wilhelm von Bode (1845–1929) and Otto von Falke (1862–1942), at the purchasing power of American collectors and the flow of artworks across the Atlantic, Meissen porcelain was relatively little collected in the United States prior to World War II; the prevailing taste was for English porcelain.[8] The lack of available objects was probably the main reason: it is likely that most of the notable prewar collections—none of which focused on Meissen exclusively—such as those of the Reverend Alfred Duane Pell (1864–1924), J. P. Morgan (1837–1913), Abby Aldrich Rockefeller (1874–1948) and her sister, Lucy Truman Aldrich (1869–1955), and George B. (1865–1940) and Georgiana (1863–1952) McClellan, were formed because the collectors could make their acquisitions outside the United States.

The arrival in the United States of German refugees around the outbreak of World War II, notably Jewish dealers and collectors, as well as surprisingly large quantities of porcelain helped kick-start a tradition of collecting Meissen porcelain in the United States that has flourished to the present day. Some immigrants were from distinguished, long-established, and very well-connected family businesses, such as Rosenberg and Stiebel (formerly J. Rosenbaum)[9] and Alexander and Richard Ball (the sons of the renowned German auctioneer and dealer Hermann Ball). They functioned as conduits between European collectors, forced by the war to dispose of their property, and wealthy American collectors, eager to benefit from their knowledge and the sudden availability of high-quality porcelain. Others, such as the Frankfurt

collector Adolf Beckhardt (1889–1962), came as refugees and had an extraordinary impact on collecting taste. Beckhardt, who had been forced to sell part of his collection when he fled Germany in the 1930s, was able to take some of his Höchst porcelain with him, which he used in 1940 to establish a gallery in New York on Third Avenue.

One of Beckhardt's first customers was Ilse Bischoff (1901–1990; see fig. 2), born in New York to a German family. She recalled her first encounter with Beckhardt:

> I knew what they were, but you wondered how on earth they suddenly got there, and it was—one German refugee from Frankfurt who had a beautiful collection, was a darling man, couldn't speak a word of English, and when he opened his shop on 3rd Avenue, I went in. [. . .] I spoke German to him, and when he opened his collection, it was put on sale, I was the first one who had a choice, and unfortunately, I didn't have enough money then to buy the whole collection in one fell swoop. Of course, now it's in all the museums.
>
> So, that's how I got started, and then I learned—you learn by collecting, and you train a very sharp eye.[10]

Bischoff also ventured that Beckhardt "started some of the great collections in this country, because people found their way there, and they were so cheap, when I think of what they were later on."[11]

Bischoff introduced to Beckhardt her friend Edward Pflueger (1905–1997), who had emigrated from Germany in the 1930s to establish the American base of the pharmaceutical company Bayer. Pflueger went on to form one of the finest postwar collections of eighteenth-century German porcelain.[12] The Swiss-born collector Hans Syz (1894–1991) also began collecting European porcelain in 1941 following a visit to Beckhardt's gallery, the Art Exchange, in 1941.[13] Other notable collectors who began collecting Meissen porcelain around this time include Jack (1897–1980) and Belle (1904–1987) Linsky, Irwin Untermyer (1886–1973), and R. Thornton Wilson (1886–1977). All of their collections were eventually donated to museums,[14] which helped establish the importance of this field of collecting in the public mind and acted as an inspiration and source of knowledge for collectors.

The strength and potential of the American collecting market also drew English dealers who specialized in eighteenth-century porcelain to New York, such as James A. Lewis and Son and D. M. and P. Manheim. Another New York dealer, William H. Lautz (1891–1973), was a key figure in the growth of interest in the United States in European porcelain. One of the "last generation of reputable and scholarly dealers—as eager to educate as to sell," Lautz encouraged and supplied collectors outside of New York, most notably Warda Stevens Stout (1886–1985) in Memphis and a circle of collectors in Seattle.[15] In 1957 the largest and most prestigious dealer in European porcelain, the Antique Porcelain Company, opened a New York branch in a townhouse on East 57th Street.[16] The company was founded in London by a German emigré lawyer, Hanns Weinberg (1900–1976), in 1945 and within a few years counted royalty and the cream of society, as well as museums and collectors, among its clients. As in prewar Europe, eighteenth-century porcelain came to be regarded as an attribute of refinement and good taste among the wealthiest circles of society, in no small part thanks to the efforts of Weinberg.

Private collectors fleeing Germany and the war in Europe were also important in establishing the taste for eighteenth-century Meissen porcelain in the United States. Siegfried Kramarsky (1893–1961), Eduard Wallach (1908–1995), Goldschmidt-Rothschild, and the Arnhold family all arrived in the United States around the outbreak of the Second World War, either bringing their collections with them or going on to collect. When Lisa Arnhold arrived in California in 1940, having left Germany in 1937, she at first lent her Meissen porcelain to the M. H. de Young Memorial Museum in San Francisco.[17] The surge in interest for porcelain as well as the financial power of United States–based collectors led the venerable English dealers Stoner and Evans to exhibit the Otto and Magdalena Blohm Collection in New York in 1948.[18] The following year, the Metropolitan Museum of Art in New York staged a major exhibition, *Masterpieces of European Porcelain*,[19] which included more than five hundred examples of porcelain from all the major European makers and filled three large galleries. The private lenders included Kramarsky, Pflueger, and Baroness de Becker (1899–1977), a granddaughter of Gustave de Rothschild who lived with Goldschmidt-Rothschild, as well as other recent collectors of Meissen porcelain who would become benefactors of the museum: Wilson, the Linskys, and Untermyer. The latter lent almost half the Meissen porcelain in the exhibition, which consisted mostly of figures and groups, while Baroness de Becker was the second-largest lender.

Although New York was home to the greatest concentration of collectors and the most important dealers, the taste for eighteenth-century Meissen porcelain spread across the United States. One of the most energetic and knowledgeable collectors of early Meissen porcelain during the 1950s and 1960s, Ralph H. Wark (1902–1987), lived in Hendersonville, North Carolina, and subsequently Saint Augustine, Florida. Wark had begun collecting around 1922 in Europe, where he lived for two decades prior to World War II, ending up in Hamburg, where he was forced to leave his collection in the care of a friend during the war. The collection survived and, in 1947, Wark moved it to the United States, where he resumed collecting, supplied mostly by European dealers with whom he had dealt before the war.[20] Wark was an influential collector who published his research and encouraged others to collect, most notably in Memphis Warda Stevens Stout, who under Wark's guidance began collecting Meissen and other German porcelain in 1949.[21] In 1951 Stout helped to found a Memphis group dedicated to the decorative arts alongside George Ryland (1889–1979) and Cleo (1890–1987) Scott, whose interest in porcelain included Chinese as well as English and European. In an effort to make the subject more accessible, the Scotts published an illustrated introduction to porcelain in 1961 with a foreword by Wark.[22]

On the West Coast, Seattle became a significant center of porcelain collecting from the 1940s, when the Seattle Ceramic Society was founded by Blanche M. Harnan (ca. 1888–1968) with the aim of collecting eighteenth-century porcelain worthy of exhibition in the Seattle Art Museum. She was also assisted by New York dealer Lautz, who regularly shipped barrels of porcelain to Seattle for division between members of the society; the barrels would then be returned with payment. The most significant collection of European porcelain in Seattle was formed by Henry C. (1899–1985) and Martha L. (1901–2000) Isaacson, who also bought from New York and European dealers. The Isaacsons were among several Seattle collectors to lend porcelain to the major exhibition *Continental Table Porcelain of the Eighteenth Century* held in San Francisco at the M. H. de Young Memorial Museum in 1965.[23] Just under half of the 280 objects in the exhibition were Meissen porcelain; in a reprise of their loans to the same museum in 1940, the most substantial lender was the Arnhold family.

The postwar recovery in Europe during the 1950s gradually created more competition and higher prices for American collectors, as a new generation of collectors emerged in Europe and elsewhere. Eighteenth-century Meissen porcelain became an international collecting taste, and today, in an age of globalization and instant communication, there are collectors as far afield as Australia, Southeast Asia, Japan, the Middle East, and Russia, as well as Europe and North America. Paradoxically, the status of European porcelain and decorative arts has—in some European museums, at least—declined. The author and ceramist Edmund de Waal observed a cultural shift as early as the 1950s away from eighteenth-century porcelain: a "fall from grace" of a material that was "obviously elitist and precious and suspiciously smacked of the connoisseurial."[24] Some museums have recently even succumbed to modish temptation and almost entirely removed their porcelain from display, perhaps in the belief that the products of an elite court culture seemingly so far removed from our own will be of little interest to their visitors. This makes the painstaking and scholarly efforts of private collectors such as Malcolm Gutter more important than ever. When Gutter's collection finds a permanent home in the Fine Arts Museums of San Francisco, his discerning eye for rarity and quality, his understanding of the historical context of early Meissen, and his interest in the provenance of his collection will all in turn fashion the narratives of Meissen collecting and be a point of reference or departure for future generations of collectors.

CATALOGUE

Maria L. Santangelo

✳

Information on porcelain marks, provenance, and
publication and exhibition history for all pieces
in the Malcolm D. Gutter Collection is included
in the catalogue checklist (pp. 241–255).

THE GUTTER COLLECTION IN CONTEXT: THE LEGION OF HONOR AND A PURSUIT OF EARLY MEISSEN PORCELAIN

The European porcelain collection at the Fine Arts Museums of San Francisco's Legion of Honor was established in 1924 with gifts of French porcelain from the French government. Founded by Alma de Bretteville Spreckels, the Legion of Honor stands as a memorial to the California soldiers who fought in World War I. Although it had a predominantly French focus to its collections and architecture due to Alma's ancestry and predilections, the money behind the establishment of the Legion of Honor came from Alma's husband, Adolph B. Spreckels, whose parents emigrated from Germany. Although Alma gifted some late eighteenth-century Meissen to the Legion in 1945, none of the early Meissen owned by the Spreckels family appears to have been passed down to Adolph or Alma.[1]

Over the years, the Fine Arts Museums displayed several notable exhibitions and loans of Meissen porcelain from the Arnhold family collection (ca. 1940–1942 and 1965); the Dresden royal collection (June 1, 1978–May 26, 1979); and the private collections of Kathy Gillmeister (November 3, 1984–December 31, 1985) and Malcolm D. Gutter (initial loans 1980). Furthermore, some significant acquisitions of Meissen were made in 1965 of a Swan service platter (1737–1741) and in 1979 of a pair of Madagascar hoopoe bird figures (ca. 1736).[2] Although the Fine Arts Museums have a respectable representation of Meissen wares and figures dating from 1730, the earliest and most experimental wares produced by the manufactory were not represented.

Remarkable examples of early Meissen, as well as several monumental blue-and-white vases, will enter the collection with Malcolm D. Gutter's promised gift. Carefully collecting over decades, Gutter has assembled an incredible array of Meissen porcelain from the earliest red stonewares to experimental white porcelains decorated with fashionable chinoiseries and Asian-inspired decorations. In addition, the gift will add twenty-one pieces of Meissen with Japanese Palace inventory numbers and royal AR (Augustus Rex) marks, bolstering the Museums' previous holdings of one single example. This group is also layered with thirteen notable Chinese and Japanese porcelains from Augustus the Strong's collection that may have directly inspired Meissen's modelers and artists. From the early to mid-eighteenth century, Meissen indisputably led the way in porcelain technology and fashion, making it the envy of all of Europe. The depth and range of the gift is evident in the illustrated checklist at the back of this volume (see pp. 241–255), which extensively lists mark, provenance, and exhibition and publication history information on each object in the collection. Plate numbers refer to extended entries for those seventy-five objects featured in the catalogue section of the book.

To celebrate the gift to the Fine Arts Museums of San Francisco, one hundred pieces from Gutter's collection were exhibited at the Legion of Honor from December 13, 2014, through March 14, 2016 (fig. 3). This exhibition, *A Princely Pursuit: The Malcolm D. Gutter Collection of Early Meissen Porcelain*, focused on the princely collection of Augustus the Strong and the golden era at Meissen, from its earliest experiments in 1709–1710 to the late 1750s, during the Seven Years' War.

Gutter has already donated one notable piece—a blue-and-white Augustus Rex vase (cat. no. 57/pl. 25), currently on permanent display in the Legion's galleries—in addition to five other pieces. He has generously lent pieces from his collection over the years to the Legion of Honor as well as to the Asian Art Museum, San Francisco (2006); the Bard Graduate Center for Studies in the Decorative Arts, Design, and Culture, New York (2007–2008); the San Francisco Airport Museum (2010); and the San Francisco Fall Antiques Show (2010 and 2012).

We are so pleased that Gutter's entire collection of Meissen and related Asian porcelains has been promised to the Fine Arts Museums of San Francisco, the city he calls home and where he began collecting more than forty years ago. Through the Malcolm D. Gutter collection, the Museums will become a destination for the study of early Meissen porcelain.

FIG. 3 Installation view of *A Princely Pursuit: The Malcolm D. Gutter Collection of Early Meissen Porcelain*, Legion of Honor, San Francisco, 2014.

CHAPTER 1

JOHANN FRIEDRICH BÖTTGER AND RED STONEWARE

East Asian porcelain techniques had eluded the West for nearly five hundred years until 1709, when alchemist Johann Friedrich Böttger (1682–1719), working with mathematician and physicist Ehrenfried Walther von Tschirnhaus (1651–1708), developed the formula, or arcanum, for creating hard-paste porcelain, often referred to as "white gold." Although the formulation would be adapted and evolve over time (eventually to other European manufactories), Böttger's discovery was the incentive for Augustus II (1670–1733), elector of Saxony (r. 1694–1733) and king of or "in"[1] Poland (r. 1697–1706), to establish the Königlich-Polnische und Kurfürstlich-Sächsische Porzellan-Manufaktur (Royal Polish and Electoral Saxon Porcelain Manufactory) at Meissen in 1710. Located near Dresden, Saxony, the manufactory was the first in Europe to produce hard-paste porcelain in imitation of the exotic and expensive Chinese and Japanese ceramics that the Dutch East India Company was importing at this time. More than three hundred years later, Meissen is still in operation.

Augustus II, or Augustus "the Strong" (see fig. 4), was a great patron of the arts and architecture, particularly in Warsaw and the newly established cultural center of Dresden. He had a well-documented mania for porcelain, and vast financial resources were spent to satisfy his *Porzellankrankheit* (porcelain sickness). Therefore, the production of porcelain in Saxony was a great financial boon as well as one of pride. From the late seventeenth century until his death in 1733, he amassed more than forty thousand Meissen and Asian porcelain objects for his personal collection and for his pleasure palace in Dresden. Originally built in 1715 on the banks of the Elbe River for the Dutch ambassador as the Holländisches Palais (Dutch Palace), it was renamed the Japanisches Palais (Japanese Palace) as part of Augustus the Strong's ambitious plan to create a true *Porzellanschloss* (porcelain palace). Extensive architectural improvements and interior decoration were undertaken at the Japanese Palace between 1715 and 1719.

The renovations were deeply influenced by the porcelain rooms at the Oranienburg Palace in Brandenburg and Friedrich I of Prussia's (r. 1701–1713) cabinet of Chinese and Japanese porcelain at Charlottenburg Palace in Berlin. However, Augustus the Strong strove to surpass his contemporaries with his vast collection

Teapot, ca. 1710, modeling by Johann Jakob Irminger (cat. no. 15)

and its display. He employed agents in Amsterdam as early as 1704 to acquire varied porcelains and ceramics,[2] and his obsession was such that an entire army brigade was traded to enhance his collection. In 1717 Augustus exchanged six hundred soldiers for 151 Chinese lidded vases that belonged to Friedrich Wilhelm I of Prussia (r. 1713–1740).[3]

Three inventories made of the royal collection—in 1721 (extended through 1727 with supplements), 1770, and 1779 (the five volumes compiled after the Seven Years' War)—survive. The 1721 inventory, *Inventarium über das Palais zu Alt-Dresden Anno 1721*, lists the various furnishings and contents of the Japanese Palace beyond Meissen, Chinese, and Japanese porcelains. Japanese Palace inventory numbers were originally painted on the underside of collection objects but were later engraved and blackened with pigment. For the inventory, red-stoneware pieces were identified with *R* for *roth* (red); white porcelain marked with *W* for *weiß* (white); black-glazed wares with *P* for *Porzellan* (porcelain); and lacquers with *L* for *lacquirt* (lacquer).

The Japanese Palace was furnished with countless wonderments, including Japanese lacquer (panels, teaware, boxes, chests, vases), ceramics (Italian maiolica, Dutch red earthenwares), French soft-paste porcelains, Chinese carved soapstones and ivories, as well as silks, mirrors, and countless brackets and shelves scaling the walls for the display of these treasures. All objects were grouped in rooms of the Japanese Palace (and consequently in the inventory) by color (e.g., celadon) or material (e.g., lacquer) to give the greatest visual and decorative effect.[4] The intended (but never fully realized) spectacular displays can be seen in the architectural designs of 1730 and 1735 (see fig. 56). The porcelain contents are further documented in the 1736 *Specification von Porcilan*, which recorded the pieces commissioned from the Meissen manufactory to furnish the palace.[5] Asian porcelains were to be displayed on the ground floor, with Meissen on the main floor above. The interiors and gardens of the Japanese Palace were completed in time for the 1719 wedding of Augustus's son, the future Augustus III (1696–1763), to Maria Josepha (1699–1757), daughter of Joseph I, Holy Roman Emperor.

After Augustus the Strong's death in 1733, Augustus III succeeded to the electoral throne and continued efforts to complete the Japanese Palace, engaging the French architect Zacharias Longuelune (1669–1748); however, the project was ultimately abandoned, and all shipments of Meissen porcelain to the Japanese Palace ended by 1738. Until that time, the royal Saxon collection was temporarily displayed in the Turmzimmer (tower room) of the Dresden castle. A 1769 inventory of the Turmzimmer survives, as well as engravings of this display.[6]

The porcelain collections of Augustus the Strong and his son Augustus III were open to the public in the Johanneum by the last quarter of the nineteenth century. Originally built as the *Stallgebäude* (stables) to the Dresden castle in the sixteenth century, Augustus the Strong had converted the structure first into a guesthouse, then into a museum for the royal painting collection in the 1730s. Following another period of rebuilding from 1872 to 1876, the royal porcelain collection was temporarily moved to the renamed Johanneum in 1875. (At this time, Japanese Palace inventory numbers were referred to as Johanneum numbers.) The royal Saxon porcelain collections (now known as the Porzellansammlung) became part of the Staatliche Kunstsammlungen (state art collections) and were moved to the Zwinger palace, Dresden, in 1962.

FIG. 4 Detail of Augustus the Strong on mounted coffeepot, ca. 1723–1724, painting attributed to Johann Gregorius Höroldt (cat. no. 46/pl. 32)

FIG. 5 Eagle-spout teapot, ca. 1710–1713 (cat. no. and pl. 8)

The story of the manufactory began when chemist and mathematician Tschirnhaus returned to Germany from Versailles to serve in the court of the young Augustus II. At Versailles, Tschirnhaus had been exposed to the secretive workings of artists' workshops. In that environment he could see how such sensitive work, like that of glassmaking, could be protected by limiting the access of employees to only their own specialized or individualized tasks. Tschirnhaus was able to implement some of these workshop practices at Meissen with his colleague Böttger. Tschirnhaus's scientific experiments in producing porcelain yielded some promising results as early as 1704. In that same year, Böttger was forcefully installed at the Saxon court after his independent experiments to make gold out of base metals had come to the attention of Augustus II. Under Tschirnhaus's guidance, Böttger turned his focus to developing a sound formula for porcelain. Kings and royalty across Europe during the early eighteenth century were racing to create porcelain in imitation of Chinese and Japanese wares. At stake were great wealth and pride for Saxony and Poland.

Some experiments took place as early as 1706 at the Albrechtsburg castle in Meissen (fig. 6). The castle's fortifications helped protect the secretive work within, and its situation above the Elbe River facilitated the transportation of raw materials and wares. Böttger was whisked away to the fortress of Königstein near Dresden (see fig. 50) in the fall of that year as Swedish troops advanced on Meissen as part of the Second Northern War. (Swedish troops would occupy Saxony for a year.) By 1708–1709 Böttger resumed work in his workshop at the Jungfernbastei fortress in Dresden. Working under a cloak of great secrecy, he uncovered the arcanum for creating porcelain and reported success to his patron by 1709. Upon the establishment of the manufactory on January 23, 1710, the workshop was moved yet again to the Albrechtsburg, where it remained until 1864.

Working alongside Tschirnhaus and Gottfried Pabst von Ohain (1656–1729), a Freiberg mining official, Böttger experimented through considerable trial and error, as he and his associates lacked any concrete knowledge of the Asian compositions. His earliest undertakings for Meissen yielded a fine-grained red stoneware (*Böttgersteinzeug*). Tschirnhaus and Böttger achieved a satisfactory paste, albeit one different from the red stonewares being imported from Yixing, China. Other manufactories in Europe also attempted to produce red wares in imitation of Asian imports. Ary de Milde (1634–1708) and Samuel van Eenhoorn (1655–1686) produced red stoneware at the De Grieksche A factory in Holland as early as circa 1658 in imitation of Yixing examples imported by the Dutch East India Company. A red ware was also produced in English workshops by the end of the seventeenth century and into the nineteenth century. Another factory was established in 1713 by a former Meissen employee outside of Berlin in Plaue (Brandenburg-an-der-Havel) and produced a red stoneware until 1730.[7]

These were all deemed to be of little competition by Augustus the Strong. Meissen red stoneware is particularly stonelike in appearance and exhibits characteristic striations. This latter detail, which is most evident on unpolished wares, is possibly due to a final sponging off of the surface prior to firing. Also, as Gutter suggests, the highly refined surface produced by Meissen is indicative of its royal production; with Augustus the Strong as the driving force, financial concerns did not impede pursuit of quality.[8]

Unlike the Yixing or Dutch red stonewares made of a single clay, Böttger stoneware is composed of one part red bolar earth (sometimes called English earth

FIG. 6 Albrechtsburg Castle, Meissen, Germany, 2015

or Nürnberg red earth) and two parts low-melting calcareous loam, fired at 1,200 to 1,300 degrees centigrade. The iron oxide in the bolar (mined locally, first from Plaue, then Zwickau) creates the material's red-brown color; however, a range of colors can be seen in the finished wares. Variations in color correspond to differences in firing temperature. Made between 1709 and 1713, these pieces of dense, fine-grained stoneware were so hard that they could be polished by lapidaries and cut and engraved by glass cutters. Employed by the factory from 1710 to 1712 for their glass-cutting skills, workers from Bohemia utilized their talents to masterful effect on the surface of some wares.

It nevertheless took about four years—from 1709 until 1713, during which time red stoneware was in production at Meissen—until early white *Kalkporzellan* was refined sufficiently to make it commercially viable. Various red stonewares, such as teawares, pipes, and tankards, were sold by Meissen as early as May 1710 at the Ostermesse (or Easter Fair) in Leipzig. Fairs were held in Leipzig three times a year, showcasing Saxon wares. Augustus the Strong and his son Augustus III were commonly present at these fairs to support and promote the skill of local producers, particularly the Meissen factory. Their presence certainly aided with the marketing of Meissen. Samuel Chladni (1684–1753), the controller at the Dresden *Warenlager* (warehouse), kept records of purchases from the 1719 Easter Fair.[9] The manufactory maintained royal sales outlets in Meissen, Dresden, and Leipzig.

The success of these early wares can be attributed to Böttger, the Dresden court silversmith Johann Jakob Irminger (1635–1724; see cat. no. and pl. 8), and the court lacquerer Martin Schnell (ca. 1675–1740; see cat. no. and pl. 9). The Gutter collection is particularly strong in these early German red stonewares, which represent the factory's first experiments to achieve true white porcelain.

Böttger continued experiments at Meissen until his death in 1719. When he finally produced a whiter, feldspathic paste around 1708, its introduction to the market in 1713 created a sharp decline in demand for Böttger's red stoneware. By 1715 *Böttgersteinzeug* production ceased altogether. By the inventory of 1719, more than two thousand pieces of red stoneware remained in the Meissen storerooms and Dresden and Leipzig warehouses. Some of the factory's unsold stocks were transferred to the Japanese Palace in 1733 (see cat. no. and pl. 6).

1 PAIR OF TEABOWLS

ca. 1709–1711

Red stoneware with black glaze

2 ¼ × 3 ⅝ in. (5.6 × 9.1 cm) and 2 ¼ × 3 ¾ in. (5.6 × 9.4 cm)

L13.62.2.1–2 (CAT. NO. 1)

•

Possibly produced in Dresden rather than in Meissen at the Albrechtsburg, before the manufactory was established in 1710, these teabowls may be among the earliest extant experimental pieces of Böttger stoneware. The form is most likely derived from Japanese and Chinese porcelain and/or lacquer prototypes. Likewise, the glossy black glaze on these teabowls is in imitation of imported Asian lacquer wares. The craze for lacquer in Europe during the late seventeenth through eighteenth century created a robust market for imitation lacquer on furniture and other decorative arts.

Scientific analysis carried out by the Institute of Ceramics, Glass and Construction Materials in Freiberg, Germany, confirms that Böttger's lacquered surface is due to "a type of glaze which contains considerable amounts of lead and which is given the opaque black colour as a result of a considerable iron-oxide and manganese-oxide content and which was fused at roughly 950 degrees centigrade to 1,050 degrees centigrade," a kiln temperature close to the 1,200 to 1,400 recognized for porcelain.[10]

These teabowls are very early examples of Böttger's invention. Both are unique wheel-thrown objects. Although contemporaneous and having some common characteristics, important and subtle differences between them can be seen under close inspection and magnification. (Such inspection and handling of many of these early red stonewares informed much of Gutter's research and collecting.[11]) Indicative of the earliest experimental wares, one teabowl (L13.62.2.1) has a lustrous maroon-colored glaze that erupted in places during firing. Such imperfections are not found on the manufactory's later black-glazed wares. Under magnification, the red stoneware of this teabowl can be seen through the glaze, which flowed over the base. However, the footrim has been cut, thus exposing a dense and dark red stoneware. This dark coloration is likely due to a high-temperature firing.

The other teabowl (L13.62.2.2) has the same early form but is slightly larger and is potted somewhat thicker than the other. The glaze is black and dense, and, while eruptions are not nearly as numerous or distinctive, it exhibits crazing. The glaze stops at the footrim, flowing over only two small areas on the inner footrim, while sagger debris remains in one of these areas and on the outer footrim. The footrim, as in the other teabowl, has been cut.

2 SAUCER

ca. 1709–1711
Red stoneware with black glaze
1 × 5⅞ in. (2.5 × 12.5 cm)
L13.62.3 (CAT. NO. 2)

•

Another rare, early experimental ware, this saucer or small dish with lacquer glaze exhibits some firing cracks on its base and crazing of its glaze. Typical of Meissen black-glazed wares, the overall glaze is thick and syrupy and is best appreciated where it pools over the unpolished, unglazed areas on the underside. The dish exhibits some slight warping due to firing irregularities. Although we assume that the form is a saucer, and thereby would be paired with a teabowl or cup, we know from contemporary prints, documentary sources, and wear patterns on some decorated pieces that tea was frequently poured into and drunk directly from a saucer (see fig. 7). Furthermore, there is no raised ring or recess on this form to support a cup or teabowl.[12] Tea had been consumed in China since the Tang period (618–907); however, it may have been first introduced to Europe (more specifically Holland) from Japan via the Dutch East India Company in the early seventeenth century. The consumption of tea, coffee, and chocolate markedly increased in the eighteenth century, which drove the market for ceramic and porcelain forms to drink these new beverages.

FIG. 7 Louis-Léopold Boilly (1761–1845), *Les Amateurs de Café* from *Recueil de Grimaces* (Collection of grimaces) (Paris: François-Séraphin Delpech, 1827). Bibliothèque nationale de France

3 SAUCER

ca. 1709–1711
Red stoneware with matte and slip decoration
1 ⅜ × 5 ⅜ in. (3.4 × 13.7 cm)
L13.62.4 (CAT. NO. 3)

•

Various unusual decorative techniques are on display on the surface of this small saucer's body. A slip glaze was brushed onto the outer rim before firing, leaving a matte (raw stoneware) center that gives it a bull's eye–like appearance. The dark brown slip has similarities to that of an *Eisenporzellan* (iron porcelain) bowl in the Gutter collection (cat. no. and pl. 4). Black iron particles are visible on the surface of the slip, and the matte center displays rings from the potter's throwing. The reverse of the saucer is glazed up to the matte, unglazed footrim, magnification of which reveals encrusted sagger debris, minute fissures, and raised clay particles (see fig. 8).

Much of Meissen's early red stoneware consisted of articles for coffee, tea, and chocolate. It is unclear from the early inventories of these stonewares if the pieces were intended to be sold in groups or as individual items. The Böttger inventory for 1711 lists service wares separately, with no inference made if they were to be assembled into usable groups;[13] however, by 1712, factory administrator Johann Melchior Steinbrück (1673–1723) reported entire services for coffee, tea, and chocolate "of five, six, or more sorts" as well as toilet garnitures that could include various covered articles for cosmetics and perfumes.[14] Somewhat contradicting himself, Steinbrück recorded in the same report "two reasons for the rapid disappearance of 'red porcelain' from the manufacturing range: for one thing only individual objects and no complete services had ever been marketed, on the other hand demand had already as early as 1713 been so concentrated on white porcelain that the production of the 'red' had not been worthwhile any longer."[15] It is perhaps prudent to assume that smaller teawares, like teabowls and saucers, could be gathered together for sale from a large, en masse group, but that larger teapots, coffeepots, and supplemental wares such as sugarbowls and tea caddies were sold separately. We know for example that Chladni sold thirty-four various chocolate beakers, each without a saucer, and only one separate saucer at the 1719 Easter Fair in Leipzig.[16]

It is not known if Meissen created a teabowl to complement this saucer. Gutter has certainly speculated whether a matching teabowl would have replicated the bull's-eye design or if one of *Eisenporzellan* (like the example featured in pl. 4) would have been more suitable.

FIG. 8 Reverse view of the saucer

4 *EISENPORZELLAN* TEABOWL

ca. 1710–1712
Red stoneware with slip decoration
2 ½ × 4 in. (6.2 × 10.1 cm)
L13.62.5 (CAT. NO. 4)

•

The surface of this bowl is referred to as *Eisenporzellan*, or iron
porcelain, a glaze probably unique to Meissen. The brushed-on, slip
decoration creates an unusual gray metallic surface. The Meissen
inventory of 1711 describes the surface as being like slate, or *Schiefer
glassurt*.[17] Formerly, the *Eisenporzellan* effect was attributed to
either an inadvertent overfiring or an intentional reduction (damp-
ing) during the firing process; however, as Gutter notes, the surface
glaze was visibly and purposefully brushed on by the potter prior to
firing.[18] The surface could then be further enhanced by polishing,
producing a slightly darker, lustrous appearance. Many examples
survive in the Porzellansammlung, Dresden.

5 TWO-HANDLED CHOCOLATE BEAKER AND SAUCER

ca. 1710–1713
Red stoneware with black glaze
Beaker: 3 ⅛ × 3 ⅜ in. (8 × 8.5 cm); saucer: 1 ⅛ × 5 ⅞ in. (3 × 14.8 cm)
L13.62.11A–B (CAT. NO. 5)

•

Composed of red stoneware, this two-handled chocolate beaker and saucer are notably large and uniform in their black glaze. Both pieces display some iridescent glaze pooling over the exposed red stoneware on their bases. The large scale of the beaker and saucer speaks to their function as wares for consuming the fashionable new drink of the time, chocolate. When it first reached Germany in the seventeenth century, chocolate was drunk for medicinal purposes, but by the next century it had become a luxury item; throughout the eighteenth century, it was subject to high customs duties and tributes. The beverage was consumed in larger quantities than tea or coffee. Since it was frequently prepared with froth on top, larger cups were designed for its consumption. Like tea, chocolate could also be cooled and drunk directly from a saucer. The high sides on this saucer are conducive to this use.

Thinly wheel-thrown, the beaker's ear-shaped handles were press-molded and luted onto the body, slightly askew. These stylized handles were possibly inspired by seventeenth-century Chinese lacquer and porcelain libation cups or, perhaps more likely, Irminger was influenced by European silver forms. Although Meissen examples with simplified double handles exist, no other red-stoneware examples with such elaborate handles appear to have survived.

The 1719 Dresden royal sales inventory recorded twenty-six black-glazed two-handled beakers (no further details on handles provided) and more than twice as many black-glazed saucers.[19] These pieces were listed individually in the inventory; still, as Gutter suggests, the stylistic and physical evidence points to the probability that they have always been paired.[20]

FIG. 9 Frontispiece depicting personifications of coffee, tea, and chocolate from Philippe Sylvestre Dufour, *Traitez nouveaux & curieux du café, du thé et du chocolate* (Lyon, 1685). Courtesy of The New York Academy of Medicine Library

6 EWER (KENDI)

ca. 1710–1712
Red stoneware
6 ⅞ × 4 ½ in. (17.6 × 11.5 cm)
L13.62.8 (CAT. NO. 6)

•

This *kendi* (ewer or wine flask) with dragon-head spout was molded directly from a Chinese prototype in Augustus the Strong's collection. The Gutter collection also contains a Chinese red-stoneware ewer (see right); such an example would have served as this *kendi*'s direct model. Expected shrinkage in the kiln would explain the slightly smaller scale of the Meissen stoneware *kendi*, if a mold had been made from the Chinese original.

Originally the *kendi* would have included a small domed cap; however, few complete vessels survive. Although the original ewers dating back to the thirteenth century were functional or ritualistic water vessels, Europeans apparently thought of them as ornamental pieces for display. Meissen produced ewers with matte surfaces, such as the example in the Gutter collection, but they were also black-glazed and lacquered, or glazed to simulate metal or slate (*Eisenporzellan*). Several Meissen examples are in the depot of the Porzellansammlung, Dresden. Chinese Yixing examples are somewhat rare.

The Meissen ewer, from the collection of Augustus the Strong, bears a Japanese Palace inventory number in black pigment.[21] After the death of Böttger in 1719, an accounting was made of the stocks of red stoneware and porcelain, including those pieces held by the alchemist himself. These sixty-one pieces from the so-called Böttger Creditwesen were transferred to the warehouses in Dresden and Leipzig, where they remained until 1733. At that time they were transferred to the king's collection in Dresden and given Japanese Palace inventory numbers. Per correspondence between Meissen scholar and archivist Claus Boltz and Malcolm Gutter, some black-glazed pieces with numbers higher than N: 42 and red pieces higher than N: 132 were not delivered into the king's collection until 1733. The fifty-nine *kendis* (including this example) were thus part of this "later" cache.[22]

Pieces from the royal Saxon collection in the Porzellansammlung, Dresden, entered the market through sales of duplicates after World War I: one in 1919 and another in 1920. The 1919 sale included eight matte *kendis* with Japanese Palace inventory number 252/R (lots 56–45), and another two black-glazed, lacquered, and gilt *kendis* with Japanese Palace number 64 (lots 54 and 55).[23] This ewer appeared as lot 56 in the 1919 duplicate sale, where it was purchased by Ole Olsen, a notable Meissen collector and general director of the Copenhagen National Museum.[24]

The *kendi* has a finely finished matte surface, and the molded decorations are clear but not crisp. The application of the surface decorations were guided by engraved outlines on the body; however, some of the applied sprigs and medallions have been lost. Press-molded in three parts, the mold lines are visible. Under magnification numerous black iron flecks, minute fissures, and tears are evident. Striations, often found on matte-surfaced Böttger stoneware, may be seen throughout. There is white sagger debris visible around the footrim and in the mouth of the spout.

6A EWER (KENDI)

ca. 1700–1710
China
Red stoneware
8 × 4 ½ in. (20.3 × 11.4 cm)
L13.62.147 (CAT. NO. 116)

•

Meissen red stoneware is composed of two clays unlike Yixing redware, which is composed of a single basic clay. No mold lines are visible on the Chinese example in the Gutter collection.[25] The Yixing example bears a clay ornament depicting a coin— one of the Eight Precious Things symbolic of good fortune in Chinese iconography—placed where the neck joins the body.

7 COFFEEPOT

ca. 1710–1713
Red stoneware
5 ⅞ × 2 ½ in. (15 × 6.4 cm)
L13.62.6A–B (CAT. NO. 7)

•

Inspired by Chinese and English prototypes, this model's form was designed by Irminger. Irminger was enlisted in 1710 by Augustus the Strong to produce designs for Meissen from 1712 until his death in 1724.[26] He also effectively acted as artistic director of the factory until Böttger's death in 1719. Irminger designed several models in hammered copper for Meissen red stonewares as well as some of its earliest white porcelain pieces. The influence of Chinese Yixing prototypes can be seen in the pagoda-like lid of this coffeepot and the curving squared spout issuing from the mouth of a sea monster, but the overall shape of the body and the scroll handle with its channeled sides are inspired by English or French silver forms.

Ulrike Weinhold, curator of the Grünes Gewölbe (Green Vault), Dresden, has noted that the form bears a certain similarity to coffeepots made by Huguenot goldsmiths; however, she also recognized the possible influence of Japanese sake bottles for the distinct four-sided body.[27] Overall, the varied influences of East and West are harmonious in detail and proportion. As Augustus the Strong was a major collector of Chinese Yixing redwares, Meissen potters certainly had access to examples imported to Europe during the seventeenth and eighteenth centuries (see cat. no. 116/pl. 6a, for example). The body of this coffeepot was left matte and faintly bears the suggestion of molded prunus (flowering plum), also inspired by Yixing wares. It is uncertain if the degree of decoration was intentional, the result of unsuccessful molds, or partially worn during the polishing. Several examples of this form and decorative motif survive in the Porzellansammlung, Dresden, with varying degrees of molding. Such coffeepots could also be polished, black-glazed, gilded, and/or lacquered with colors.

This coffeepot was press-molded in sections—including spout, handle, and base—then luted together. The matte surface was probably partially polished, giving the piece a satiny appearance. Striations on the red clay are evident, especially on the base of the bulbous body. These striations result from the use of a sponge to smooth the porcelain body during the pre-firing finishing process.[28] Under magnification, whitish sagger debris are evident on the footrim and in the crevice between two of the facets on the handle. Furthermore, blemishes such as minute tears may be noted.

8 EAGLE-SPOUT TEAPOT

ca. 1710–1713

Red stoneware with black glaze

4⅜ × 4⅜ in. (11 × 11 cm)

L13.62.7A–B (CAT. NO. 8)

•

Although many of their earliest red-stoneware forms were initially influenced by Asian examples, Meissen potters also looked to European silver shapes for inspiration. The elaborate Baroque shape of this teapot was probably designed by Irminger.

A single (interior) pouring hole may be seen where the curved spout, in the form of an eagle, issues forth from a grotesque mask applied to the body (see fig. 5 for alternate view). Meissen produced this teapot design with two variant handles and decorative surfaces. Some retain a polished stoneware surface, while others were lacquered and could be even further enhanced with gilding and enamel decoration. The overall gilding on this teapot is very faint but visible in areas around the spout, the molded base edge, and the spout's eagle head.

9 TEAPOT

ca. 1710–1713
Red stoneware with black glaze, lacquer, and gilding
3 ¾ × 3 in. (9.5 × 7.5 cm)
L13.62.9A–B (CAT. NO. 9)

•

Displaying varied decorative techniques on red stoneware, this jewellike miniature teapot is covered by a lustrous black glaze that is further enhanced by lacquer colors and gilt accents. Black-glazed red stonewares were sold as early as 1710 at the mercantile fair in Leipzig.[29] Eighteenth-century collectors' interest in lacquer was so great that Meissen enlisted Martin Schnell, who led a Dresden workshop for lacquered furniture; he was listed on the Meissen paymaster's list of 1721. Three varied techniques were employed at Meissen to achieve gilding: a true gilding (with gold); gold with mercury; and an alloy of copper and zinc.[30]

This teapot form, identified in the Meissen inventories as a *Chinesisches Exportmodell* (Chinese export model),[31] was inspired by a Chinese model but adapted to a German aesthetic and sense of design. Its molded swags, enhanced by gilded tassels and drapery, can be seen on Saxon silver of the period. The hexagonal form of the teapot was press-molded in sections and then luted together. A single (interior) pouring hole may be seen where the spout connects to the body—a characteristic found in all red-stoneware teapots. The rich, thick black glaze also covers the base. Patches of thin gray-black glaze may be seen on the base, possibly where the pot was held in the sagger. Under magnification, scratches and fissures may be seen overall, as well as a few minute bare patches, especially on the footrim, where the glaze did not take. Upon close inspection, one can see where the gilding and lacquer colors have been rubbed by wear. The gilding and red enamel survived the best, but the brown and iridescent emerald green of the lambrequin design on the shoulder has rubbed off or deteriorated.

COLLECTOR'S STORY: TEAPOT

2001 was a banner year for me; pieces just seemed to fall into place in my cabinets, sometimes quite fortuitously. This was one of them. In January I had purchased a magnificent and highly important blue-and-white vase (cat. no. 36/pl. 24). I also looked forward to traveling to New York, where Sotheby's was offering the remnants of Martha Isaacson's great collection; a great and rare *Böttgersteinzeug* dish was first on my go-after list. In addition, Colonial Williamsburg had deaccessioned an equally rare Böttger white porcelain teapot, and the sale was some months away.

One Friday night in April, I perused the latest issue of the English trade rag *Antiques Trade Gazette*. My eyes suddenly lit upon a full-page advertisement for a single-owner sale of more than two thousand miniature pottery and porcelain teapots. They had been amassed since the 1960s by a lawyer named Joseph Jackson. A habitué of London's Portobello Road market, he almost always left the market on Saturday mornings with teapots filling the many pockets of his jacket. After his death in 1975, his wife boxed them up, and they remained for his daughter to consign to an auction house, Law Fine Art, at the time completely unknown to me. The sale was to be held April 24. Among thirty mostly English examples featured in the ad, a photo showed a Böttger piece, identified as such and estimated at £2,500–3,500. My reaction to this serendipitous discovery was mixed: on the one hand, my wonderment at this very rare teapot—likely the real thing—popping out of the woodwork; on the other, needing my checkbook once more at the ready. The teapot was similar to one of my all-time favorites (and frustrations), the *Böttgersteinzeug* example sold at Sotheby's, London, in 1975.

Here is when a rich library of books and catalogues is indispensable to a collector. My instinct induced me to paw through some of my old catalogues, and by the next day I had discovered the sale at which Jackson had purchased the pot (Sotheby's, London, July 8, 1969). An introductory call to Law Fine Art the following Monday morning provided the confidence to set up a phone bid. It was in good condition, with only a bad repair to part of the cover finial and a minor chip to the tip of the spout. Some rubbing (wear) had also occurred to the gilding and lacquer colors. One more thing: I phoned dealer and friend Errol Manners in London, knowing he—probably only he—would have seen the advertisement. Sure enough, he knew about the teapot and was planning a brief reconnoiter to Berkshire to examine it, figuring that, among two thousand teapots, there might be another diamond or two. Knowing that I was going

after it, he relinquished active interest, but happily agreed to give it a once-over for me.

On the day of the auction, Nicholas Lyne, one of the partners of the auction house, made the early morning call to me; the teapot was knocked down to me at an incredible £2,900. It turns out none of the German trade or other Meissen collectors had learned of the sale, my underbidder being a member of the English trade. Evidently—even though Law Fine Art had adequately catalogued it and its provenance—the piece was so unusual that nonspecialists shied away. An added element of delight and charm: Nick confided he had allowed Jackson's nine-year-old grandson, sitting next to him, to execute my bid by raising his hand after a prompting squeeze. The boy was ecstatic when he "won."

—MALCOLM GUTTER

10 MOUNTED TANKARD (*WALZENKRUG*)

ca. 1710–1713
Polished red stoneware with gilding and pewter mounts
9 ⅞ × 5 ⅛ in. (25 × 13 cm); height without cover: 7 ⅝ in. (19.5 cm)
L13.62.12 (CAT. NO. 10)

•

Throughout the relatively short period of red-stoneware production, Meissen continued to experiment with its possibilities. Böttger red stoneware can be divided into four ware types: matte, polished, black-glazed, and *Eisenporzellan*.[32] Some of these polished stonewares, termed *Jaspisporzellan* (jasper porcelain), simulate natural materials such as unpolished red stone, porphyry, slate, and marble. The unique marble-like appearance on the body of this tankard was achieved through the use of variegated clays. Gutter has identified fifteen known Meissen vessels with such marbled bodies—eleven of which are tankards—making this piece exceedingly rare. All but one of the tankards mounted in the eighteenth century have pewter mounts.

This tankard is composed of predominantly red-hued clays, but other examples display a range of clay colors from cream to yellow and dark brown. The varied compositions of these wares proved difficult to produce, "as the differing degrees of hardness of the light-coloured and dark-coloured paste made reworking by means of grinding and polishing extremely difficult. But without polishing, the marbleized surface does not really come into its own."[33] The outer surface of the Gutter tankard has been polished to a high shine, enhancing its marble-like appearance; however, the unpolished inner surface reveals another, more natural character of the body.

The tankard is engraved on the side with a shield-shaped emblem surmounted by a coronet. Enclosed in the emblem is a rampant lion below the Latin motto "audaces juvat" (brave are the bold). The same emblem can be found on another pewter-mounted tankard in the Staatliches Museum Schloss Schwerin, Mecklenburg-Vorpommern. The Gutter tankard is slightly taller and tapering in shape than the Schloss Schwerin example, and, although the motto appears to be by the same hand, the first letter, *A*, is capitalized on the latter tankard but is lowercase on the former. There also appear to be some slight differences to the pewter mounts. It is indeed difficult to determine if the engravings were done contemporaneously with the tankards' production.[34] It is also uncertain if such highly decorated tankards were used. Many red-stoneware tankards were produced at Meissen, as grain-based beer and ale was a common beverage drunk throughout the day, and numerous examples survive in the collections of the Porzellansammlung, Dresden.

COLLECTOR'S STORY: MOUNTED TANKARD

The story begins in late March 2012, when I received an email from a friend that included a link to a provincial—and yet unknown to me—Hanover auction house, HannoVerum. A tankard was to be sold there in a fortnight, and my brain was being picked regarding its authenticity. Ordinarily I shy away from such queries, especially when there is the potential for competition. However, when I opened the link, all defenses dropped. What to do? Yes, this tankard was authentic; it was also one of my holy grails. The friend was not himself a collector of early Meissen but was inquiring on behalf of another friend, so I would not be competing against him directly. An added and powerful inducement of confusion for a potential buyer: the tankard, dated late eighteenth century, was estimated a low €170–190! One of Meissen's true rarities and offered practically as junk. I decided to go for it, knowing if it had fetched a low price and I had demurred I'd never forgive myself, and if it tore the house down, at least I had been in the game. So as not to lose the friend, I enlisted another to bid on my behalf, my offering up to €20,000.

The tankard proved, as it turned out, to be no wallflower. It had not gone unnoticed, fetching €26,500. (My bidder had gone to €24,000.) But for whom did success shine? Six months later, while perusing the online preview of coming attractions for the ceramics sale at Antiquitäten Metz, the Heidelberg auction house, the tankard caught my eye; the estimate now €40,000—what I would have expected. The Metz brothers had paid (including premium) approximately €31,000; apparently German law allows an auction business to bid at other sales and reoffer properties.

I phoned Mike Metz, a colleague and one of the two principals, requesting a catalogue, a condition report, and photos. Just prior to the sale, I requested a phone bid for the lot, this time resolving the fish would not get away (would I dare to go to €60,000?). Around 2:45 a.m. on December 1, my phone rang: "Your lot. It's now at €38,000." In the next second, the hammer came down at that price. Shockingly good fortune: I was apparently the sole bidder. The Metz sale, in fact, was a rather important one, and included pieces belonging to the

Hoffmeister brothers that went unsold from the three sales in 2009 and 2010 at Bonhams, London.

A final tantalizing and mysterious question: who originally consigned the tankard to the Hanover salesroom? Probably he or she and HannoVerum were unaware of its value and importance as a masterpiece. It was another case of an important work of art coming out of the woodwork.

—MALCOLM GUTTER

COLLECTOR'S STORY: TEAPOT

In the summer of 1995, I was approached by a relatively recent appointee of Bonhams auction house in London, Jane Brown. She had recently acquired for her forthcoming November British and Continental porcelain and pottery sale a rare Böttger stoneware miniature teapot (see p. 22 for alternate view). Would I like to come over to Montpelier Street, Knightsbridge, to examine it? Excited, I made an appointment for the following week. Ushered into the storage section of the building, I sat in front of a table upon which this little vessel was placed. A masterpiece of Baroque sculpture, I was dazzled by its diminutive size yet crisp detail, as well as its contrasting and variegated polished red and black hues. However, an unusual, and not particularly attractive, metallic brown glaze on parts of the pot, distracted—and detracted—from its otherwise amazing beauty. I nevertheless left Bonhams determined that it would go into my collection: a very rare thing (I count only eleven in existence), a real prize.

How had she obtained this phenomenal object? To quote from a notice in the *Antiques Trade Gazette* following the sale, the pot "came from a private source and was discovered by the auctioneers' representative at a Buckinghamshire valuation day. The vendor, who used it for her dolls' tea parties when she was a child, reckoned it had been in her family for at least one hundred and fifty years, possibly coming via an ancestor who was a tea trader." In order to protect my anonymity, I enlisted my dealer friend Errol Manners to bid on my behalf, mindful of potential competitors in London and in Germany. Alas, the day before the sale, I received a disconcerting phone call from Errol, informing me that he had just been enlisted to bid on behalf of another client, who would go considerably higher than my bid, thus precluding any success on my part. Severely disappointed, I swallowed my pride but went on with my collecting life.

Sources later identified Marjorie West of Atlanta as the high bidder. I met her a few times over the years, at American Ceramic Circle symposia and at antiques fairs, but we never became close porcelain friends. I had known, however, that she had a wonderful collection of Meissen and other Continental porcelains. In 2011 fortune presented the opportunity of seeing her collection, as the American Ceramic Circle was to hold its

annual meeting in nearby Birmingham. Rather than flying directly to Alabama, I decided to go through Atlanta; my close friend Jody Wilkie, head of Christie's Continental ceramics department, arranged a visit to West's home. Already at an advanced age, West was nevertheless most gracious, giving me carte blanche to examine and photograph any and all pieces. She passed away in the autumn of 2016, alas without arranging for dispersal of the collection. Her children decided to divide it between museum gift and public auction sale; Christie's, New York, was chosen as the purveyor.

The auction was slated for October 2017. Should I go back to New York City, preview the sale of about eighty pieces, and then stay for the fireworks? I decided to stay at home and bid by telephone, having already examined and photographed the pieces during the 2011 visit. I put four of her pieces on my wish list. After twenty-two years, this teapot ranked as the top priority, beckoning me with a second chance to enter my collection.

The porcelain part of the sale commenced with lot 713; happily, lot 715, a delicious Böttger stoneware scent flask (cat.

no. 14; see p. 223), was an early winner for me—a good omen. Two lots later, the little teapot was on. Having worked myself into a frenzied state, I entered the bidding—the $50,000 level already reached. $55,000, my bid, was countered by $60,000. $65,000: a very long and extended silence was finally ended with the not-to-be-believed sound of the hammer coming down in my favor. Ecstasy propelled me into securing my other two lots from West's collection, topped off by a superb and documentary dish from another collection at the same sale. I soon boarded the plane to New York to collect my trophies, chest expanded and head held high in triumph.

—MALCOLM GUTTER

CHAPTER 2

EARLY WHITE BÖTTGER PORCELAIN

Ehrenfried Walther von Tschirnhaus and Johann Friedrich Böttger's efforts achieved a white, hard-paste porcelain by 1708. Following his mentor's death that same year, Böttger eventually developed a usable glaze and presented his findings to the king in 1709.[1] By 1713 Böttger's ongoing experiments finally produced a commercially viable white porcelain. A mixture of kaolin (china clay) and gypsum (alabaster, or hydrated calcium sulfate) fired at 1,350 to 1,400 degrees centigrade, the new composition and higher firing temperature produced a hard-paste porcelain with the translucency and strength found in the much-coveted pieces from Asia. Unlike Asian porcelain—which is composed of china clay (kaolin) and china stone (petuntze, a mixture of quartz, feldspar, and mica)—Böttger and Tschirnhaus's earliest experiments used gypsum in lieu of china stone. Their use of kaolin allowed the composition to be considered as hard-paste porcelain, albeit a hybrid one. It has a relatively high lime content (calcium oxide) and little potassium (potassium oxide) unlike the "true" hard-paste porcelain produced in Asia and later at Meissen. Termed *Kalkporzellan* (chalky or lime porcelain), its chemical composition fluoresces pale pink-white under an ultraviolet, or short-wave, lamp, whereas a feldspathic paste fluoresces pale violet. By 1720 Meissen developed a feldspathic paste that yielded a brighter white body with even greater translucency (see chapter 4).

Through Meissen, Augustus II had finally achieved the pure white porcelain coveted and imitated throughout the West for five hundred years. This discovery led to a great period of experimentation at the manufactory. In addition to working out the clay formulation, Böttger also recognized the limitations of the kilns at Albrechtsburg as early as 1711. In order to increase the scale of objects produced, they would need to introduce new kilns.[2] White porcelain samples were first shown by Meissen at the Leipzig Easter Fair in 1713; however, red stoneware was still offered in great number in the fall of that year. In fact, according to Dawson, "no fewer than 70,200 [red-stoneware] pipes were delivered to the 1713 Michaelmas Fair."[3]

Wassermann teapot, ca. 1719–1720
(cat. no. 18/pl. 15)

FIG. 10 Two-handled chocolate beaker and saucer
with applied rose sprays, ca. 1718–1721 (cat. no. 19)

Meissen's earliest white porcelain boldly showcases its brilliant white quality, albeit with a few irregularities and firing flaws. Early experiments in decoration and gilding were commissioned by Meissen from artists and gilders in Dresden and Augsburg. Many of these workshops employed distinctive decorative styles, motifs, and palettes, such as those used by the Dresden workshop of Johann Georg Funcke (active 1692–1727). Chapter 3 will explore the Funcke workshop and *Hausmaler* (home or independent painters) in greater detail. The manufactory took back control of its entire production once the painter Johann Gregorius Höroldt (1696–1775) was employed by Meissen in 1720. The warm tones of the early *Kalkporzellan* were an ideal palette for Höroldt's brilliant early chinoiseries and landscapes (see chapter 5).

11 PAIR OF SINGLE-HANDLED BEAKERS

ca. 1709–1713

Decoration by Johann Georg Funcke, ca. 1718–1720

Hard-paste porcelain

3 × 2 ½ in. (7.5 × 6.2 cm) and 2 ¾ × 2 ⅜ in. (7.1 × 6.1 cm)

L13.62.24.1–2 (CAT. NO. 16)

•

These beakers are among the earliest hard-paste porcelain pieces produced in Europe. Comparable beakers can be found only in the Porzellansammlung, Dresden; the Bayerisches Nationalmuseum, Munich; and the Schlossmuseum Arnstadt. Several clues point to their early manufacture at Meissen, including their unique grayish paste and experimental irregularities of form and composition. The first deposit of clay with kaolin used by Meissen was from Colditz; it was satisfactory but produced a slightly smoky cast to the wares. In 1710–1711 a superior clay deposit was discovered at Aue, near Schneeberg. Both clays were used in combination until 1717, at which date clay sourced from Aue was used exclusively until the middle of the nineteenth century.[4]

The beakers also display various irregularities in their potting, paste, and glaze. Imperfections in the paste produced air bubbles erupting through the glaze on both pieces. The glaze of one beaker (L13.62.24.1; pictured here on the right) also exhibits a great number of minute black particles and suffered from a major firing crack, most visible from the interior. Unlike their Asian prototypes, these beakers have simple molded and applied strap handles (see p. 61 for alternate view). They were luted on in somewhat irregular positions.

The numerous imperfections of these beakers are telltale clues to the highly developmental nature of early Meissen wares. Gutter suggests that the experimental, and therefore imperfect, nature of these beakers made them undesirable for sale or presentation to the court. They were therefore shelved and later sent upriver to Dresden, around 1718–1720, to be decorated by the Funcke workshop.[5] In his characteristic style, Funcke decorated each beaker with a single gilt chinoiserie scene outlined in iron-red enamel. The placement of the scenes varies on the two works. One beaker charmingly depicts a steatopygic figure crouched in the grass pointing to a snake, but the scene extends nearly to the rim of the beaker while a lone insect punctuates the lower, empty third, possibly obscuring some kiln dirt or an imperfection. The fisherman scene with a thatch-roofed brick house on the second beaker is more harmoniously placed.

Meissen scholar Maureen Cassidy-Geiger has identified a pattern book for lacquers by Paul Decker (1677–1713) as a print source for some of the Funcke, and later Höroldt, chinoiserie scenes for Meissen.[6] The Nuremberg artist certainly inspired Funcke with his contemporary print source; however, these beakers could also have been based on German, English, or Dutch japanning (a technique for imitating Japanese lacquer and surface ornament) on late seventeenth- and early eighteenth-century furniture.

COLLECTOR'S STORY: SINGLE-HANDLED BEAKERS

The eminent English porcelain collector and scholar Geoffrey Godden once lamented, "The bargains you most regret are the ones that got away." The background to the acquisition of these extraordinary objects fits this sentiment quite well. In 1976 I had the opportunity to purchase a very early and exquisite Böttger porcelain beaker for £650. It had been left unsold from a 1975 sale of white porcelain Robert Williams held. I had demurred from the purchase due to financial considerations; the beaker is now in the British Museum. It would remain my number one piece-that-got-away for thirty-four years.

Fast-forward to early July 2009. In storage in the Bayerisches Nationalmuseum, Munich, I spied a remarkably early Böttger porcelain beaker; it was poorly fired, reflecting its experimental nature, as well as thinly potted and highly translucent. I was bowled over by its numerous potting and firing flaws, including countless embedded particles and the profuse volcanic-like eruptions of its glaze. This beautiful object—the imperfections only enhancing to my eye—represented stage one in the history of Western hard-paste porcelain. In July—perhaps presciently—I enthusiastically sent a photograph of the beaker to Errol Manners in London as a stump-the-expert exercise.

In early May 2010, I found myself in Europe again, this time at the beginning of a two-month sojourn to celebrate Meissen's jubilee in Dresden and to attend the London fairs and sales—especially part two of the Hoffmeisters' collection sale at Bonhams; I also assisted Errol in packing for the Haughton Ceramics Fair. En passant I made a quip about the Hoffmeisters' Funcke-decorated Böttger beaker not being auctioned days earlier—Sebastian Kuhn deciding instead to put it up with the final (third) part of the collection in November. To this Errol replied, "Come downstairs, I want to show you something." With me dutifully following, he opened his secret—usually pregnant—chest drawer, revealing one bubble-wrapped parcel, then another. Out popped these breathtaking beakers—their form identical to that in Munich, replete with similar, thrilling flaws. A minute's examination pointed up their contrasts, but I was still unable to choose a favorite, realizing part of the excitement was in "playing" one against the other. I should have both—and at any price.

The beakers had been included in the second part of the sale of the Mario Leproni collection at Sotheby's the previous November; they had been miscatalogued and were embedded

in a lot of seven Doccia porcelain beakers, circa 1750–1760. I—as others, of course—had seen the lot in the catalogue. As all beakers were photographed "face on"—their decoration facing the reader—they looked identical in form, telltale handles hidden. (Truth to tell, to any but acutely astute on-site previewers, these gilded Böttger beakers could quite easily have been mistaken for the lot's accompanying grayish-paste and "similarly" gilded Doccia cups and saucers.)

Errol initially would give me only right of first refusal; he had not firmly decided how to handle his extraordinary prizes—and what price to ask for them. As for me: three angst-ridden weeks. How would it turn out? On the Thursday before my flight back to San Francisco, the subject was broached: "Errol, I'd like to carry the beakers home; I don't trust their being shipped." A lovely response: "Yes, do so . . . let's discuss price; I have to have £16,000." Sigh of relief, having feared a far more complicated, financially painful transfer. Sheepishly but quickly, I asked, "How about £15,000?" Sealed. A moment later, Errol replied, "Malcolm, these beakers really do belong in your collection; and I'm so happy they have remained together." My thought while writing the check: this has been a bargain concluded with a

truly fair and noble friend and colleague. On Friday I dropped by to collect the treasures; the Böttger beaker that had gotten away so many years before had been reincarnated as equally beautiful twins.

A follow-up: In mid-July I received news from Sebastian Kuhn through Errol of an incredible find pertaining to the beakers. Kuhn, while perusing some recently acquired old catalogues, had discovered five beakers sold in 1911 at Hugo Helbing, Munich—three of which were pictured, one "ours"—that were catalogued as early Vienna (Du Paquier). They had been part of a foreign (outside Germany) nobleman's collection; the two beakers had indeed been part of a larger set, filling a major piece of the provenance puzzle.

—MALCOLM GUTTER

12 INCENSE BURNER

ca. 1710–1713
Red stoneware
Height: 3⅞ in. (9.7 cm)
L17.46.1 (CAT. NO. 13)

·

13 INCENSE BURNER

ca. 1718–1720
Hard-paste porcelain
4⅛ × 2⅞ × 2⅝ in. (10.4 × 7.4 × 6.6 cm)
L13.62.13 (CAT. NO. 17)

·

14 INCENSE BURNER

ca. 1715–1717
Enameling by Johann Georg Funcke
Hard-paste porcelain
Height: 3⅞ in. (9.7 cm)
L17.46.3 (CAT. NO. 33)

·

These charming seated figures inspired by Chinese prototypes were used as incense burners. The open mouth and pierced ears provide clues to their purpose. No exact model is known in Chinese porcelain; however, Meissen modelers may have been inspired by Chinese soapstone examples. Like other chinoiserie decorations, these Oriental figures are seen through a Western filter. Gutter has identified a similar seated figure in the engraving *Chinese Idols* illustrating Thomas Salmon's (1679–1767) *Modern History: or, the Present State of All Nations* (1724–1739; fig. 11), but a similar contemporary print source could have provided the inspiration for Meissen's model.

FIG. 11 Detail of *Chinese Idols*, illustration in Thomas Salmon's *Modern History: or, the Present State of all Nations* (London: Bettesworth & Hitch, 1759)

These Buddha figures—often and misleadingly referred to as "pagodas," following their identification as such in the Japanese Palace inventory—were initially produced in red stoneware and later adapted in white porcelain. Occasionally the same molds were used. These incense burners were press-molded in two or possibly three (in the case of the red-stoneware version) parts. The seam line is still visible on the back of the red-stoneware and undecorated porcelain figures' heads. The model may be attributed to the Dresden court sculptor Johann Benjamin Thomae (1682–1751). All three figures exhibit particularly fine modeling, as seen in the detailing of the teeth, hands, and feet.

Ten red-stoneware figures are included in the Japanese Palace inventory under N=180/R. All ten have been identified by Gutter; three are matte stoneware, and seven are *Eisenporzellan*.[7] The white porcelain model was produced at Meissen with several variations in scale and decoration well into the 1720s. A similar incense burner in the Arnhold collection depicts the seated figure surrounded by various tewares.[8] Many of these figures were listed in the Japanese Palace inventory. One of these entries, for N=220/w, reads, "Acht und Dreyssig Stück detto (Pagoden), differenter Grösze, No. 220" (thirty-eight pieces [pagodas], different sizes).[9]

Meissen also produced a related figure, as seen in the Gutter collection (cat. no. 33/pl. 14), further enhanced by enamels. The enamel colors and decorative motifs on this figure as well as its distinctive and liberal use of luster suggest a rare attribution to Johann Georg Funcke. Funcke and his workshop provided decoration and gilding on various wares for the Meissen manufactory, but almost no figures survive.[10]

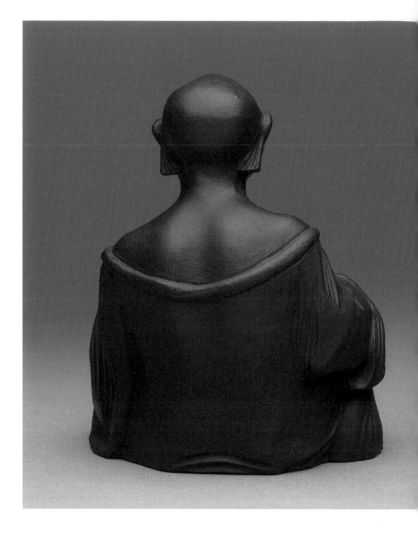

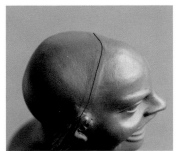

FIG. 12 Detail of T-shaped mold seam lines on head of red-stoneware figure

FIG. 13 Line following mold seam along the ear of red-stoneware figure

FIG. 14 Line following mold seam behind the ear of undecorated porcelain figure. Note the different proportions: the front of the head (distance from ear to forehead) is much longer in this figure than the red-stoneware figure (fig. 13)

COLLECTOR'S STORY: INCENSE BURNERS

The idea of assembling this wonderful and rare collection of sculpture for the collection started with my 2016 acquisition of the Funcke-decorated incense burner (cat. no. 33/pl. 14). When it joined a superb white porcelain example already in the collection (cat. no. 17/pl. 13), thoughts turned to the possibility of making the trifecta: completing the group with one of Böttger red stoneware would be unmatched. I did, in fact, have knowledge of a superb example still in private hands. It had been sold at Christie's, London, in 2004, adding to its rarity a royal provenance. The figure—elegantly detailed, beautifully chiseled, and typically idiosyncratic, as was each sculptural object in this early period of Meissen's development—had been sold from the Dresden royal collection at the first *Dubletten* (duplicate) sale in Berlin in 1919; it had been purchased by collector Ole Olsen, and was now on offer by an anonymous consignor. As a complement to my white porcelain example it had at that time

intrigued me; I went so far as to request a condition report. Estimated at £8,000–12,000, its hammer price proved beyond my pocketbook: £26,000. With buyer's premium that summed to more than £31,000, or $60,000! So there I was: the possessor of two superb paradigms of Böttger porcelain incense burners, the lacuna a stoneware example known to me with an impeccable provenance.

In October 2016, in connection with the European Fine Art Fair (TEFAF) New York art and antiques show—complemented by a symposium at the Frick Collection—I broached the subject of acquiring the piece privately with staff from Christie's. The discussion continued the following week during the American Ceramic Circle meeting/symposium in Hartford, Connecticut. Happily the prognostication expressed by my friends at Christie's was upbeat: nothing is impossible, let's give it a try. Negotiations had to be orchestrated with the utmost

delicacy and intricacy—as pride and my relationship were at stake. If the owners knew the identity of the buyer, would they even think of selling?

In mid-November I received an eye-popping email from Christie's Dominic Simpson. "Malcolm, I received a positive response; they will accept £55,000." Could I believe it, so soon a communication? Their willingness to sell was surprising on its face; at an actual in-the-ballpark price was even more reassuring. Encouraged, we began negotiations and quickly settled. With a hunter's pride, I had now achieved a remarkable goal: deepening and strengthening my collection with three superb versions of Meissen incense burners, each representing apogees of their form and decoration.

—MALCOLM GUTTER

15 *WASSERMANN* TEAPOT

ca. 1719–1720

Hard-paste porcelain

6¼ × 6¾ in. (16 × 17.3 cm)

L13.62.18A–B (CAT. NO. 18)

•

When first recorded by Meissen in 1722, this fantastic anthropomorphic or "grotesque" teapot was identified as *Wassermann* (water man).[11] Arguably conceived as a cabinet piece and not a functional ware, it features a helmeted old man standing upon a scallop shell and grasping a dolphin, which forms the spout (see p. 54 for alternate view). The teapot is completed by a handle composed of an atlantid hemi-figure supporting a female satyr on his shoulders, and the cover takes the shape of the man's helmet, surmounted by a frog. The model was inspired by various sources including Françoise Bouzonnet's (1638–1691) engravings in *Livre de vases* (Paris, 1657), a compilation of design illustrations conceived by Jacques Stella (1596–1657) (fig. 15). Cassidy-Geiger has also recognized the possible influence of Jean Le Pautre's (1618–1682) series of vase engravings, *Vases d'ornement* (Paris, seventeenth century).[12]

Until the late twentieth century, this model was attributed to Johann Gottlieb Kirchner (1706–after 1737). In his article on the work reports of turners and formers at Meissen from June 1722 to December 1728, Boltz cites evidence that numerous *Wassermann* teapots were produced during this period, prior to the arrival of Kirchner at the factory.[13] It is now suggested that Irminger played a part in the *Wassermann* teapot's design.[14] Furthermore, the paste of this teapot is of the earlier Böttger *Kalkporzellan*, not the later feldspathic paste found later in the 1720s.

The *Wassermann* model is found in numerous public and private collections; however, there are many variations in modeling and decoration. Two of these teapots in the Porzellansammlung, Dresden, bear the Japanese Palace inventory number N=442/w. A highly decorated and gilded example is in the Arnhold collection.[15] The Gutter example is quite experimental in nature. The body was clearly but erratically press-molded in quadrants, with visible seams on the sides, luted together and then glazed. The handle and spout were applied in a similarly idiosyncratic manner. The spout has a single interior pouring hole. This example has particularly fine, hand-finished features in the old man's face. Characteristic of early Böttger porcelain, there are some eruptions or bubbles visible through the glaze. The helmet cover is a later replacement.

FIG. 15 Plate 17 from Françoise Bouzonnet's *Livre de vases* (Paris, 1657). Rijksmuseum, Amsterdam, RP-P-OB-8728

CHAPTER 3

HAUSMALER- AND FUNCKE-DECORATED MEISSEN PORCELAIN

The demand for decorated Meissen porcelain created a market for independent enamelers, known as *Hausmaler* (home painters). These artisans would purchase blank, white wares and enhance them with gilt and enamel decoration before reselling them. Particular *Hausmaler* were in special favor with the Meissen manufactory, and in some cases their work can be identified based on stylistic acumen or even pigments used. Furthermore, the Augsburg goldsmith workshop of the Seuter brothers, Bartholomäus (1678–1754) and Abraham (1689–1747), provided much gilding and some metal mounts for Meissen from 1722 to 1746.

Distinctive enamel decoration and gilding was also produced by Johann Georg Funcke's Dresden workshop for Meissen. Technically not considered a *Hausmaler* but more an extension of the factory, the goldsmith Funcke had a close relationship with Meissen and was recorded as an enamel decorator as early as 1710. By 1713, his work included gilt decorations. Per this arrangement, Funcke's workshop would receive pieces for decoration or gilding directly from Meissen. Following firing in a muffle kiln, they were then returned, downriver, to Meissen. His workshop's enamels are characterized by a soft pastel color palette and were not particularly durable.

Funcke's decoration is very different from the bright, luminous enamels coming from Johann Gregorius Höroldt (see chapter 5). After Höroldt arrived at Meissen in 1720 from Vienna's Du Paquier manufactory (1718–1744), along with former Meissen employee Samuel Stöltzel (1685–1737), the outsourcing to Funcke sharply declined. By 1725, Stöltzel and Höroldt were able to produce a number of durable enamel colors such as iron red, puce, black, yellow green, sepia, capuchin brown, and gray blue as well as a satisfactory gold. This work was also continued by Thuringian enamel artist and gilder Christoph Conrad Hunger (1717–1748) after his own return to Meissen in 1727. (Nearly concurrent with Funcke's work for Meissen, Hunger had been supplying the gilt decoration for the newly established [and competing] Du Paquier Porcelain manufactory.[1])

The relationship between Meissen and the Funcke workshop ended with Funcke's death in 1727. As the manufactory was no longer dependent on the *Hausmaler* for decoration and gilding, Meissen ended the sale of undecorated porcelain to independent painters by the 1730s.

Silvered cup and saucer, porcelain 1713–1715, silvered decoration by Johann Georg Funcke, ca. 1715 (cat. no. 32)

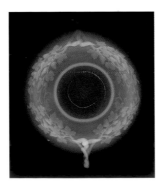

FIG. 16 X-radiograph of waste
bowl (parameters 50 kV, 5 mA,
30 seconds)

CONSERVATION NOTE

The two blue curved branches at the base of the bowl's interior cleverly disguise two firing cracks. The cracks are visible in an X-radiograph (fig. 16) as two bright white semicircular lines in the center. A repaired handle is also distinguishable at the top as being less dense—that is, not as radiopaque—as the rest of the ceramic body, including the other handle.

The overglaze enamels were generally applied with a brush. However, in the case of all of the red flowers, a finger was used to adjust their appearance (see figs. 17 and 18). The placement of the leaves, red flowers, grass, and large flower at the end of the branch were all outlined first with a thin black line. The small bright pink and blue flowers, in contrast, were done freehand, with no outlines to guide their placement. —COLLEEN O'SHEA

16 TWO-HANDLED WASTE BOWL (*SPÜLKUMME*) WITH APPLIED GRAPEVINES

ca. 1715–1720
Enameling by Johann Georg Funcke
Hard-paste porcelain
4 × 8 ¾ in. (10.2 × 22.4 cm)
L13.62.14 (CAT. NO. 23)

•

This *Spülkumme* (waste bowl, used for waste tea or tea leaves) is decorated on the outside with applied grapevines that continue on to form the naturalistic, plaited-vine handles. The 1719 inventory describes two similar waste bowls but decorated with the more common sprays of flowering roses.[2] An early white porcelain teapot and lidded vase in the Wark collection are similarly decorated, with the unusual grapevines and clusters of grapes and a naturalistic handle and knop.[3] Gutter has suggested that the Wark teapot may have been part of a tea service along with this waste bowl.

The painted decoration inside this bowl (see fig. 19), cleverly disguising a firing crack, is the work of Funcke. Certain decorative motifs, such as the four-petaled flowers, or milkwort, and distinctive leaves are characteristic of his workshop. These devices are frequently applied to the inside or underside of his bowls or cups (see also cat. no. 25/pl. 18). Painted in the workshop's distinctive palette of green, blue, black, yellow, dark magenta, and rose, the enameled flowering plant provides clues in dating this piece. All of Funcke's early green enamels exhibit numerous black flecks under magnification. Lesley Bone, former head objects conservator at the Fine Arts Museums of San Francisco, proposes that the black particles are poorly ground copper-oxide particles that clump or blotch together (see also cat. no. 27/pl. 20).

The waste bowl was wheel-thrown, and the handles and decoration were applied prior to glazing. Some warping to the bowl occurred during firing, and one handle has been replaced.

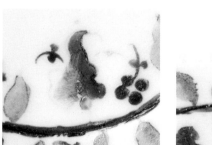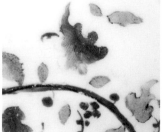

FIGS. 17 AND 18 Details of finger marks in red flowers

FIG. 19 ABOVE Detail of interior of waste bowl

17 BEAKER VASE

ca. 1715–1720
Gilding by Johann Georg Funcke or the Augsburg workshop
of Bartholomäus Seuter
Hard-paste porcelain
5¼ × 4 in. (13.4 × 10.3 cm)
L13.62.48 (CAT. NO. 24)

•

The lacelike gilt ornamental border (*Goldspitze*) inside and outside the slightly flaring rim of this cylindrical beaker is suggestive
of work done by Funcke. The form was first produced in Böttger
red stoneware and adopted in white porcelain circa 1713. The vase,
here decorated with applied grapevines and two female masks, was
produced in various sizes with different surface and applied decorations. Some examples of this beaker vase are enameled and gilded
while others, such as Gutter's, are only gilded, but the decorative
patterns can provide clues to pairings. Gutter believes that the
number of pairs, or near pairs, suggests that these beakers were
likely intended for display as part of a garniture.[4]

The modeling of the original form is attributed to the Dresden
court goldsmith Johann Jakob Irminger; however, he was certainly
inspired by Baroque silver and related contemporary architecture.
Numerous related atlantes (male figures) can be seen on the facade
of the Zwinger, Augustus II's palace in Dresden (see especially the
atlantes on the Zwinger's Wall Pavilion, fig. 20). The Zwinger was
built between 1710 and 1728 by court architect Matthäus Daniel
Pöppelmann (1662–1736) in collaboration with Dresden sculptor
Balthasar Permoser (1651–1732). Permoser provided figural models
to the Meissen manufactory as early as 1710.

FIG. 20 Atlantes by Balthasar Permoser on the Wall
Pavilion, Zwinger palace, Dresden

18 TWO-HANDLED CHOCOLATE BEAKER

ca. 1717
Enameling and gilding by Johann Georg Funcke
Hard-paste porcelain
3⅛ × 3 in. (7.8 × 7.5 cm)
L13.62.22 (CAT. NO. 25)

•

Meissen produced this chocolate cup with Chinese-inspired, ear-shaped handles in white porcelain as well as red stoneware (see cat. no. and pl. 5). The style and composition of the enamel and gilt decorations all suggest Funcke's hand. Furthermore, the interlaced ornament of foliate strapwork (*Laub- und Bandelwerk*) and a small quatrefoil flower, or milkwort, inside the cup (fig. 21) are motifs utilized by his workshop. Distinctive blue, green, and puce enamels were documented by Funcke's workshop by 1717 and can be seen on this beaker.

Also notable on the large leaves and flower heads is the lavender luster commonly referred to as Böttger luster. As a trained goldsmith, Funcke may have independently, or in collaboration with Böttger, developed it for Meissen. The luster, originally referred to as mother-of-pearl glaze, was made by covering already-glazed porcelain with a substance that Höroldt described in his 1731 handwritten book of recipes as a volatile gold compound. Factory manager Johann Melchior Steinbrück reported on the collaboration between Böttger, Funcke, and Johann Gottfried Mehlhorn (1671–1735) in developing the lustrous glaze.[5] Its formulation was passed down at Meissen and continued by Höroldt upon his arrival at the manufactory in 1720.

FIG. 21 Detail of milkwort at the bottom of the beaker's interior

19 TWO-HANDLED CHOCOLATE BEAKER

ca. 1718–1720
Gilding by Johann Georg Funcke
Hard-paste porcelain
3 × 2½ in. (7.3 × 6.5 cm)
L13.62.23 (CAT. NO. 26)

•

Equipped with two ear-shaped handles, this chocolate beaker features applied laurel-leaf decoration above the footrim. Its interior is entirely gilded, and its base, rim, and handles are further enhanced by gilding. The beaker is decorated with gilt birds on flowering branches, all lined in iron red (see fig. 22 for a teabowl and saucer in Gutter's collection with comparable iron-red outlines on birds and branches). Under magnification, it appears that the red enamel was applied prior to the gilding. Iron red was first introduced and billed to Meissen by Funcke's workshop in 1718. On the basis of invoices presented to the manufactory, Boltz has identified when certain colors were introduced by Funcke's workshop. These include purple, green, blue, and yellow (all 1715), followed by deep purple/puce (1717), black (1718), and red (1718).[6] Prior to 1719, many Meissen enamels can be attributed to Funcke; however, this all changed upon Höroldt's arrival in 1720 from Du Paquier.

Gutter has identified a probable pair to this beaker in the Ernst Schneider Collection, Schloss Lustheim (Bayerisches Nationalmuseum, Munich).

FIG. 22 Teabowl and saucer, ca. 1715, enameling and gilding by Johann Georg Funcke, ca. 1718–1720 (cat. no. 34)

20 TEAPOT

ca. 1718–1720
Enameling by Johann Georg Funcke
Hard-paste porcelain
4⅞ × 4⅜ in. (12.5 × 11 cm)
L13.62.21A–B (CAT. NO. 27)

•

First made at Meissen in red stoneware and in undecorated white porcelain,[7] this globular teapot with domed lid was enameled by Funcke. Irminger was responsible for the original design, which was influenced by shapes in silverware. The teapot is wheel-thrown, with a press-molded handle and spout. The spout has a single interior pouring hole. Variations of this teapot have different molded surface decorations, lid designs, and sizes. The Gutter teapot is decorated with molded rose and floral sprays at front and back as well as a tasseled lambrequin border along the top rim. A curved spout extends from a mask applied on the teapot body. The lid is further decorated with scattered florals and branches. All of the molded decorations are colored with the Funcke enamels of green, red, yellow, black, purple, and blue. The presence of black enamel, in use at Funcke's workshop by 1718, provides guidance for dating.[8] Also, characteristic to his green enamels, black particles are apparent in this teapot (see conservation essay, pp. 227–231).

In an unusual move, the enameling on the molded decoration extends, in a single sprig, beyond the raised areas to the porcelain body. Gutter has identified three other teapots with this characteristic: one with a ribbed, domed lid in the Schloss Favorite, Rastatt;[9] another from the ex-Oppenheimer collection;[10] and one in the Schneider collection, Schloss Lustheim. Like the Gutter teapot, the Schloss Lustheim example was from the Blohm collection.[11] This teapot was part of a partial tea service, which it was separated from shortly after their 1960 sale at auction.

FIG. 23 Detail of sprigged flowers on one side of teapot

FIG. 24 Detail of similar flowers painted directly on surface of other side of teapot

CONSERVATION NOTE
The teapot and cover were likely wheel-thrown, with the handle, knop, and spout added separately. The surfaces of both the teapot and cover are decorated with sprigged elements, or those applied to the main form with additional clay. The moldmade sprigs on this teapot form flowers, leaves, chevrons, tassels, and the head at the bottom of the spout, and are applied to the main surface with gentle pressure. They are recognizable as being slightly raised from the otherwise smooth surface. However, the sprigged elements are not quite the same on both sides. A branch of pink flowers is a sprigged component on one side (fig. 23), whereas a similar branch is painted directly on the teapot body on the other side (fig. 24). Perhaps the delicate molded flowers broke before they could be applied to the surface, or the artist simply forgot to make a second set. —COLLEEN O'SHEA

21 EAGLE TEAPOT (*ADLERKANNE*)

ca. 1720–1725
Gilding possibly by Augsburg workshop of Bartholomäus Seuter
Hard-paste porcelain
5¼ × 5⅛ in. (13.3 × 13 cm)
L13.62.50A–B (CAT. NO. 28)

•

One of Meissen's iconic models, this eagle-spout teapot's prototype was designed by Irminger and was originally produced in red stoneware. Some slight changes were made to the model's proportions as it was interpreted for porcelain. Variations can be seen in the roundness of the domed lid as well as the overall size of the teapot. The spout is composed of an eagle with outstretched wings, whereas other models feature only the eagle head. The domed lid with mushroom finial is connected by a silver gilt chain to an ear-shaped handle with a putto-head thumb rest.

The unusual *Goldchinesen* (gilded chinoiserie) scene depicts on one side a Renaissance clock, which was possibly modeled after an actual clock made by Augsburg's great clockmaker Hans J. Buschmann (after 1591–1662).[12] Buschmann was commissioned by the Holy Roman emperor Ferdinand III to produce a large clock, or *Türmchenuhr* (little tower clock), for the first Qing emperor of China, Shunzhi (r. 1644–1661). Missionaries delivered the clock to the emperor in 1655.[13] The chinoiserie scene on this teapot might be an imagined one referring to this historic occasion of East–West trade. The appearance of the Augsburg *Türmchenuhr* piece may also suggest an attribution to Bartholomäus Seuter's workshop in Augsburg.

The teapot body and cover are wheel-thrown, with a press-molded and applied handle and spout. The eighteenth-century silver gilt chain is a later replacement; however, the metal collars on the handle and knop appear to be original.

COLLECTOR'S STORY: EAGLE TEAPOT

Eagle teapots are among Meissen's grandest creations, a paragon of Baroque porcelain sculpture. Their appearance in stoneware represents one of the manufactory's clarion calls of excellence, rivaling high-fired ceramic ware from the Far East. As was true for most of the great forms in stoneware, it was translated into white porcelain sometime during the Böttger period. Although eagle-head spouts became during the 1720s one of the standard "organic" orifices for the manufactory's teapots—along with grimacing mask terminals and S-shaped faceted spouts—the full eagle treatment was and remains by far the rarest and most commanding. Such teapots are a signpost of importance in the psyche of Meissen collectors, and so it was with me. Only two examples had been offered at auction since the time of my plunge into Meissen in 1971: the yellow-ground *Hausmaler* specimen sold in 1982 from the Schnyder von Wartensee collection (now in the Wark collection), and one surfacing at Sotheby's, New York, in October 1994. It was frustration over that piece that truly sparked a passion for having one of my own.

I begin my story with the preview of the 1994 Sotheby's, New York, sale under Tish Roberts, which featured among many wonders an eagle teapot that had popped up from a Virginia source. Consigned with other *Goldchinesen* from the collection, the teapot nevertheless had no relation to them other than similar decoration, opening the way to it being offered as a single lot. Inquiries over the next several months about its being sold in a group or as a single piece elicited nothing but coyness; Tish had in fact fated it going to a dealer, who could thereupon break it up for a good profit. I hit upon the idea of calling Alfredo "Freddy" Reyes of Röbbig, Munich, the most likely interested party to make a deal. But he was very cool; in fact, he already had a client lined up, so I never heard from him again on the matter.

In April 1998 I was once more in New York, previewing upcoming sales when I ran into Michele Beiny, granddaughter of Hanns Weinberg, now dealing herself. Exchanging pleasantries, she ventured, "Anything you're looking for?" With a chuckle I came back, "Oh, an eagle teapot." Not missing a beat, she offered, "I just happen to have one." About a week later, I received pictures of the teapot—with a $75,000 price tag. I turned it down several weeks later.

Four weeks after that, I was in London for the antiques shows. On the afternoon of my arrival, I took a short walk to Phillips to see the upcoming sales. Pleasant surprise, the schedule board at the entrance stated a sale of Continental and English ceramics and glass to be held in two days, with previews going on that day and the following. I spied this teapot in a crowded case and examined it. But was the lid correct? Although it fit perfectly—well proportioned to the pot—the decoration conforming to the flange was different from that on the shoulder of the teapot, a necklace of arrowheads versus C-scrolls around the shoulder. Even if right, I had just spent almost $10,000 on my bird tankard (cat. no. 83/pl. 60); the teapot's estimate at £14,000–18,000 ($27,000–35,000) I knew to be ridiculously low. Ecstasy mitigated by ambiguity: uncertainty of its purity, as well

as financial constraints, I left the room and phoned Errol. He knew about the teapot and thought it was a great one, figuring it would fetch about £30,000. That evening I phoned Anton Gabszewicz: "Yes, I know about the teapot, and I think it has the wrong lid." This admonition I took quite seriously—so much so that he virtually talked me out of it. The next morning I spent a good half hour with it, the doubts nagging. The teapot was being sold the following afternoon, very soon into the session.

Talk about being a nervous wreck! The salesroom the next day was quite bare. I still didn't know what I would do (although I had written "to £28,000" beside the lot in the catalogue). After about fifteen minutes the teapot came up; curiously and significantly, nobody was on the phones. John Sandon, head of the department, started at £12,000; I immediately countered and continued to pursue, already in increments of £1,000. The conflict involved me against his commission bid, all the way up to £25,000. John looked at me, frozen with fear was I. I looked at the pot in the case—how could that cover be wrong? I nodded once more for £26,000—and the hammer came down.

What had I done? I had purchased a teapot with a wrong cover for $50,000! In a fit of buyer's remorse, I jumped up and caught the attention of Jo Marshall: "I'd like to rescind the sale." Alas, that evening Jo informed me John's decision was negative—the teapot was mine. For the next eleven days, I could not get myself to go near Phillips.

The "breakthrough" occurred some weeks later at the preview for the sale of the Herbert Wolfe collection at Bonhams,

Knightsbridge. The first several lots included Wolfe's library, including the seminal two-volume Siegfried Ducret study of Augsburg *Hausmalerei*. How it takes a crisis to focus one's attention on detail! While perusing the first volume, I began to see numerous examples—including the eagle teapot in Schwerin—with "mismatched" covers such as mine. I just had never noticed such minutiae. My heart soared to the heavens—my lid was right after all!

So who had provided John Sandon with the commission bid? It seems the grand master Bob Williams, "retired" in East Sussex, had learned of the teapot and contacted Marjorie West of Atlanta. He had been physically unable to come up to London to bid for her, hence the necessity for a commission bid—working in my favor as long as I was willing to top her "fixed" target. Days after its purchase, at a party for Lady Davson, which counted among its guests porcelain collectors, dealers, and experts, it became clear nobody had known of the teapot, accounting for the absence of phone calls at the sale. Sandon, it seems, had received it at the last minute, although in time to include a color photograph of it on the catalogue's back cover. However, no advertising was done for the piece, his great love always for English porcelain.

—MALCOLM GUTTER

22 TEAPOT

ca. 1725–1730; gilt decoration slightly later
Gilding probably by Augsburg workshop of
Bartholomäus Seuter
Hard-paste porcelain
5⅜ × 4½ in. (13.8 × 11.3 cm)
L13.62.47A–B (CAT. NO. 29)

•

Surmounted by a round knop finial, this pear-shaped teapot has a C-shaped handle and a domed lid. The curved spout erupts from a male mask (*Fratzenkopf*) on the teapot body. This model has some variations in size and subtle differences in shape, as seen in other pieces in the Gutter collection (see cat. no. 27/pl. 20 and cat. no. 64/pl. 47).

The diffused underglaze-blue rocks and birds decoration (*Fels und Vogeldekor*) lacks the clarity of some of the early pieces executed under metallurgist David Köhler's (ca. 1683–1723) tenure at Meissen.[14] The underglaze blue of this teapot is freely enhanced with an incongruous yet detailed *Goldchinesen*. Engraved details were achieved with an agate tool. Augsburg *Hausmaler* painted gold decoration on white Böttger porcelain as well as those ornamented in underglaze blue. The *Goldchinesen* is probably the work of Bartholomäus or Abraham Seuter of Augsburg.[15]

The gilded scenes on the teapot were derived from etchings created by Höroldt in 1726 and were completed either at the Seuter workshop in Augsburg or the Funcke workshop in Dresden. Emblematic of the close relationship between these two workshops and Meissen, both the Seuters and Funcke had access to Höroldt's etchings. The figure depicted holding two festooned poles is taken from one of Höroldt's chinoiserie etchings (see chapter 5 for more on Höroldt's source books and etchings). It is notably and frequently repeated on numerous occasions, including Höroldt's blue-ground AR vase in the Porzellansammlung, Dresden (PE 666), and on a *Hausmaler* saucer attributed to Abraham Seuter in the Schneider collection, Schloss Lustheim (ES 242a).

In 1723, thirteen years after the factory was founded, Meissen's crossed-swords mark was introduced; derived from the arms of Saxony, the symbol is now widely recognized and is still in use today (see fig. 55, for example). This teapot is marked in underglaze blue with this early factory mark. (The earliest pieces of Böttger stoneware and porcelain are unmarked.)

FIG. 25 Detail from reverse of teapot

CHAPTER 4

KÖHLER AND RIPP: UNDERGLAZE-BLUE DECORATION

T he output of blue-and-white-decorated porcelain, including many monumental vases (see cat. nos. 35–37/pls. 23–25), surged during Meissen's second decade, 1720–1730. Emulating the coveted Asian porcelains in Augustus the Strong's collection, underglaze blue was first offered for sale by the manufactory at the 1720 Easter Fair in Leipzig. Augustus, desperate to add to his growing collection of blue-and-white Chinese and Japanese porcelain, spurred the manufactory to produce such wares, offering a monetary prize of 1,000 thaler (about $30,000 today) to the person who could solve the technical problems to produce clear and vibrant underglaze-blue decoration on porcelain. Meissen finally achieved success after uncovering the closely guarded research of scientist and paste compounder David Köhler after his death in 1723. Protecting highly specialized knowledge of the manufactory's porcelain production was common and deliberate as a means to guard the formula from rival manufactories; special skills or knowledge could even provide security or favor to key Meissen employees. Köhler came to Meissen from Freiberg, working closely with Johann Friedrich Böttger in the Albrechtsburg at Meissen as early as 1704. In addition to his early experiments with blue, Köhler worked with the paste, glaze, and firing at the manufactory. He was appointed *Obermeister*, or technical director, in 1719.[1]

By 1719–1720 Köhler recognized that "if the outlines were to be prevented from running, what had to be changed was not the color itself but rather the porcelain paste of the glaze."[2] It was this change, from the *Kalkporzellan* to a special feldspathic paste (*Blaumasse*), that ultimately led to the success of underglaze blue. In tandem with these adjustments in the porcelain formula, Köhler also developed a clearer blue with a paste composed of an improved cobalt mixed with a kaolin clay. This was sponged onto the porcelain body prior to glazing and created a bright clear blue. Samuel Stöltzel, another early colleague to Böttger, continued experimentation with underglaze blue after Köhler's death.

Much of the underglaze-blue decoration during this early period was completed by Johann Caspar Ripp (1681–1726). An experienced German faience painter, Ripp came to Meissen in 1720 and worked intermittently with Höroldt until 1723. As a highly skilled painter, Ripp apparently chaffed under Höroldt's direction, and ultimately, due to personal politics, he left the factory in disgrace.[3]

Reverse view of baluster vase and cover, ca. 1725–1730 (cat. no. 37/pl. 25)

23 BALUSTER VASE

ca. 1720–1721
Painting by Johann Caspar Ripp
Hard-paste porcelain
21⅜ × 9 in. (54.8 × 23 cm)
L13.62.26 (CAT. NO. 35)

•

Based on a Chinese baluster form, this monumental vase was originally part of a pair. It is one of the largest surviving blue-and-white vases made in the eighteenth century at Meissen.[4] The vase is decorated with densely populated chinoiserie scenes accented with large willows on the upper and lower sections of the piece. All scenes are articulated in a clear and refined underglaze blue. The painting is attributed to Ripp. A prolific painter of vases, his underglaze-blue decorations, influenced by his experience with faience, were particularly accomplished (a vase in the Museumslandschaft Hessen Kassel, Germany [KP 1956/173] is a particularly good example). He and other blue-and-white painters at Meissen made use of Höroldt's print sources for inspiration, including the engravings of Pieter Schenk the Elder (1660–1711), published in Amsterdam in 1702.

The provenance of this piece is of special interest, as its first-known owners were notable Meissen collectors Margarete and Franz Oppenheimer. We know Franz Oppenheimer was present at the 1919 *Dubletten* sale of the royal collection held at Rudolph Lepke's Berlin auction house and that he purchased at least two Augustus Rex vases.[5] Dresden held these sales of "duplicate" pieces in their collection in 1919 and 1920. Additional Meissen porcelains from the former royal family, the Wettins, also came up on the market in 1926. From these public auctions and private sales, numerous pieces from the royal collection entered the market. The Oppenheimer collection was acquired in total by another notable Meissen enthusiast, Fritz Mannheimer, around 1936;[6] much of that collection in turn ultimately went to the Rijksmuseum upon Mannheimer's death in 1939. (The collection was forcibly detoured in between, when it was bought by Adolf Hitler in 1941; after repatriation from Germany, it was finally acquired by the Rijksmuseum in 1952, following Mannheimer's wishes for the collection.)

The pair to the Gutter vase, along with other porcelains from the Oppenheimer/Mannheimer collections, were sold at Frederik Muller & Cie, Amsterdam, in 1952.[7] In conversation with Jan Daniël van Dam and Abraham L. den Blaauwen, former curators at the Rijksmuseum, Gutter discovered that his vase was likely sold off by Mannheimer—along with other duplicates, or pieces deemed lacking in quality or condition—between the time he acquired his collection in 1936 and his death in 1939.

Due to technical necessity, this vase was thrown in parts and luted together. It is apparent that the piece suffered a significant loss of approximately four inches from the neck. One can speculate that this loss occurred prior to the publication of Ludwig Schnorr von Carolsfeld's 1927 catalogue of the Oppenheimer collection, as this vase was not illustrated with its pair. The piece has also suffered some contusions to its body and irregularities in the glaze during the firing process.

24 NARROW-NECKED VASE (*ENGHALSVASE*)

ca. 1720–1721
Painting by Johann Caspar Ripp
Hard-paste porcelain
16 ½ × 6 ½ in. (42 × 16.5 cm)
L13.62.29 (CAT. NO. 36)

•

The grandest Meissen vases, such as the examples seen here (cat. nos. 35–36/pls. 23–24), were reserved for Augustus the Strong's personal collection or for use as diplomatic gifts. This monumental vase is decorated with an Asian scene, including figures and willows painted in clear blue tones. The palette and decoration bears some similarities to the Ripp baluster vase (cat. no. 35/pl. 23).

This vase is possibly one of seven blue-and-white vases gifted in 1725 from Augustus the Strong to Vittorio Amedeo II, king of Sardinia.[8] They would have likely been displayed as part of a garniture, or *Aufsatz*. Samuel Chladni, controller of the Dresden *Porzellan-Warenlager* (warehouse), was notified between July 4 and August 28 to select numerous pieces for the king of Sardinia in Turin, including "1 grosser Blau und Weisser Camin Auffsatz von 7. stck. Vasen" (one large blue-and-white chimneypiece garniture of seven vases).[9] A related group of narrow-necked vases can be found in the Porzellansammlung, Dresden,[10] and another pair is in the collection of Henry Arnhold, New York.[11]

This form was influenced by seventeenth-century German faience and Dutch delft models, which in turn may have been influenced by sixteenth- or seventeenth-century Chinese vases. At Meissen the model was first developed in red stoneware by Irminger. The elongated, narrow neck extends to a bowl or saucer shape. Originally the vase would have had a lid, relatively few of which survive.

FIG. 26 Reverse view of narrow-necked vase

25 BALUSTER VASE AND COVER

ca. 1725–1730

Hard-paste porcelain

16¼ × 8½ in. (41.3 × 21.5 cm);

height without cover: 13¼ in. (33.5 cm)

GIFT OF MALCOLM D. GUTTER, 2015.66A–B (CAT. NO. 37)

•

Augustus the Strong's AR monogram (for "Augustus Rex," see fig. 27) was in use at Meissen from around 1725 to 1740 for pieces produced for the court or presented as diplomatic gifts. This baluster vase, bearing such a mark, was likely intended as part of a garniture.

Unlike the early-production underglaze-blue vases (ca. 1720–1721; cat. nos. 35–36/pls. 23–24), this vase was produced after 1723, following Köhler's death and Ripp's departure from Meissen. A stronger, more defined gray blue was adopted here. The floating world of chinoiserie landscapes has hardened into scenes of identifiable Asian florals, such as chrysanthemums and prunus branches. One side depicts a container supporting erupting flowers that is somewhat reminiscent of a European commode in form, possibly inspired by seventeenth-century faience and delft bulb pots whose demi-lune shapes often took on the appearance of commodes. Cleverly, the commode form echoes the shape of the lower vase. The other side is decorated with rockwork supporting a large spray of riotous flowers and prunus (see p. 88 for alternate view). Each side is accented with a butterfly. The neck of the vase is decorated with a band of lambrequins, and the domed cover with a flat rim is similarly decorated in florals.

An AR vase with an identical cover is in the Nieborów Palace, Poland. Formerly of the Radziwiłł Palace, it was possibly included in the 1840s description of seven vases in the rooms on the first floor of the palace.[12] The garniture may have also included AR vases now in the Mint Museum, Charlotte, North Carolina; the Victoria and Albert Museum, London (C.1 1943); and a clobbered vase (one with added, later decoration) in the British Museum (1941,0708.1).

FIG. 27 Detail of AR monogram from underside of baluster vase

26 SAUCER

ca. 1722–1724
Painting by Johann Caspar Ripp
Hard-paste porcelain
1 × 4¾ in. (2.5 × 12 cm)
L13.62.31 (CAT. NO. 38)

•

The exterior of this saucer (fig. 28) was wheel-turn engraved in Dresden. The rare etched design (*Schnittdekor*) of an olive-branch-and-dove pattern reveals the white porcelain body underneath. The pattern is very rare—possibly unique—for Meissen but has precedent in Chinese examples. The thick, "dead-leaf" brown glaze (also known as capuchin glaze, or *Kapuzinerbraun*) appears under magnification to have been applied or brushed on thickly, rather than dipped. The iron oxide–rich glaze was likely brought to Meissen by Samuel Stöltzel from the Du Paquier manufactory. Once he joined Meissen in 1720, Stöltzel shared this formula with Köhler.[13]

The prototype decorative motifs on the inside well of the saucer, later developing into the *Fels und Vogeldekor*, are also inspired by Chinese sources.[14] The underglaze-blue decoration may be attributed to Ripp, the only notable blue painter at the factory at this time. According to the inventory supplied by Ripp to the factory commission, he decorated numerous saucers and a brown-glazed and etched service.[15] The underside of this saucer displays the Meissen caduceus mark of a single serpent and staff, possibly in reference to the Greek healer Asclepius or even as a pseudo-Chinese mark (*Peitschenmarke* or *Merkurstab*; see cat. no. 39/pl. 27).

A related Chinese bowl in the Gutter collection was formerly in the Dresden royal collection and is marked with the Japanese Palace inventory number N=531-/~ (fig. 29).[16] A description of the bowl in the 1779 inventory reads: "Ein detto auswendig mit eingeschnitt- enen Vogeln und Blumen 3 Zoll tief, 6½ Zoll in Diam: No. 531" (One bowl the same as above, the outside engraved with birds and flowers, 3 inches high, 6½ inches in diameter: No. 531).[17] As Gutter points out,

> these entries [on the Chinese piece] provide proof the engraved decoration was applied early on, before a piece's registration and entry into the king's collection—possibly on direct commission from him. Moreover, the relatively few examples finished in this fashion points, in my opinion, to a single artist responsible for the work; there is likelihood he was working in Dresden—rather than in another part of Saxony or in Bohemia—drawing on experience engraving glass, stone, and probably Böttger red stoneware.[18]

26A BOWL

ca. 1700–1720
China, Jingdezhen
Porcelain
2⅝ × 6 in. (6.7 × 15.2 cm)
L13.62.105 (CAT. NO. 117)

•

The *Kapuzinerbraun* glaze on the underside of this blue-and-white Chinese bowl, etched with doves and olive branches, was made by a Dresden artist. The rare, and possibly unique, Meissen example at left was probably engraved on the underside by the same hand.

FIGS. 28 (BOTTOM LEFT) AND 29 (BOTTOM RIGHT) Underside views of Meissen saucer (pl. 26) and Chinese bowl (pl. 26a)

27 COVERED FISH TUREEN

ca. 1722–1723
Painting by Johann Caspar Ripp
Hard-paste porcelain
9 × 12 ⅜ in. (23 × 31.5 cm); height without cover: 4 ⅜ in. (11.2 cm)
L13.62.30A–B (CAT. NO. 39)

•

Probably the earliest example of the form in porcelain, this covered circular tureen features leaping carp handles on its sides and lid. The body of the tureen and lid are decorated overall by Ripp with underglaze-blue rockwork, *indianische Blumen* (East Indian flowers, a term inspired by Chinese and Japanese wares imported in the 1700s by the Dutch East India Company), birds, and insects. The porcelain form was inspired by the red-stoneware tureens (*Pastetennäpfe* or *terrine grosse*) designed by Irminger that were later copied at other German factories, including Fulda.[19] Three related tureens are in the collection of the Porzellansammlung, Dresden (one PE 605, others unpublished); however, the Gutter tureen appears to be unique in that its interior base bears the Meissen caduceus (see fig. 30),[20] which was applied to some of the manufactory's porcelain as early as 1721–1722. In 1723, thirteen years after the factory was founded, the caduceus was replaced with crossed swords deriving from the arms of Saxony; the now-famous and immediately recognizable mark is still used today. (The earliest pieces of Böttger stoneware and porcelain are unmarked.)

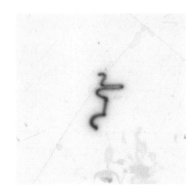

FIG. 30 Detail of caduceus mark from inside the tureen

CHAPTER 5

HÖROLDT AND CHINOISERIES

From 1720 to 1731, Meissen established a semi-independent studio where painted decoration was applied to porcelain. Placed under the direction of Johann Gregorius Höroldt, this atelier was located within the premises of the Albrechtsburg castle, the fortress site of the porcelain manufactory, by 1722. Höroldt came to Meissen in 1720 from the Du Paquier manufactory in Vienna. He was brought to Meissen by Samuel Stöltzel, who had defected earlier from Meissen. Stöltzel, working alongside David Köhler, made blue for the manufactory. Höroldt made the other colors, possibly bringing some colors and knowledge with him from Du Paquier. He authored a number of fundamental styles of painting on porcelain and developed the first palette of sixteen usable enamel colors for overglaze decoration at Meissen by 1731. Höroldt was appointed *Hofmaler* (court painter) in 1724, and in that role was paid on a per-piece basis for nearly a decade. In 1731 a reorganization took place at Meissen, and his business was integrated into the manufactory as a result of the Hoym-Lemaire scandal (see chapter 7 [pl. 61] for more on the affair). Höroldt assumed the position of *Hofkommissar* (court superintendent and factory director)[1] and would later retire from the manufactory in 1765.

Höroldt also produced drawings designed to serve as graphic sources that reflected the image of China held by Europeans in the early eighteenth century. The products of his imagination, when committed to Meissen porcelain, would fan a China mania throughout Europe. Höroldt's sketchbook, known as the Schulz Codex, contains 132 sheets filled primarily with chinoiseries, fanciful and primarily fabricated European idealizations of life in China and Japan. The pencil, ink, and wash drawings by Höroldt and his painting apprentices were compiled between 1723 and 1726.[2] Six additional documented chinoiserie engravings were made by Höroldt in 1726 (see pl. 22). Although it is generally believed that he produced these drawings as a source for his artists to work from, some argue that his sketchbook could have documented scenes painted by Meissen artists. Nonetheless, his imaginative designs were painted on Meissen porcelain and would go on to influence Asian-inspired decorations at ceramic and porcelain manufactories across Europe.[3]

Reverse view of mounted coffeepot, ca. 1723–1724, painting attributed to Johann Gregorius Höroldt (cat. no. 46/pl. 32)

At Meissen these fanciful chinoiseries are surrounded by gilt Baroque-scroll cartouches highlighted in iron red (later in purple and black) and frequently luster. Several pieces in the Gutter collection include scenes and figures that are featured in the Schulz Codex. Höroldt's studio occasionally combined its chinoiseries with harbor scenes (*Kauffahrtei*) and visual references to European exploration. Some of these harbor scenes are attributed to Meissen painter Christian Friedrich Herold (1700–1779). Under Höroldt's direction and strictures, pieces were rarely signed by painters at Meissen; however, a few signed works and stylistic comparisons can suggest attribution to some notable painters, such as Herold, Johann Christoph Horn (1692–1760), Johann Ehrenfried Stadler (1701–1741), Adam Friedrich von Löwenfinck ((1714–1754; fig. 31), and Höroldt himself.

FIG. 31 Saucer with Löwenfinck-contour chinoiserie, ca. 1740 (cat. no. 53/pl. 39)

28 MOUNTED TANKARD

ca. 1722–1723

Painting attributed to Johann Gregorius Höroldt

Hard-paste porcelain and silver-gilt mount

6½ × 3½ in. (16.5 × 8.8 cm); height without cover: 5⅞ in. (15 cm)

L13.62.44 (CAT. NO. 42)

•

Probably decorated by Höroldt, this tankard depicts trade in the age of discovery, around the early eighteenth century. The fanciful chinoiserie scene can be found in the Schulz Codex (fig. 32) and depicts an exoticized Asian figure holding a colorful parasol, greeting a European figure standing in a boat recently pulled ashore. The European offers a bowl to his host, while his other objects of trade, including a barrel of coral, are visible in his boat. Another pair of Asian and European figures in the foreground is presumably involved in a trade discussion. The broad expanse of sky is decorated with fluffy blue clouds, two soaring birds, and a butterfly.

This painterly effect, in use until circa 1725–1726, suggests an early date of decoration and manufacture. An underglaze-blue band encircles the tankard along the top and bottom and outlines the gilt-edged cartouches. The cartouches are also enhanced by surrounding foliate strapwork (*Laub- und Bandelwerk*). Furthermore, the shield-shaped cartouche surround is enhanced with Böttger luster (possibly developed in collaboration between Höroldt and Funcke; see chapter 3). The luster also enhances select decorative elements, including the underside of the parasol. Unlike later chinoiserie-decorated tankards, this piece is relatively undecorated beyond the central cartouche (see p. 109 for alternate view). A single spray of iron-red *indianische Blumen* decorates the strap handle.

FIG. 32 Detail from sheet 30 of Johann Gregorius Höroldt's Schulz Codex. Grassi Museum für Angewandte Kunst, Leipzig

29 WASTE BOWL WITH CHINOISERIES

ca. 1722–1724

Painting possibly by Johann Christoph Horn or
Johann Gregorius Höroldt

Hard-paste porcelain

3⅛ × 7⅛ in. (8 × 18 cm)

L13.62.36 (CAT. NO. 43)

•

A small group of Meissen works produced between 1722 and 1724 was decorated in chinoiseries influenced by the Chinese *wucai* and *doucai* styles. *Wucai* (or five-color decoration) is clearly represented in the use of red, green, and yellow enamels with underglaze blue on a white porcelain ground. The *doucai* (or contrasting colors) technique employs the use of underglaze blue to create an outline for the overglaze enamels. Overglaze or enamel blue was still problematic for the factory during this period, so Höroldt and his studio still relied on underglaze blue. Therefore, these pieces display a blending of underglaze blue, colored enamels, and gilding.

Numerous Asian figures and vignettes appear on this bowl, interspersed with flowering trees. The inner rim of the bowl is further decorated with an underglaze-blue band enameled with red flower heads and enhanced with gilding. A dentil gilt band encircles the foot of the bowl. *Mischtechnik* (mixing of decorative techniques) pieces are frequently marked with the caduceus mark. The shape and profile of this waste bowl (*Spülkumme*), with a high footrim, is characteristic of those made in the mid-1720s.[4]

Johann Christoph Horn was credited with this distinctive mixing of underglaze blue and colored enamels at Meissen, where the blue was painted on to provide the outline for the decoration. An example of this technique can be clearly seen on the flowering trees to the left of the squatting figure. Horn came to Meissen in 1720 and was employed as an underglaze-blue painter. Prior to his arrival at Meissen, he worked as a blue decorator at the Dresden faience factory of Martin Eggebrecht (active at Meissen 1708–1784) for nearly ten years.[5] His work frequently depicts Chinese figures in landscapes featuring rocks and flowers, as seen on this waste bowl. A jug and cover in the Rijksmuseum, Amsterdam (BK-17460), share many of these decorative techniques.[6] However, another frequently cited characteristic of Horn's hand is the large scale of his figures and/or elongated heads and faces, which is not seen on this work. Overall, there are several characteristics of this waste bowl that might suggest an attribution to Horn; however, the high quality of painting may also suggest Höroldt's hand. Some elements depicted, such as the vessel for boiling water and the table, can be found in the Schulz Codex, although no human figure depicted on the waste bowl appears in this source.

30 TEA CADDY WITH CHINOISERIE FIGURES

ca. 1723
Painting attributed to Johann Gregorius Höroldt
Hard-paste porcelain and gilt-bronze mount
3¾ × 1¾ in. (9.6 × 4.5 cm) (porcelain only)
L13.62.46 (CAT. NO. 44)

•

The hexagonal shape of this tea caddy accommodates the gilt and channeled frames around six individual chinoiserie figures. The Johann Jakob Irminger–designed form was inspired by silver sources. Meissen adopted this form in red stoneware and Böttger porcelain. A red-stoneware example is in the Arnhold collection, New York.[7] The body is slightly warped and is fitted with a late eighteenth- or early nineteenth-century gilt-bronze mount.[8]

Four of the six large-scale figures depicted, like those on the teabowl in the next chapter (see cat. no. 57/pl. 40), are copied directly from engravings in Carel Allard's *Orbis habitabilis oppida et vestitus* (*The Towns and Costumes of the Inhabited World*), published in a circa 1695 edition in Amsterdam.[9] The Allard figures include those representing "Mongul" (Mongolia); "Honan" (Cathay or China; fig. 34); "Benin" (Republic of Benin); and "Macassar" (Macassar straits, now part of Indonesia but then a major Dutch trading post).

The vignettes are further enhanced by rockwork, flora, and flying insects not seen in Allard. The unusually high quality of the painting as well as the prominence placed on the figures may suggest an attribution to Höroldt. The entire palette of colors and Böttger luster available to Meissen was utilized on this tea caddy. It also exhibits the early experimental green enamel employed by Höroldt and his painters.

FIG. 33 Alternate view of tea caddy

FIG. 34 *Honan* (Cathay or China) from Carel Allard's *Orbis habitabilis oppida et vestitus* (*The Towns and Costumes of the Inhabited World*), ca. 1695 edition (Amsterdam)

FIG. 35 (RIGHT) Reverse view of teabowl

FIGS. 36 AND 37 (OPPOSITE LEFT AND RIGHT) Details from sheets 51 and 100 of Johann Gregorius Höroldt's Schulz Codex. Grassi Museum für Angewandte Kunst, Leipzig

31 TEABOWL AND SAUCER WITH SCENES OF PORCELAIN PRODUCTION

ca. 1723–1724

Hard-paste porcelain

Teabowl: 1¾ × 3 in. (4.5 × 7.5 cm); saucer: 3 × 5 in. (2.5 × 12.8 cm)

L13.62.32A–B (CAT. NO. 45)

•

The scene on this teabowl portrays three Chinese figures working in various stages of porcelain production—one at a table, forming a vessel through the use of a hammer and a cutting or chasing tool (see opposite top), and two others firing and supplying oxygen to a muffle kiln (see fig. 35). Various elements decorating this teabowl can be found in Höroldt's sketchbook (see figs. 36 and 37). The scene on the accompanying saucer depicts two figures in a landscape enjoying tea, with one tending a steaming kettle; it can also be seen in sheet 92 of the Schulz Codex. This outdoor scene is framed by a border of double red lines, standard for these early wares.

An exotic bird perched amidst rockwork and *indianische Blumen* is featured in the interior of the teabowl. The porcelain body itself is transitional and displays some characteristics of early Böttger porcelain and the later feldspathic paste.

32 MOUNTED COFFEEPOT

ca. 1723–1724

Painting attributed to Johann Gregorius Höroldt (mounting probably Augsburg)

Hard-paste porcelain and silver-gilt mounts

8½ × 4⅝ in. (21.5 × 11.8 cm)

L13.62.43A–B (CAT. NO. 46)

•

Developed under Böttger, the form of this Baroque, pear-shaped coffeepot with an S-handle and domed lid is seen with some variations. Here, it provided an ample field for Höroldt's decorations and chinoiseries.[10] Scenes on the front and back are framed by gilt-edged quatrefoil cartouches of iron red, Böttger luster, and gilt *Laub- und Bandelwerk* (see p. 102 for alternate view). Great skill and detail can be seen in the chinoiserie scenes. Delicate passages of shading on the figures' garments were accomplished with thin washes of enamels. An elaborate and varied palette was also employed.[11]

The chinoiserie scene on the coffeepot depicts a crowned personage with strikingly Western facial features who lovingly receives, or is in the act of gifting, a porcelain vase. His tell-tale dark, bushy eyebrows suggest that this may be a rare depiction on porcelain of Augustus the Strong.[12] The incredible care in decoration combined with the important subject matter suggests Höroldt's own hand. Beyond the decorative cartouches, the white porcelain body is further enhanced by *indianische Blumen*.[13]

This exact cartouche surround can be seen on a teabowl and saucer in Gutter's collection (at top right). Furthermore, both pieces are enhanced with related gilt borders (*Goldspitzenbordüre*) around their neck and rims. Decorative similarities and identical gilding patterns provide evidence that these pieces were originally part of the same coffee service. Neither scene on the coffeepot appear to be illustrated in the Schulz Codex, unlike those of the teabowl and saucer.[14]

33 TEABOWL AND SAUCER

ca. 1723–1724

Painting attributed to Johann Gregorius Höroldt

Hard-paste porcelain

Teabowl: 2 × 2⅞ in. (5 × 7.3 cm); saucer: 1 × 5 in. (2.5 × 12.6 cm)

L13.62.33A–B (CAT. NO. 47)

•

The scene on this teabowl, which depicts a Chinese figure blowing into a pipe to stoke the fire for a kettle, can be found in the Schulz Codex (fig. 38). The scene on the saucer, also taken from the Schulz Codex (sheet 2), portrays a mother seated next to a cradle, nursing her child.

FIG. 38 (BOTTOM) Detail from sheet 108 of Johann Gregorius Höroldt's *Schulz Codex*. Grassi Museum für Angewandte Kunst, Leipzig

34 TEA CADDY AND COVER

ca. 1723–1725

Hard-paste porcelain

4 × 3⅛ in. (10 × 8 cm)

L13.62.39A–B (CAT. NO. 48)

•

Like the tea caddy featured in plate 30, this example was part of a larger service. Designed by Irminger, the hexagonal baluster body with flat cover was inspired by European silver forms. Six recessed panels outlined in gilding depict complementary, but not continuous, *Kauffahrtei* (harbor scenes). A prominent and colorful sky dominates all six fields. Harbor scenes first appeared at Meissen under Höroldt in the early 1720s and were fashionable through the 1730s.[15] Based on their apparel, the figures appear to be Mongolian rather than Chinese. However, one panel incorporates a European friar. The engraving sources for the figure and scenes have not been identified.

35 SAUCER WITH CHINOISERIE AND HARBOR SCENE

ca. 1724–1725
Painting possibly attributed to Christian Friedrich Herold
Hard-paste porcelain
1 × 5 in. (2.6 × 12.7 cm)
L13.62.34 (CAT. NO. 49)

◦

The highly developed scene on this saucer depicts the production and sale of porcelain in the Japanese island port of Dejima and its export by the Dutch. The background harbor scene, including a Western galleon and Eastern junk, is painted in a neutral, pastel palette, whereas enamels used for the chinoiserie figures in the foreground are much stronger in tone. The chinoiserie scene is dominated by an Asian figure in black holding a parasol, but also features a seated figure decorating porcelains before an elaborate outdoor structure occupied by two standing figures and topped by a dog on its roof. The entire palette of enamels available, except luster, was used on this saucer. Possibly unique, this scene does not appear in the Schulz Codex, nor has any print source been identified.

Possibly attributed to Herold, this saucer shares some distinctive characteristics of his work as identified by scholars such as former Meissen archivist Otto Walcha, Ingelore Menzhausen, and Siegfried Ducret, including the tranquility of the scene, grouping of figures, low horizon line, and sunburst in the sky. Herold joined Meissen in 1725; he was previously trained as an enamel painter in Berlin. He was noted for his harbor scenes, a few of which were signed. The enameled scene here is encircled by two iron-red rings, and the rim of the saucer is decorated by a wide gilt band. As of yet, no other pieces from this service have been identified.

36 TEABOWL WITH CHINOISERIE AND HARBOR SCENE

ca. 1726–1728
Painting possibly attributed to Christian Friedrich Herold
Hard-paste porcelain
1¾ × 3 in. (4.5 × 7.5 cm)
L13.62.35 (CAT. NO. 50)

•

The decoration on this service, represented in the Gutter collection by this teabowl and a sugar box (cat. no. 51/pl. 37), combines *Kauffahrtei* and chinoiserie scenes populated by Asian and Western figures. The service displays the same gilding pattern (*Goldspitzenbordüre*) throughout. The interior of the waste bowl and teabowls in the service are all decorated with an elaborate enameled diaper pattern accented with chrysanthemums (fig. 39). The underglaze-blue crossed-swords mark on this teabowl is notably off-center (fig. 40).[16]

FIGS. 39 AND 40 Details of interior and underside of teabowl

37 SUGAR BOX AND COVER WITH CHINOISERIES AND HARBOR SCENE

ca. 1726–1728
Painting possibly attributed to Christian Friedrich Herold
Hard-paste porcelain
3⅛ × 4½ × 3⅜ in. (8 × 11.3 × 8.5 cm)
L13.62.42A–B (CAT. NO. 51)

•

Related scenes and identical gilding patterns indicate that this sugar box and the previously discussed teabowl (cat. no. 50/pl. 36) were originally part of the same porcelain service. Although the crossed-swords mark was first introduced in 1723, the KPM (for Königliche Porzellan-Manufaktur) mark (fig. 42), or its KPF (Königliche Porzellan-Fabrik) or MPM (Meissener Porzellan-Manufaktur) variations, were used on sugar boxes and teapots produced from 1722 to 1725. Although a royal decree was declared in 1723 for all Meissen works to bear the crossed-swords mark, it was not enforced until 1731. This favored sugar-box form was first produced in Böttger red stoneware.[17]

FIGS. 41 AND 42 View from above sugar box and detail of KPM mark on underside

38 TUREEN AND COVER (*OLIOTOPF*)

ca. 1723–1725
Painting possibly attributed to Johann Gregorius Höroldt
Hard-paste porcelain
5 ⅜ × 6 ⅝ in. (13.8 × 16.7 cm)
L16.30A–B (CAT. NO. 52)

•

Displaying a tour de force of decoration, this small tureen comprises a circular bowl, supported by tripod feet and equipped with squared strap handles, and a domed lid with a flattened rim surmounted by a gilt knop finial. The form, originally modeled on a Japanese seventeenth-century incense burner (*koro*), lost its original function once it made its way to Europe, where it became a small tureen for soup or stew (*Oliotopf* or *Olitätentopf* in German, *olla podrida* in Spanish, or *pot à oille* in French). Some of these European models even adopted stands or underplates. An even earlier inspiration for the form might have come from Chinese bronzes. At Meissen the form was likely inspired by a Japanese example, as one such model was included in Augustus II's collection by 1723.[18] It was first adopted at Meissen in white undecorated Böttger porcelain. A circa 1715–1718 example survives in the Porzellansammlung, Dresden (PE 2911 a,b).

The model was also taken up by the Du Paquier manufactory in Vienna. Many variations in decoration and form can be seen in the Du Paquier collection of Melinda and Paul Sullivan.[19] Another Du Paquier *Oliotopf* (ca. 1720) in the Museum of Applied Arts,

Budapest (15.646.a,b), with a continuous chinoiserie scene may have influenced a very similar Meissen pair (ca. 1725–1730) in the collections of Ernst Schneider at the Schloss Lustheim (ES 306a–b) and the Rijksmuseum (BK-17355).[20] Most surviving examples at Meissen, however, are decorated with chinoiseries or in Kakiemon style. One such early *Oliotopf* decorated with chinoiseries was illustrated by Elias Baeck (1679–1747) and published by Jeremias Wolf (1663–1724) in Augsburg circa 1720–1724.[21]

The dazzling chinoiserie of this *Oliotopf* is supplemented with a fanciful "salami" decoration. The Meissen sobriquet "salami" refers to a densely decorated field of medallions surrounded and interspersed on an iron-red patterned ground. The majority of the body is decorated with three large quatrefoil cartouches decorated with chinoiserie scenes framed by gilt and Böttger luster; *indianische Blumen* ornament the remaining space on the piece (see p. 216 for alternate view). The lid (fig. 43) is further decorated with three cartouches and bordered on the rim by three clusters of chrysanthemum heads and peonies. The extended lip of the *Oliotopf* is decorated with iron-red *ruyi* (ceremonial scepter design motif). Some elements depicted on this *Oliotopf* can be found in the Schulz Codex; however, no precise scene appears to be the source.

The pair to the Gutter *Oliotopf* is in the Kunstkammer of Schloss Friedenstein, Gotha (P 36 I).[22] Gutter has identified another pair, which supports the suggestion that these *Oliotopfs* may have been made in pairs at Meissen.[23]

FIG. 43 View from above tureen

39 CUP AND SAUCER WITH LÖWENFINCK-CONTOUR CHINOISERIE

ca. 1740
Hard-paste porcelain
Cup: 2 ¾ × 3 ¾ in. (7 × 9.5 cm); saucer: 1 ⅝ × 5 ¾ in. (4 × 14.5 cm)
L13.62.41A–B (CAT. NO. 53)

•

The distinctive painting style of this chinoiserie cup and saucer is characteristic of the work of Adam Friedrich von Löwenfinck. Abraham L. den Blaauwen first used the term "contour" to describe Löwenfinck's chinoiserie style of simple black lines to delineate facial features and to outline figures unmodulated by shadowing, and pointed to the influence of the Augsburg-published prints by Baeck, Pieter Schenk the Elder (d. 1711), and Wolf.[24] Löwenfinck's designs took inspiration from Pieter Schenk the Younger's (1698–1775) engravings, particularly his *Nieuwe geinventeerde Sineesen* (Newly invented chinoiseries; Amsterdam, ca. 1720).[25]

Löwenfinck joined Meissen as an apprentice to Höroldt in 1727 and initially worked on underglaze-blue and floral painting. Before long he expanded his repertoire and developed an identifiable and distinctive style in Höroldt's studio. He left Meissen in 1736 to pursue a career in faience painting at Bayreuth and continued work at manufactories at Ansbach, Höchst, and Hagenau. His signed work at these centers has helped identify his decorations at Meissen.[26] The manufactory continued to decorate a large group of pieces in the Löwenfinck style even after the artist's defection.

The form of this large cup and saucer was inspired by European silver; however, the decoration and palette were influenced by Japanese Kakiemon porcelains. Frolicking children at play are painted in bright enamels on a primarily undecorated ground. A similar treatment of figures and sparse design, with rims edged in brown, can be seen on a teabowl and saucer in the Rijksmuseum (BK-17352-A/B).[27]

CHAPTER 6

HÖROLDT AND EUROPEAN DECORATION

Detail of teabowl and saucer, ca. 1726–1727
(cat. no. 66/pl. 49)

P rint sources were commonly used as inspiration for eighteenth-century European porcelain decoration. In them Meissen painters found visual examples for many decorative elements, including botanical specimens (such as the prevalent German flowers, or *deutsche Blumen*), insects, commedia dell'arte figures, dwarfs, mythological figures, and *Veduten* (landscape scenes), to name a few. In 1720, soon after he arrived at Meissen, Johann Gregorius Höroldt began to acquire books and sheets of engravings for himself and members of his studio to consult. One such publication was the circa 1695 Amsterdam edition of Carel Allard's early pictorial compilation of "exotic" cultural geography, *The Towns and Costumes of the Inhabited World*, which was widely distributed. Höroldt was also influenced by and collected popular seventeenth-century travel literature by such engravers as Dutch author Johannes Nieuhof (1618–1672), Augsburg printmaker Martin Engelbrecht (1684–1756), and Nuremberg publisher Johann Christoph Weigel (1654–1725). Select source books were produced directly for the Meissen and Du Paquier manufactories, such as Jeremias Wolf's pattern book, published in Augsburg circa 1720.[1]

By 1745 the manufactory contained more than five thousand of these reference materials; however, due to changing fashions and heavy usage, many items were not retained.[2] Prints were purchased and borrowed by both *Hausmaler* and Meissen decorators. Apparently, a few prints borrowed by Höroldt from Augustus the Strong's library in Dresden were not returned.[3]

Several porcelains from the Gutter collection produced under Höroldt's tenure at Meissen are painted with European figures, landscapes, and harbor scenes (*Kauffahrtei*) inspired by various distributed print sources. Meissen widely used print sources by German engraver Johann Schmischek (1585–1650); French artists Jacques Callot (1592–1635), Jean-Antoine Watteau (1684–1721), and François Boucher (1703–1770); Italian engraver Stefano Della Bella (1610–1664); and English artist William Hogarth (1697–1764). Such materials continued to be of great relevance to decorators of the factory as well as modelers such as Johann Gottlieb Kirchner (arrived in 1727) and Johann Joachim Kändler (arrived in 1731), who were instrumental in moving the focus of the manufactory away from painterly decoration and toward sculpture.

40 TEABOWL

ca. 1721–1722

Hard-paste porcelain

1⅞ × 3 in. (4.8 × 7.5 cm)

L13.62.45 (CAT. NO. 57)

•

The figures on this teabowl, in the earliest depiction of colonial Americans on European porcelain, derive from seventeenth-century travel engravings. The primary source, by an unidentified engraver, dates to circa 1642–1643.[4] This engraving, *Nieu Amsterdam*, "is probably the earliest view of New York and is therefore of the highest interest and importance,"[5] according to architect and historian I. N. Phelps Stokes, who later cited it in his *Iconography of Manhattan Island, 1498–1909* (1915–1928; fig. 44). This engraving was reinterpreted by Aldert Meijer (ca. 1664, active until ca. 1690) and appeared in Allard's *Towns and Costumes of the Inhabited World* as plate 88. Meijer's engraving was copied and subsequently published as *Engelse Quakers en Tabak Planters aende Barbados* (English Quaker tobacco farmers in Barbados)[6] in a 1726 publication.

In addition to appearing in seventeenth-century travel literature, both figures on the Gutter teabowl are featured on folio 88 of the Schulz Codex alongside chinoiseries, grouping the new Americans with other exotic peoples. This teabowl was most likely part of a chinoiserie tea service, as Gutter has identified a related teabowl and saucer in the Musée Ariana, Geneva, with Asian figures.[7]

The two portraits are framed within gilt cartouches highlighted with Böttger luster, most likely executed by Johann Georg Funcke's workshop. Interspersed between the cartouches are Buddhist symbols of immortality or good omens. Some of these emblems also decorate the interior of the teabowl.

FIG. 44 Nieu Amsterdam, 1642–1643, reproduced as plate 5 in I. N. Phelps Stokes, *The Iconography of Manhattan Island, 1498–1909* (1915), vol. 1. Bancroft Library, University of California, Berkeley

COLLECTOR'S STORY: TEABOWL

I had received the catalogue for the Sotheby's, London, sale "Property from a Distinguished Swiss Collection" in advance of my spring 2009 trip. Perusing it in San Francisco, I discovered nothing of interest. Though I resolved a brief visit to the salesroom to see the show, an invitation to attend a boardroom luncheon at Sotheby's King Street rival, Christie's, was enough inducement to quit before the porcelain came up. One of Sotheby's lots, in fact, contained fourteen items of odd *Hausmalerei*—cups and saucers—only seven of which were illustrated in the catalogue (all could be seen online, I later discovered, but only with due diligence; in any case, a proper description of this teabowl was absent).

Monday afternoon following the sale, I found time to pay greetings to Errol and Henriette Manners at their Kensington Church Street shop. The entire fourteen-item lot from Sotheby's was strewn before me on a table in their basement inner sanctum. There among the porcelain odds and ends was this fantastic teabowl. Errol had purchased the lot specifically to have it. He had understood its importance immediately at the preview—or before. Some fifteen years prior, Errol had purchased another small important piece with early Canadian figures. The

artistic and historical significance of the piece was not lost on me. I eventually ventured, "I hope you make me a good price." Errol's reply: "It will be pretty expensive—you wouldn't be able to afford it."

At Christie's auction the following morning, I naively broached Henriette for price mercy. She informed me that photos of the teabowl had already been sent to another client. Out of the salesroom, a call to Errol confirmed this; he responded by stating the price was £4,000—take it or leave it. The client in fact was Henry Arnhold in New York, who, since the 2008 exhibition of his collection at the Frick Collection, New York—and concomitant publication of his catalogue—had retired from collecting. Errol had received a phone call from him inquiring about the impending sale of the Hoffmeister brothers' Meissen collection. Impulsively, Errol had blurted: "Henry, I have a piece that will take you out of retirement." Arnhold's acceptance the following day—deciding to buy the piece for the Metropolitan Museum of Art as a gift befitting the quadricentennial of Henry Hudson's voyage up the river that now bears his name—was in the end too late; my noon consummating telephone call to Errol in London was in Manhattan a too-early 7 a.m. The teabowl

indeed was to come to America—but west of the Rockies, not the East Coast.

Prior to sale at Sotheby's, the teabowl was in the collection of Mario Leproni, an eminent Swiss porcelain collector and friend of the renowned ceramic historian, connoisseur, and collector Siegfried Ducret. Several of Leproni's pieces were included in a 2001 exhibition of Meissen from Italian museums and private collections, held in Turin, *I fragili lussi*. In the catalogue entry for the object, however, no connection is made to Carel Allard's travel/geography book and the figures being from the New World. Possibly influenced by W. B. Honey's insightful comments—but mistaken identities—on the related saucer in the Victoria and Albert Museum, they (and their costumes) were instead considered Oriental types. It is still unknown where and when Leproni obtained this incredible object.

—MALCOLM GUTTER

FIG. 45 Reverse view of teapot

FIG. 46 (OPPOSITE LEFT) Bernard Picart, *Salmacis and Hermaphroditus*, 1708. Etching, 5¼ × 5¾ in. (13.5 × 14.5 cm). Rijksmuseum, Amsterdam, RP-P-OB-51.281

41 TEAPOT WITH MYTHOLOGICAL SCENES

ca. 1721–1722
Hard-paste porcelain
4.⅞ × 4 in. (12.3 × 10 cm)
L13.62.58A–B (CAT. NO. 58)

•

Inspired by a silver shape, this teapot form was first produced in red stoneware.[8] The shape is a rare, simplified variant of an *Adlerkanne*, or eagle teapot (see also cat. no. 28/pl. 21). Although there do not appear to be any early Böttger white porcelain examples of this form, the teapot was produced in porcelain frequently decorated with Höroldt's chinoiseries. The decoration of this teapot is unusual for its period; even though *Hausmaler* explored mythological scenes, they rarely did so during Höroldt's tenure at the manufactory.

Taken from Ovid's *Metamorphoses*, the mythological scenes depict the story of Artemis/Diana and Callisto. Callisto, who had taken a vow of celibacy along with her fellow nymphs of Artemis, was seduced by Zeus/Jupiter. A cartouche on one side of the teapot illustrates the moment when Callisto's pregnancy was revealed while bathing (see fig. 45); on the other side, a cartouche shows an enraged Artemis, discovering the deceit, banishing Callisto from her fold.

The central scenes are surrounded by a gilt cartouche enhanced with Böttger luster and an iron-red foliate medallion on its handle, identifying the decoration as factory, not *Hausmalerei*. Interestingly, however, the decoration and palette of the lid suggests that it was enameled at the Funcke workshop, but contemporaneous with the teapot's gilding.[9] As mentioned

in chapter 3, Funcke was responsible for gilding factory wares until 1726/1727, but his enamel decorations for Meissen sharply declined after Höroldt's arrival in 1720.

Subject matter from Ovid's *Metamorphoses* is also featured on a cup and saucer (see below right) in the Gutter collection. The same painter may have been responsible for both the teapot and the cup and saucer; however, we know these pieces are not from the same service. The figures on the cup possibly portray Zeus seducing Callisto in the guise of Artemis. A circa 1710–1750 etching by Jacopo Amigoni (1682–1752), *Jupiter in the Guise of Diana Seducing Callisto* (British Museum, 2002,0728.67), may have served as a possible print source for the teabowl. The saucer depicts Salmacis, another nymph of Artemis, spying on Hermaphroditus as he bathes his feet in a stream; Bernard Picart (1673–1733)'s etching *Salmacis and Hermaphroditus* (fig. 46) may have been a possible print source.[10]

Although the teabowl and saucer are somewhat simply decorated with gilt cartouches, without luster, several characteristics strongly suggest manufactory decoration. These clues include an iron-red landscape inside the teabowl and the iron-red floral sprays on the reverse, as well as early experimental greens on the saucer and a luster 4 on its underside.[11]

42 CUP AND SAUCER WITH MYTHOLOGICAL SCENES

ca. 1721–1722
Hard-paste porcelain
Cup: 1¾ × 3 in. (4.5 × 7.8 cm); saucer 1 × 4.⅞ in. (2.5 × 12.5 cm)
L13.62.153A–B (CAT. NO. 59)

•

43 TEABOWL AND SAUCER

ca. 1722–1723
Painting probably by Johann Gregorius Höroldt
Hard-paste porcelain
Teabowl: 2 × 3⅛ in. (5 × 7.9 cm); saucer: 1 × 5 in. (2.4 × 12.7 cm)
L13.62.60A–B (CAT. NO. 60)

•

Probably the first of Höroldt's such depictions, this teabowl and saucer feature, respectively, Scaramouche and Pantalone, characters from the commedia dell'arte, a form of improvisational theater that developed in Italy during the mid-sixteenth century. Commedia figures were first seen in red stoneware at Meissen and were later famously depicted by the modeler Johann Joachim Kändler (1706–1775).[12] Modelers frequently used the same print sources as the decorators. Under Höroldt's tenure, Meissen decorated commedia-themed services between 1722 and 1724.[13]

The likely print source for the saucer is Callot's etching *Pantalone* (ca. 1618–1620; fig. 47), from a performance of the commedia dell'arte. The image of Scaramouche on the teabowl appears to be taken from a late seventeenth-century engraving, *Joseph Tortoriti faisant le personnage de Scaramouche* (fig. 48), published in Paris by Jean Mariette (1660–1742), although the image is reversed. The teabowl and saucer depict single figures against "landscaped" stages within cartouches framed with luster and *Laub- und Bandelwerk*. Insects, birds, and *indianische Blumen* further enhance the teabowl. The inside of the teabowl is also decorated with an iron-red landscape. Iron-red rings encircle the footrim on the underside of the saucer.[14]

FIG. 47 Jacques Callot, *Pantalone*, ca. 1618–1620. Etching with some engraving, 8½ × 5¾ in. (21.5 × 14.7 cm). The British Museum, X,4.511

FIG. 48 *Joseph Tortoriti faisant le personnage de Scaramouche*, late seventeenth century. Engraving, 12¼ × 8⅜ in. (31.2 × 21.3 cm). Victoria & Albert Museum, London, Given by Dame Marie Rambert, E.4952-1968

44 SAUCER

ca. 1722–1723

Painting probably by Johann Gregorius Höroldt

Hard-paste porcelain

1 × 5 in. (2.6 × 12.7 cm)

L13.62.66 (CAT. NO. 61)

•

Like the commedia dell'arte, another popular subject adopted by Meissen modelers and decorators alike was dwarfs. The dwarfs illustrated on this saucer were adapted from a series of twenty-one etchings by Callot published in Nancy known as the "Grotesque Dwarfs," or *Varie figure gobbi di Iacopo Callot* (ca. 1621–1625). Callot's work was widely distributed and interpreted by other artists in the seventeenth and eighteenth centuries. One of Callot's pupils, François Collignon (1609–1657), took up the subject in his series of etchings *Facétieuses inventions d'amour et de guerre* (Facetious fabrications of love and war, 1631–1637; fig. 49), published in Paris. This appears to be the closest print source for the image on the Gutter saucer.[15]

The central scene of a pair of dwarfs dancing is contained in an oval gilt cartouche.[16] A luster mark a//. on the underside of the saucer and the lack of Böttger luster on the cartouche surround suggest the hand of Funcke's workshop.[17]

FIG. 49 François Collignon after Stefano Della Bella, plate from the series *Facétieuses inventions d'amour et de guerre*, 1631–1637. Etching, 4⅛ × 4¼ in. (10.5 × 10.9 cm). Fine Arts Museums of San Francisco, Achenbach Foundation for Graphic Arts, 1963.30.57488

45 COVERED BOWL AND STAND (*OLIENBECHER*)

ca. 1723–1725

Hard-paste porcelain

Bowl: 3 × 3¾ in. (7.5 × 9.4 cm) without cover, height with cover 4¼ in. (10.8 cm); stand: 1⅛ × 6¾ in. (2.9 × 17 cm)

L13.62.65A–C (CAT. NO. 62)

•

Known in German as an *Olienbecher*, this round *écuelle*, or covered bowl and stand, was used to serve soup or stew. Probably inspired by a silver model, its form was first adopted by Meissen in red stoneware and then in early Böttger white porcelain. This model also has affinities to the *Oliotopf* form, but is not raised on three feet (see cat. no. 52/pl. 38). Meissen produced several variations to the *Olienbecher*; the Gutter piece includes angular strap handles and a coral/twig finial. The favored decoration for this model was chinoiserie or European landscape (*Veduten*) and harbor scenes, examples of which are well represented in the Meissen print archives.[18]

Aside from its high artistic quality, the decoration is a remarkable document of its time, marking the set as one of the most important pieces of the Gutter collection. A man on horseback and a fisherman on the river Elbe in the foreground are depicted on one side of the covered bowl. Dresden's cityscape—including the Residenzschloss and the Jungfernbastei fortress (see fig. 50), the site of the earliest experiments of Böttger and Tschirnhaus—beckons in the distance. Likely inspired by seventeenth-century Dutch landscape painting or prints, the appearance of the Elbbrücke (now the Augustusbrücke) in its pre-reconstruction state indicates a date before 1727 for the print source and porcelain decoration.[19] This is possibly the earliest depiction of Dresden on porcelain. The verso of the *Olienbecher* is equally significant (see p. 145 for alternate view), featuring a scene of Leipzig, including the tower of the Pleissenburg, a Renaissance electoral castle/fortress (later demolished in 1900), and the Thomaskirche, site of Johann Sebastian Bach's (1685–1750) final appointment as cantor.[20] To the left of the Pleissenburg tower is another church, possibly the Matthäikirche, now demolished.[21] The saucer, or stand, is decorated with a riverside scene with a village in the distance. These *Veduten* are framed within quatrefoil cartouches of iron-red *Laub- und Bandelwerk* enhanced by gilding and Böttger luster, with gilt lacework around the rims of both the bowl and its lid.

According to Claus Boltz's article on Meissen turners and formers, *Olienbecher* with *Baumäste* (twig) finials first appeared in the manufactory's records in 1726.[22] However, Gutter's inspection of the cup's paste with a short-wave ultraviolet lamp points to a Böttger (*Kalk*) porcelain body, suggesting an earlier date of manufacture, circa 1723–1725.

FIG. 50 *Jungfernbastei in Dresden, painting after a reconstruction by Friedrich Hagedorn, 1887*

143

COLLECTOR'S STORY: COVERED BOWL AND STAND

Over the years I have attempted to acquire pieces reflecting Meissen's extraordinary creativity and range, both in ceramic form as well as decoration. The *Olienbecher* had eluded me, partly due to cost but also to the scarcity of very early examples. The earliest specimens date to 1723; production continued through the 1730s and 1740s, its forms and decoration evolving to reflect changing tastes. I preferred to bide my time rather than jump on a later example that would merely fill a gap in my collection.

A 2004 *Olienbecher* underbidding fiasco at Sotheby's, New York, had popped a dream: obtaining an example now seemed illusory, beyond my means. And even if not the case, when would one again surface? During a catch-up trip to San Francisco's Bonhams and Butterfields in August 2005, I spied a catalogue resting on the front desk for the London Bonhams English porcelain sale, the first of the season, to be held in a few weeks time. Thumbing through, an advertising page toward the end jumped out at me; this *Olienbecher* was a featured item of a mid-November sale of Meissen and other Continental porcelain.

What a glorious piece, so similar in form and composition to the one lost a year and a half earlier. The baroque shape of this example—for me one of Meissen's sexiest objects, with its angular handles—accompanied especially by early landscape (as opposed to chinoiserie) painting appealed to me. An added element: a conservative estimate of £10,000–12,000.

In October the online catalogue was posted. There it was—lot 21—but now with a lower estimate of £6,000–8,000. I asked John Sandon, head of Bonhams's porcelain department, what he knew of its provenance, for more photos, and an explanation for the change in estimate. The *Olienbecher* had been consigned by a member of a moneyed family at Bonhams's office in Bath. At the time of consignment, John had not been aware of the worn gilding, hence the lowering of the estimate. The photos he sent me, however, only whetted my appetite: the scenes on both sides of the cup conjured memories, although at the time elusive. Despite my funds being drained by recent purchases, I resolved to hunt for this *Olienbecher*, its demerits I hoped working in my favor toward finally snaring one. Securing funds from my

home equity account would be necessary, and I was prepared for that. (Having retired from teaching, I became quite shy about financially overextending myself.)

A few days before the sale, a revelation: I happened upon a waste bowl in the catalogue for a February 2005 Christie's auction. Part of the Benedict XIV service, the bowl featured a familiar depiction of Dresden, the famous Augustus bridge the same as on the Bonhams *Olienbecher*, albeit the latter's scene was from farther downriver. An added excitement: the prominent building on the left bank of the river—could it be the Japanisches Palais? Never had I seen it depicted on Meissen; I resolved the piece had to come into my collection.

Acquisition of many wonderful things over that year in no way mitigated the unbearable state of anxiety over the *Olienbecher*'s potential success or failure. On November 16 the call from Bonhams came about 2:45 a.m. after a sleepless night. (I had penciled in £13,000–15,000 as an expected price, but feared having to go to £20,000; after all, Freddy Reyes had paid the equivalent of £34,000 for the example lost in 2004.) The

bidding started at £4,000. In a minute it was at £6,500, when I was asked by my contact to enter the fray. All the counterbidding came from the floor; at £8,000 another floor bidder joined in. A gentleman was against me through £9,000. My £9,200; long pause, hammer down, victory. The piece was mine. What a battle, and what an even greater triumph! A phone call the following day to John confirmed what I had suspected, my competition members of what I call the German trade mafia. A phone call to Klaus Kuhlemann and Jeffrey Tate also revealed they had noticed the piece in the sales catalogue. But I was nevertheless bemused: happily they seemed to have quite overlooked its exceptionalness.

—MALCOLM GUTTER

46 TEABOWL

ca. 1723–1724
Hard-paste porcelain
1¾ × 2⅞ in. (4.5 × 7.4 cm)
L13.62.63 (CAT. NO. 63)

•

This teabowl depicts the royal fortress Château de Vincennes just outside of Paris. The Vincennes porcelain manufactory would be established there in 1740 and eventually move to Sèvres as the French royal porcelain manufactory, thereby making this an important document in the study of French porcelain as well. The print source for this decoration is probably from a series of 244 etchings by Sébastien Le Clerc (1637–1714), *Vues des faubourgs (ou des environs) de Paris* (Scenes of quarters of Paris and its environs, ca. 1696–1700). Plate 38 depicts a horse-drawn coach and riders going past the castle of Vincennes (fig. 51). Although the painter took some fantastical liberties by depicting a swan-inhabited moat and two figures on its banks in the foreground, the keep of the château is a true copy, albeit reversed from Le Clerc's engraving.[23]

The scene of Vincennes is contained in a quatrefoil cartouche of iron-red *Laub- und Bandelwerk* enhanced by gilding and Böttger luster with gilt lacework around the inner rim of the teabowl. The reserves, or white ground areas outside the cartouches, are decorated with *indianische Blumen*.[24]

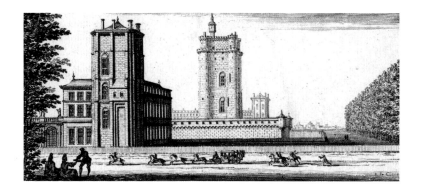

FIG. 51 Sébastien Le Clerc, *Quelques figures, chevaux, paysages*, ca. 1696–1700. Etching, 2⅞ × 6⅛ in. (7.2 × 15.6 cm). British Museum, 1917,1208.1727

47 TEAPOT

ca. 1725–1728

Hard-paste porcelain

4¼ × 4¼ in. (11 × 11 cm)

L13.62.57A–B (CAT. NO. 64)

•

This teapot with *Schwarzlot* (black monochrome) harbor and riverside scenes is one of the earliest pieces in the Gutter collection to display the crossed-swords mark (introduced in 1723). (It is also marked with *K.P.M.,* for Königliche Porzellan-Manufaktur.) A gilder's numeral, 29, is also applied to the base of the teapot.[25]

For more on this model, introduced by Irminger for Meissen, see cat. nos. 27 and 29/pls. 20 and 22. The *Fratzenkopf* mask where the spout emerges from the body of this teapot is highlighted with luster. The *Schwarzlot* landscape scenes on either side are dominated by vast expanses of sky framed by puce/purple cartouche surrounds and enhanced with Böttger luster and gilding. The same monochromatic puce palette is used on the *indianische Blumen* scattered over the teapot body and lid. *Schwarzlot* was primarily employed for harbor scenes and landscapes, many of which were inspired by seventeenth-century Dutch seascapes.[26]

FIG. 52 Reverse view of teapot

48 TEABOWL

ca. 1722–1723

Hard-paste porcelain

1 ¾ × 2 ¾ in. (4.6 × 7 cm)

L13.62.62 (CAT. NO. 65)

•

Night scenes are extremely rare at Meissen. The very thinly potted Böttger porcelain and the treatment of the flowers decorating the back side of this teabowl has led Gutter to believe it is one, if not the earliest, of the nocturnes produced at Meissen. The dusky scene is dominated by two figures and their boat sitting on the shore in the foreground. Two additional figures next to the boat are illuminated by a blazing campfire issuing billowing black smoke over much of the composition. Three ships at sail are silhouetted in the background.

The gilt cartouche surround is enhanced with iron-red *Laub- und Bandelwerk* and Böttger luster. The rim of the teabowl is painted with a single gilt band, and the interior is decorated with an iron-red scene of a galleon at sail surrounded by birds, framed within double iron-red bands (fig. 53). The back of the teabowl is decorated with *indianische Blumen*, thinly painted in a limited palette.

It is interesting to compare this work with another teabowl and saucer featuring nocturnal scenes (see below right). The present example is more limited in palette, and the painting quality is somewhat less refined. Its scene is probably inspired or taken from a print, although the exact source has yet to be identified.

49 TEABOWL AND SAUCER

ca. 1726–1727

Hard-paste porcelain

Teabowl: 1 ¾ × 3 in. (4.3 × 7.5 cm); saucer: ⅝ × 4 ⅞ in. (1.7 × 12.5 cm)

L13.62.61A–B (CAT. NO. 66)

•

As discussed at left, nocturnal scenes are unusual on Meissen, and European porcelains in general, and are rarely seen on forms other than teabowls or saucers. Like that teabowl, this teabowl and saucer depict a scene alongside a riverbank, although the painting here is of greater detail and refinement. The saucer depicts a highly detailed fireside encampment with several figures and animals, possibly goats. Two of the figures cast fishing nets at water's edge, illuminated in part by a bright yellow, full moon. The moon, emerging from a cloudy sky, is reflected upon the water. The scene on the teabowl features a horseman crossing a bridge, visible through a glowing campfire. The other side of the teabowl features a daytime river scene (see p. 130 for alternate view). The scene was likely inspired by a seventeenth-century Dutch print or painting, although a source has not been identified.

The scenes on both the teabowl and saucer are framed in gilded quatrefoil cartouches surrounded with puce *Laub- und Bandelwerk* and Böttger luster. Their rims are further enhanced with a broad band of gilt lacework.[27]

FIG. 53 (ABOVE) Detail of interior of teabowl

51 SAUCER

ca. 1727–1730

Hard-paste porcelain

$\frac{7}{8} \times 4\frac{3}{4}$ in. (2.2 × 11.9 cm)

L13.62.59 (CAT. NO. 68)

•

The decoration of this saucer is quite unusual and can be seen in the context of two related coffee and tea services produced by Meissen circa 1727–1730. The central scene depicts a stag and doe among trees set with stylized Baroque devices. The design is surmounted by a crown motif. The cavetto, or inner border, is of Böttger luster and is interspersed by four oval, gilt-framed medallions decorated with puce *camaïeu* (or monochromatic) scenes, three of chinoiseries and one of a hunt. The outermost rim of underglaze blue is further enhanced with gilding. The underside of the saucer is decorated with polychrome floral sprays and four underglaze-blue rings flanking the footrim (fig. 55). The source for the central scene is derived from Schmischek and his *Neues Groteschgen-Büchlein* (1630).[29]

Other teabowls and saucers from this service are well documented and include related examples in the Victoria and Albert Museum (202&A-1854); the Wark Collection at the Cummer Museum (AG.2000.2.398a–b[30]); and the Nationalmuseum Stockholm (NMK 233/1921). Other forms from the service have also been identified, such as a jug in the British Museum (1955,0708.1). Slight variations in the characters of the central hunt scene occur on each.

Scholars are of varying opinions as to whether the decoration of these services was produced at Meissen or by *Hausmaler* decorators. Although the prominent Böttger luster, available only at the manufactory, as well as the floral sprays on the underside certainly suggests Meissen decoration, it would be interesting to confirm this theory through scientific enamel analysis.

FIG. 55 Detail of underside of saucer

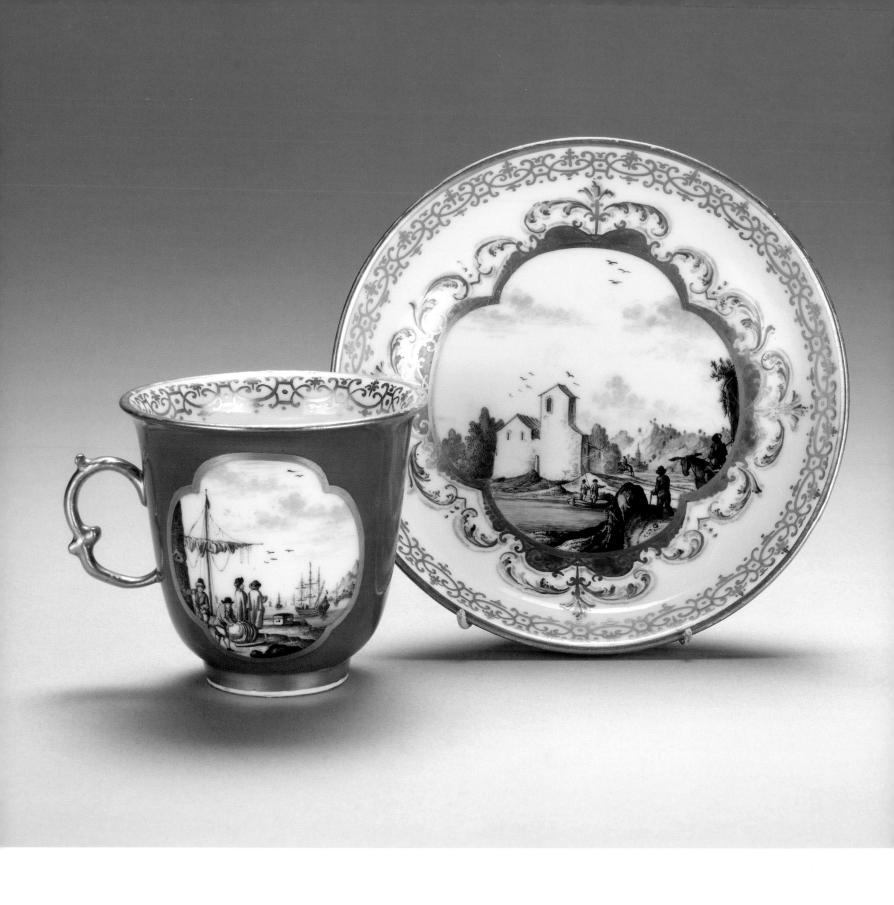

52 COFFEE CUP AND SAUCER

ca. 1740–1750
Painting possibly attributed to Christian Friedrich Herold
Hard-paste porcelain
Cup: $2\frac{3}{4} \times 2\frac{3}{4}$ in. (7×7.1 cm); saucer: $1\frac{1}{8} \times 5\frac{1}{8}$ in. (2.9×13 cm)
L13.62.55A–B (CAT. NO. 69)

•

Höroldt introduced a variety of ground colors at Meissen in the 1720s, but red was first achieved in the mid-1730s and continued to be developed into the 1740s. This coffee cup is a rare example of red-ground ware. The color proved to be a problematic one to produce in the kiln. Among Meissen works, the reds range in shade from those resembling a tomato to that of a persimmon. Gutter explored the subject of red-ground wares in his 1989 article for *Antique Collector*. At that time he identified all the red-ground pieces known to him, but he has since come to believe that Meissen produced seven distinct red-ground services for coffee, tea, and chocolate. Another coffee cup and saucer from the same service as Gutter's is in the Gardiner Museum, Toronto (G83.1.686a–b).[31]

On the coffee cup, a quatrefoil gilt band frames a seascape with a scene of maritime trading (*Kauffahrtei*) in the foreground. In general, elaborate cartouches are not employed on pieces with ground colors. The scene on the saucer features in the foreground two figures, one on horseback, overlooking a bay of water with two fishermen in a small boat. The majority of the field is dominated by a large building on the shore and a village nestled in a distant mountainous landscape. The scene is contained in a gilt quatrefoil cartouche enhanced with luster and iron-red *Laub- und Bandelwerk*. (See also p. 10 for alternate view.) The scenes on this cup and saucer are probably derived from a seventeenth-century Dutch engraving, although the exact source has not been identified. The saucer and inner rim of the cup are bordered with identical gilt lacework.

Although it is difficult to attribute the decoration to any painter with certainty, the subject matter and quality of painting suggests the hand of Herold. After discussions with Julia Weber—formerly curator of the Bayerisches Nationalmuseum, Munich, and now director of the Porzellansammlung, Dresden—regarding comparable pieces with the gilder's mark S in the Lustheim collection, Gutter has extended the possible date of production beyond the previously accepted date of circa 1740 to circa 1740–1750.

CHAPTER 7

HÖROLDT AND FAR EASTERN DECORATION

Covered tureen, ca. 1730 (cat. no. 87/pl. 64)

FIG. 56 (ABOVE) Zacharias Longuelune, wall arrangement plan for the porcelain collection at the Japanese Palace, ca. 1735. Sächsisches Staatsarchiv, Dresden, SächsStA-D, 10006 Oberhofmarschallamt, Cap. 2, Nr. 15, Bl. 26d/1

I n 1717 Augustus the Strong purchased the Holländisches Palais in Dresden on the banks of the river Elbe, the former residence of the Dutch ambassador. Augustus expanded the palace to display his vast collection of Chinese, Japanese, and Meissen porcelain, which eventually grew to more than forty thousand pieces, and he renamed it the Japanisches Palais (Japanese Palace) in recognition of these valuable holdings. Although it was never fully achieved, tantalizing glimmers of the ambitious porcelain arrangements for the Japanese Palace can be seen in surviving documents (fig. 56).[1] In these fantastic displays, plates densely line the walls, punctuated by larger wares and vases resting on brackets, further enhanced by garnitures of vases upon the mantelpieces.

Johann Gregorius Höroldt and his contemporaries at Meissen found great inspiration in the forms and decorations of Augustus's Asian porcelain. Sometimes the Meissen artists copied the Asian versions exactly as special commissions for Augustus the Strong; at other times, interpretations were based loosely on originals. Meissen capitalized on the high demand in Europe for Asian decoration, such as the prevailing Kakiemon style. Augustus the Strong favored the style so much, he set aside one of the largest galleries in the Japanese Palace for Kakiemon-decorated Meissen porcelains.

Many pieces in the Gutter collection bear engraved and blackened inventory numbers for the Japanese Palace, making it one of the largest repositories of such numbered works in private hands (see p. 257). Surviving royal inventories of the Japanese Palace were taken from 1721 to 1727 and in 1770, and of the porcelain room in the Turmzimmer (tower room of the Dresden Residenzschloss) in 1769, 1780, and 1783. At the time of the 1721 inventory, Augustus had thirteen thousand pieces in his Asian collection. By 1727 that collection had grown to twenty-one thousand pieces. Only the 1770 Japanese Palace and 1769 Turmzimmer inventories survive. Claus Boltz's 1996 article "Japanisches Palais-Inventar 1770 und Turmzimmer-Inventar 1769" is invaluable for studying Meissen and Asian porcelain in the collection.[2]

In addition to works bearing Japanese Palace inventory numbers, several pieces in the Gutter collection bear the AR monogram (for "Augustus Rex"; see fig. 58), reserved for pieces produced for the court of Augustus the Strong or his son Augustus III. Such works were also presented as diplomatic gifts.

53 BEAKER VASE

ca. 1725
Painting attributed to Johann Ehrenfried Stadler
Hard-paste porcelain and nineteenth-century French
gilt-bronze mount
15¾ × 8 in. (40 × 20.3 cm)
L13.62.90 (CAT. NO. 76)

•

Known as a *Flötenvase*, this Meissen beaker-vase form was inspired by seventeenth-century Japanese porcelains. Overglaze enamel colors were used for the rich flora and birds in combination with underglaze-blue decoration for the rock formations. The combination of overglaze and underglaze decoration on Meissen objects is very rare; it was most likely done out of necessity, as the difficulty of producing a successful blue enamel was not resolved until circa 1726. The combination is used to rich decorative effect, as seen on earlier Chinese *wucai* decoration.[3] It blends influences taken from Japanese Kakiemon and Chinese *famille verte* porcelains.

Dominated by a polychrome *Kaiserkrone* (imperial crown lily) growing out of the rockwork, the decoration is attributed to Johann Ehrenfried Stadler. Stadler came to Meissen circa 1724 from Martin Eggebrecht's Dresden faience works. He developed an identifiable painting style in Höroldt's workshop, particularly for his florals (or *Bluhmen-Werck*) and use of underglaze blues combined with enamels. The vase also exhibits an unusual brown-enamel band around its base.

Although there was a tradition of producing grand vases at Meissen (see three underglaze-blue examples, chapter 4 [cat. nos. 35–37/pls. 23–25]), few grand polychrome and underglaze-blue vases are known. It appears that Stadler had a hand in all eleven known examples.[4] As the majority of surviving related works were made for Augustus the Strong, one can suggest that these polychrome vases were made in pairs for display in the Japanese Palace, as seen in the design plans. There is, however, the possibility that some were made as a garniture.

FIGS. 57 AND 58 Reverse view and detail of AR monogram
on underside of beaker vase

54 FRAGMENTS OF A BOTTLE-GOURD VASE

ca. 1726–1730

Painting attributed to Johann Ehrenfried Stadler

Hard-paste porcelain

Reconstructed vase: height 14⅛ in. (36 cm),
base diameter 4½ in. (11.5 cm)

L13.62.91 (CAT. NO. 77)

•

Many pieces from the renowned collection of Meissen assembled by banker Gustav von Klemperer (1852–1926) were in transit through Dresden on February 13, 1945, when the city was fire-bombed by Allied forces.[5] The surviving pieces and fragments were discovered after the war and were transferred to the Dresden Porzellansammlung. A group of fragmentary and restored works was returned to the Klemperer family and subsequently consigned to Bonhams, London, for auction in 2010. It is from this sale that the fragments of this bottle-gourd vase were acquired. The vase was reconstructed through careful examination of its companion, now in the Ernst Schneider Collection, Schloss Lustheim, Munich (ES 75; fig. 59), which is marked with *AR* for "Augustus Rex."[6] Although the early provenance of both vases remains unknown, Klemperer was present at the second sale of duplicates from the royal collection of the Johanneum in October 1920, where he may have acquired these pieces.[7]

Many other great eighteenth-century German porcelain collections met similar fates as the Klemperers'.[8] Due to the persecution of the Jews, the Klemperers abandoned their collection when they fled Dresden following the anti-Jewish pogrom Kristallnacht on November 9, 1938. Their property was seized and transferred to the state of Saxony as part of its collection. To protect it from air raids, the state collection was stored outside of Dresden; however, the approach of the Russian army provoked the Germans to move it to another location. The truck transporting part of the Klemperers' collection was in front of the Dresden Residenz when the city was bombed.

The bottle-gourd form and its lotus decoration are derived from both Chinese and Japanese prototypes and further influenced by late seventeenth- and early eighteenth-century German faience.[9] Chinese and Japanese examples in the Porzellansammlung provided direct inspiration to Meissen's artists for both the vase shape and lotus decoration. The bottle-gourd form was also used for three large, early blue-and-white vases, all circa 1722–1724 (a pair in the Ludwig collection, Bamberg, and another—indubitably also one of a pair—in the Bayerisches Nationalmuseum, Munich). The fantastic and colorful lotus decoration in *famille verte* style lavished on the Gutter vase and its Lustheim pendant is unique, yet quintessentially Meissen in palette and decorative technique.[10] Of the related lotus-decorated pieces noted here, the academic consensus is that they are the work of a single artist, most likely Stadler. As noted in the discussion of the beaker vase above, Stadler achieved artistic and technical mastery circa 1727–1730.

The palette used for this pair of bottle-gourd vases is sea green, yellow green, brown, iron red, yellow, gold, purple, and luster (used for some stripes to depict water), with black for the leaf veins. As Höroldt was not able to obtain a satisfactory blue enamel until 1726 or 1727, its absence might be definitive for dating.

FIG. 59 Gourd vase with lotus decoration, ca. 1730. Hard-paste porcelain, 13⅝ × 6⅞ in. (34.6 × 17.5 cm). Bayerisches Nationalmuseum, Munich, Oberschleißheim, Schloss Lustheim, Meißener Porzellan-Sammlung, Stiftung Ernst Schneider ES 75

56 SAUCER

ca. 1727–1730

Hard-paste porcelain

1 ⅛ × 7 ½ in. (2.8 × 19 cm)

L13.62.92 (CAT. NO. 79)

•

In 1726–1727 Höroldt experimented with ground colors, undoubtedly influenced by Chinese examples in the king's collection. The body of this saucer is composed of an experimental porcelain paste that is tinted pale violet-pink with metallic oxides. In contrast, the flattened handles are composed of an untinted white paste, as are the raised floral sprigs on the reverse. Kakiemon decoration of enameled *indianische Blumen*, a phoenix, and a bug is enhanced by a gilt lacework border and rim. The phoenix (or *feng-huang*) is stripped here from its traditional symbolism in Chinese mythology, in which it represents femininity or the Chinese empress.

Few examples of tinted wares survive in various shades of gray blue and pale violet-pink. Other identified tinted pieces, as well as the Japanese Palace inventory, suggest that this saucer would have been accompanied by a spouted cup, monogrammed with an applied *AR* for Augustus Rex. (For nearly identical examples, see two saucers and a cup, Porzellansammlung, Dresden;[14] cup and saucer, Seattle Art Museum [69.198];[15] cup and saucer, Metropolitan Museum of Art, New York [1977.216.12, .13; fig. 60]; and cup, British Museum [Franks.42], probably the companion to Gutter's saucer.)

Gutter's saucer is decorated on the underside with applied prunus enhanced with enamels (see p. 169 for underside view).[16] The shape for these cups and saucers was possibly inspired by silver forms. The saucer has two distinct flattened handles to facilitate drinking coffee or tea directly from it.

FIG. 60 Pitcher and stand, ca. 1725–1730. Hard-paste porcelain, pitcher 2 ⅜ × 4 ¼ in. (6 × 10.8 cm), stand width 7 ½ in. (19.1 cm). The Metropolitan Museum of Art, New York, Bequest of R. Thornton Wilson, in memory of his wife, Florence Ellsworth Wilson, 1977, 1977.216.12, .13

COLLECTOR'S STORY: SAUCER

Tinted-paste porcelain's special technology and the scarcity of examples may have inhibited its research over the years; I know of no article specifically devoted to its development. The objects remain a rather mysterious group, which for me only enhances their allure, their rarity a source of delight and envy. The three gorgeous blue-paste vases in the Metropolitan Museum of Art, the three small examples in the British Museum, and certainly not least the Augustus portrait tankard in the Porzellansammlung, Dresden, stand out as spine-tingling examples.

A collector of limited financial resources must constantly be aware of parameters: some pieces seem destined to be forever tantalizing, through ravishing illustrations or museum glass. Imagine my surprise and giddiness when, in June 2010, I spied this tinted-paste saucer waiting in the wings at Christie's, South Kensington, one of many leftovers from the Roy Byrnes collection, one hundred seventy or so of his "best" pieces having sold a month prior at King Street. (During my 1996 visit with Roy at his home, this piece was somehow overlooked.)

Dominic Simpson had chosen not to include this piece among Roy's best. My good luck: if it had been included in the main sale, he would perforce have done considerable research, noting findings and references in the catalogue for all to see. As it was, once he had relegated it to South Kensington, the people there took over, Dominic relinquishing all interest. Catalogue entries for South Kensington sales are sparse, lots with little or no "follow-up" material.

And where had Roy obtained the saucer? I phoned him Sunday before the sale. (He fortuitously kept a notebook of provenance and concordance with the numbered labels on the underside of his pieces.) Roy revealed without any qualms he purchased the saucer, together with a married early Meissen teabowl (damaged and not particularly important), at Sotheby's, New York, in October 1994. (Interestingly, Tish Roberts had added a footnote for that lot, correctly identifying the saucer as "perhaps" belonging to the solid paste family, the "stand" for an AR cream cup in the British Museum collection.) Although in

esteemed company—the sale was one of the most distinguished held since the Second World War, and included the collection of Edward G. Schiffman   the lot had been listed under the always-tempting-but-useless category "Property of Several Collectors."

I had been told by Dominic that Roy's "seconds" would be offered in groups—it turned out three—during the first half of 2011. The saucer showed up, estimated at £700–1,000, as one of four pieces, in lot 165 of the April Interiors sale. Confident of his virtually unerring eye, especially for rarities, I confided my interest to Errol Manners; always the gentleman, graciously withdrawing from bidding, he promised to perform a once-over on the saucer when and if he viewed the sale. I registered to bid online rather than by telephone. I had penciled in £5,500 as tops—very high, but as Errol had opined, "you'll never have another chance for something like this." The lot came up at about 3:30 a.m., but a minor crisis arose: my internet connection partially failed, the picture frozen, the sound mute. At £700 my connection, though still lacking sound, suddenly revived—the

bidding bar now active—and I clicked for £750. One more increment against me, another click by me for £850, and then verification ("bid is in your favor"). I had won—another skin-of-my-teeth success: an amazing catch. But where were the other collectors? Sadly, the imperfect computer connection will forever hold the mystery of the bidding give and take. In the end, it was the fantasy of every collector—the piece had slipped through the cracks, nobody catching on. I called Roy to let him know his saucer was to remain in California and was greeted by happy congratulations.

—MALCOLM GUTTER

57 BEAKER VASE

ca. 1726–1730
Painting attributed to Johann Ehrenfried Stadler
Hard-paste porcelain
15¾ × 9½ in. (40 × 24.1 cm)
L13.62.93 (CAT. NO. 80)

•

A dragon wrapping his tail around an umbrella of wild and bright fruits and *indianische Blumen* highlights the dramatic and opulent decoration of this vase.[17] Complementing the central image is an exotic, brightly colored bird perching on a thin branch (see fig. 62). The lower section of the vase is decorated simply, with random sprays of flower heads and leaves, and the luster footrim (found on a few other large vases of this period) provides a final flourish. Likely created by Stadler, this vessel displays the wide range of enamel colors that the Meissen manufactory developed during Höroldt's tenure. Nine distinct enamels are used in the decoration of this vase: iron red, green, turquoise, purple, black, yellow, brown, brownish gray, and the recently introduced (overglaze) blue. Höroldt achieved success with the deep, blue enamel around 1726.

The Gutter collection contains three of these early polychrome pieces decorated by Stadler under Höroldt's tenure. He quickly achieved mastery both in personal style and technique after joining the manufactory in 1724. His large vases, painted in both underglaze-blue and polychrome enamels, were executed within a limited period, between about 1725 and 1730. He specialized in flower painting, or *Bluhmen-Werck*, and the Gutter vase displays his wildly fantastic, dramatic, and opulent best.

The form of the vase, with its flaring, trumpetlike rim and lower bowl section, was introduced at Meissen around 1725 and was taken from seventeenth-century Arita prototypes. It was

wheel-thrown in three pieces—the upper beaker section in two pieces, and the lower, bowl-like section—and luted together by slip before firing.

The vase has a pendant, now in the Porzellansammlung, Dresden.[18] Both pieces exhibit matching, underglaze-blue AR monograms, accentuated by a small dot at their lower right (see fig. 61).[19] Probably conceived as a pair, they also could have been part of a larger, five- or seven-piece garniture. As discussed in the chapter introduction, surviving documents of the planned displays of the Japanese Palace show large vases arranged on wall brackets. Another visual clue to their display can be found in the vintage photographs of the porcelain room of the Turmzimmer of the Dresden Residenzschloss. In these photographs, pairs of such vases are mounted symmetrically on wall brackets around doorways or mirrors.[20]

The Meissen manufactory produced a copy of the Gutter collection vase in 1922, identified by an AR monogram and 1922 in underglaze blue. It measures 14⅝ inches high, about 1 inch shorter than the original. Iron-red inscriptions—*Schauhalle* (exhibition hall) and *Originalkopie unverkäuflich* (original copy, not for sale)—have been added to its base. The luster on the footrims of the originals were not duplicated on the 1922 copy.[21]

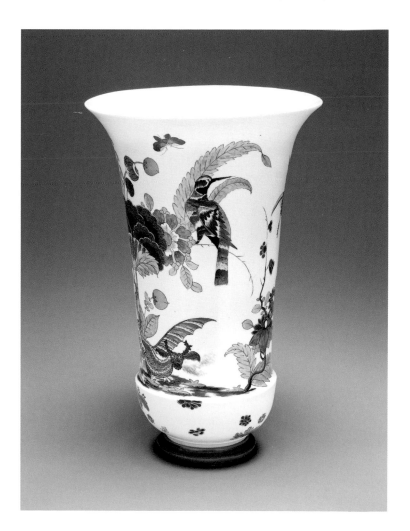

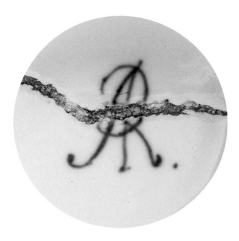

FIGS. 61 (ABOVE) AND 62 (RIGHT) Detail of AR monogram on underside and reverse view of beaker vase

58 BEAKER AND SAUCER

ca. 1726–1727

Hard-paste porcelain

Beaker: $3\frac{1}{4} \times 3\frac{1}{8}$ in. (8.3×7.9 cm);
saucer: $1\frac{3}{8} \times 5\frac{1}{2}$ in. (3.5×14 cm)

L13.62.83A–B (CAT. NO. 81)

•

A Chinese example made in the kilns of Dehua, which produced wares known in Europe as *blanc de chine* (white china), certainly served as the model for this beaker. Around 1726–1727, Samuel Stöltzel was experimenting with the Meissen paste and glazes in an attempt to whiten the body in imitation of Chinese and Japanese examples. (The Japanese referred to the fine white porcelain body as *nigoshide* [milky white].) Pursuing this direction, Meissen would eventually adopt an increasingly feldspathic body, confirmed by pale violet fluorescence under a short-wave ultraviolet lamp.

Although the exact Chinese model for the beaker has not been identified, the Meissen workshop had access to comparable Chinese prototypes in Augustus the Strong's collection. Other elements visible on the underside, such as the three applied prunus branches on the saucer (fig. 63) and the double footrim on the beaker, are directly inspired by Chinese examples. The saucer, however, did not have a Chinese precedent and was created by Meissen for a European market. The crazing on the saucer reflects the experimental nature of the paste on this piece.

In correspondence with Gutter, Claus Boltz proposed an interesting hypothesis regarding the saucer. Boltz believed it was one of Stöltzel's early experiments (with a new body that was not fully compatible with the glaze) that was taken by Meissen general director Count Karl Heinrich von Hoym circa 1728–1731 to Rodolphe Lemaire in Paris to be copied for Kakiemon porcelain. For more on the Hoym-Lemaire scandal, see the entry for plate 61.

As seen in the inventory, the number of beakers made far outpaces the saucers.[22] Other known beakers, and a few saucers, with the inventory number N=397-/w: are found in several public and private collections.[23]

FIG. 63 Detail of underside of saucer

59 TEAPOT

ca. 1724–1730
Hard-paste porcelain
4⅛ × 4⅜ in. (10.5 × 11.2 cm)
L13.62.76A–B (CAT. NO. 82)

•

Inspired in form by Chinese Yixing red-ware teapots, albeit a bit flattened, this globular teapot has a domed lid and straight spout. Boltz noted three teapots with this form made at Meissen between June 1722 and December 1728.[24]

Lustered laurel leaves (*Spitzlaub*) were applied to the lid, neck, and base of the teapot. Kakiemon decoration further enhances the vessel, including designs of a boy in a blue kimono pulling a peony along with a red string and of a blue kylin (a Chinese mythological animal; fig. 64). Gutter has noted a Japanese bowl—with Japanese Palace inventory number N=254-/w, in the Porzellansammlung, Dresden—that may have inspired the decoration on this teapot.[25]

This combination of Chinese form with Japanese Kakiemon on a transitional *Kalk*-feldspathic body is quite unusual. As mentioned in the previous entry, Stöltzel was modifying the factory paste by 1726–1727, in part to achieve a whiter body for fashionable Kakiemon decorations. The Böttger porcelain (or *Kalk*) paste was still in use through the 1720s, and many wares exhibit a transitional paste, as one sees here. The rare synthesis of paste, form, and decoration suggests that this teapot is a rare experimental object.

FIG. 64 Reverse view of teapot

60 MOUNTED TANKARD

ca. 1727–1728
Painting attributed to Johann Ehrenfried Stadler
Hard-paste porcelain with silver-gilt mount
6⅞ × 3¾ in. (17.5 × 9.4 cm); height without cover: 6⅜ in.
(16.2 cm)
L13.62.81 (CAT. NO. 83)

•

Decorated with riotous flowering branches of *indianische Blumen*, this tankard is composed of feldspathic paste. On the body opposite from the handle resides a large bird with fanciful plumage perched upon a branch supported by an outcropping. He is surrounded by three additional birds. The commanding decorative treatment of these birds and flowers are indicative of Stadler's work. The scene can perhaps be most closely compared to one of the blue-ground-and-gilt-vases in the Porzellansammlung, Dresden (PE 666), as well as a related dish (PE 1466).[26]

The inclusion of blue enamel decoration, introduced circa 1726, and the contemporary green-ground diaper band design around the base facilitate the dating of this tankard. Three concentric lines of iron red flank the diaper band.

61 TEN-SIDED BOWL

ca. 1729–1730

Hard-paste porcelain

3⅜ × 7¾ in. (8.6 × 19.7 cm)

L13.62.77 (CAT. NO. 84)

•

One of the great highlights of the Gutter collection, this ten-sided bowl is based in form and decoration on a Kakiemon prototype in the Dresden royal collection. As mentioned in previous entries, the new, whiter feldspathic paste was developed in part by Meissen alchemist Stöltzel to showcase Kakiemon decorations. The outside of the bowl is embellished with a pastoral scene of horses cavorting among flowering grasses; inside the bowl are *indianische Blumen* and coiled phoenixes, or ho-ho birds in Japanese terminology. A pair of Japanese prototypes for this bowl survive in the Ashmolean Museum, Oxford (fig. 65).[27] The ten quadrants are outlined in bright blue enamel, and the shaped rim features a tied-ribbon motif and a brown trim. Meissen's brown enamel was in imitation of the Japanese brown-pigmented clay used to decorate rims, known as *kuchibeni* (mouth rouge). In addition to the crossed-swords mark and Japanese Palace inventory number, the underside (fig. 66) also displays the rubbed, somewhat illegible, inventory number 119 of its Japanese prototype, signifying ownership by Höroldt himself and its use as a model for his painters.

In the late 1720s, a duplicitous scheme was hatched between Count Karl Heinrich von Hoym (1694–1736), the director general of Meissen, and the Parisian merchant Rodolphe Lemaire. Japanese porcelains in Augustus the Strong's collection were copied by Meissen and then sold as valuable Japanese wares by Lemaire to the Parisian market. Some of the porcelains were

unmarked, while others exhibited the blue crossed swords in overglaze enamel that could be easily removed. A Kosel mark could also be used to cover or obscure the crossed swords (see fig. 69 for an example of such a mark). (It was once believed that this mark was named after Augustus the Strong's mistress Countess Constantia von Cosel, but this explanation is now accepted as false.) This illegal manufacture of Kakiemon-decorated porcelains at Meissen took place between 1729 and 1731. By 1731, Hoym and Lemaire's duplicity was discovered, and both were arrested. Pieces were seized from Hoym's palace and taken to the royal collection, where they were inventoried and accessioned. Unfortunately, the Japanese Palace inventory does not note which works were confiscated in 1731 by Augustus the Strong.[28] (For other pieces in the Gutter collection with possible ties to the Hoym-Lemaire affair, see cat. nos. 81, 87–89, and 91/pls. 58, 64–66, and 68.) This bowl is a particularly important document to the scandal.

Although Höroldt must have been intimately aware of this elaborate arrangement as director of the manufactory, he avoided prosecution. However, immediately following these events his comfortable workshop was absorbed within the manufactory, possibly as a result of his involvement. With this move Höroldt's title changed from *Hofmaler* (court painter) to *Hofkommissar* (court commissioner). Running an independent workshop, Höroldt had been paying for his own pieces of Meissen, which his workshop copied or drew inspiration from. In 1731 Höroldt sold many of his own Meissen models back to the manufactory, including this rare bowl.[29] This explains the Japanese model number 119, incised into the paste under the glaze on the footrim on the bowl, and the partially obliterated black number on the underside probably made by Höroldt.[30]

FIG. 65 Pair of octagonal bowls with horses and English Empire-style mounts, ca. 1700. Japan, Kakiemon workshops. Porcelain and nineteenth-century mounts. Ashmolean Museum of Art and Archaeology, University of Oxford, EA1978.664.a–b

FIG. 66 Detail of underside of bowl

COLLECTOR'S STORY: TEN-SIDED BOWL

In 1993 Christie's held three European porcelain sales, a monumental diminution from the monthly or bimonthly offerings of the 1950s, '60s, and '70s, reduced further by the late 1990s. That year I took a sabbatical leave from teaching, allowing attendance in London for the June follies—the Olympia, Grosvenor House, and Ceramics antiques fairs. I would also travel by train from London to Dresden to begin research on red stoneware. Before leaving for the Continent, I had made an appointment with Louise Newman to go into the Christie's catacombs to view the upcoming sale. She may have actually thrust this bowl into my hands, fearing my not spotting it on the cluttered shelves. Dazzling: those incredible horses on the outside and the phoenixes on the interior in a brilliant orange-red, blue, and yellow palette. It just sang to me, damage notwithstanding (quite noticeable then), exuding such sumptuous decoration contained within a sensual form.

Turning it over I noticed both the overglaze swords mark and perfectly good Japanese Palace inventory number. I will confess that although noticing the error in the Christie's catalogue—the so-called *Dreher's* incised number listed as 1195 was in fact 119—I failed to grasp its significance. (Nor should I have, as my study of Claus Boltz's 1980 article on the Hoym-Lemaire scandal was still in the future.) The crudely scraped surface around another area on the underside, however, was at first a bit puzzling. There had been an attempt to obliterate numbers in black, the remnants of which were still observable. It took but a moment, however, to recall where I had seen another such example: the underside of an Imari Meissen box in Dresden. I could not precisely recall the configuration of the "scraping," but I was most eager to revisit it in its case in the Porzellansammlung. How fortunate I had planned this trip to Germany!

More than I could imagine, the box in Dresden allowed the Christie's bowl to reveal its secret. On the glazed flat bottom, as with the bowl, there was a crossed-swords mark, along with a Japanese Palace inventory number (N=170-/w) for Meissen porcelain. In addition, the remnants of another inventory number could be more clearly seen, partially remaining after being scraped on the bottom. (See pl. 61 for more on the Hoym-Lemaire scandal.) Most significantly a clearly defined square, designating Kraak porcelain (Chinese wares imported by the Dutch, often decorated with paneled borders; Kakiemon ware is customarily categorized as such and bears this mark), convincingly suggested this partially obliterated number to be, in fact, the number of the Arita prototype from which the Meissen was copied. The obliterated number on the bowl at Christie's had to be as well, providing that much more incentive to bring it into my collection.

Damage had most likely relegated the photo of the bowl in the sales catalogue to humble black-and-white, the "humiliation" compounded by it being placed with three lesser Meissen

pieces and given a very modest estimate of £1,200–1,800. I have learned that a "proper" frame of mind is an essential ingredient for successful bidding, germinating in turn price anticipation far exceeding a catalogue estimate. In the case of this bowl I had originally feared paying £5,000, based upon its rarity and beauty. On the train from Heidelberg to Cologne, the horrific thought crossed my mind it could fetch £10,000—would I be prepared to pay that much? The kernel proved to be both psychologically important and prescient.

The sale took place about a week after my return to San Francisco. Anticipating a phone ring at about 4 a.m., I nevertheless was awake most of the night. Bidding started somewhere around £1,000 and quickly rose to well above the high estimate. I do not remember exactly when I came in, but I soon realized I was in a duel with only one other bidder. It was then that my earlier premonition of having to surrender a £10,000 bid became reality. I still remember the shock when the bowl was being knocked down in my favor, intense buyer's remorse even now quite palpable. What had I done?

But a rather dramatic sequel, not without its ironies, was still to come. I had decided to have the bowl sent home through Christie's shippers. As was the custom when one of my "babies" arrived, the box sat by the dining table, waiting for a ceremonial opening after dinner. That evening I proceeded to cut the tape. The usual protecting material was removed, but I could not feel the bowl. Moving my hand around the box, now with some apprehension, I finally arrived at a small bubble-wrapped item. Much too small for a bowl; could something additional have been included? An elongated item was unwrapped, mummy-like, and out popped an American Indian doll! No further rummaging in the box produced the bowl. It seems the packers had inadvertently misdirected the two objects into containers nevertheless correctly addressed, thereby shipping my bowl to Hamburg and the American doll to San Francisco. I drove to Christie's San Francisco office the following morning. Christie's had to keep its fingers crossed that my much more valuable bowl on the other side of the Atlantic be acknowledged and given up. Letters of apology; the bowl arrived after a few days.

—MALCOLM GUTTER

62 DISH

ca. 1729–1731
Hard-paste porcelain
2 ⅛ × 9 ½ in. (5.4 × 24 cm)
L13.62.88 (CAT. NO. 85)

•

Featuring a Japanese Kakiemon design on a distinctly European form, this deep dish (*Schüssel*) depicts a ho-ho bird flying toward an outcropping of flowering branches and a meandering banded hedge. The decoration is sparse, following the Japanese aesthetic, and the new Meissen feldspathic white paste is shown off to great effect.

Objects with Japanese Palace inventory numbers following 66[31]—numbers 67 through 70—incorporate the same or similar decoration, but on somewhat different forms. Meissen also produced dishes with a more typically Japanese flattened profile and a gently sloping rim, such as those labeled *N=69-/w*, identified as *Schaalen* in the Japanese Palace inventory. Such examples are in the holdings of the Fine Arts Museums of San Francisco (fig. 67) and the Schneider collection, Schloss Lustheim (ES 342). Following the Japanese prototype, the decoration on these dishes extends to the edge. There are a few subtle differences in enamel colors (e.g., banding on the hedge) and floral design between the Japanese and Meissen porcelains.[32] The Gutter collection also contains a recently acquired dish of scattered Kakiemon sprigs with the Japanese Palace inventory number 65 (see top right). It is interesting to note that the paste and glaze on that dish are more experimental and irregular in nature than the present example. (The caduceus mark on the 65 dish is an early example of the nefarious marks used in the Hoym-Lemaire affair.[33])

62A DISH

ca. 1729–1730
Hard-paste porcelain
1 ⅜ × 9 ⅞ in. (3.6 × 25 cm)
L17.46.4 (CAT. NO. 103)

•

FIG. 67 (BOTTOM) Dish, 1728–1730. Hard-paste porcelain; diameter: 8 ¾ in. (21.4 cm). Fine Arts Museums of San Francisco, Museum purchase, California Arts Society Grant, 69.3.2

63 SAKE BOTTLE

ca. 1730
Hard-paste porcelain
Height: 7⅝ in. (19.5 cm)
L13.62.79 (CAT. NO. 86)

•

Though Japanese in form and Kakiemon decoration, this sake bottle has a pale turquoise-green ground, developed by Höroldt in 1725, in imitation of Chinese celadon wares. Augustus the Strong clearly favored celadon, as demonstrated by the dedication of a second room of the Japanese Palace for the sole display of these wares.[34]

The Japanese Palace inventory for N=291-/w reads: "Neun und Fünfzig Stück diverse Aufsatz-Bouteillen, Celadon-Couleur, mit weissen Feldern, darein kleine Blümgen und Zierrathen gemahlt, auch vergoldten Rändgen, No. 291" (Fifty-nine various celadon bottles for display sets with gold-framed white reserves containing small flowers and ornaments, no. 291).[35] The inventory record includes a celadon bottle of rounded shape, or *Sakeflasche* (like this one), as well as ones of quadrangular and octagonal form.[36] Numerous examples from the original fifty-nine bottles listed in the inventory remain in the Porzellansammlung, Dresden (see PE 5255 and PE 529 in the rounded form). The quadrangular variant shape was first adopted at Meissen in red stoneware.

Imported Asian wares with solid ground colors inspired Meissen to produce wares of various colors including brown, blue, yellow, and green, with reserved areas of white surrounded by gilt cartouches. The celadon-ground vase is decorated with three quatrefoil cartouches of gold-banded dentil borders decorated with *indianische Blumen* and insects. Although the decoration is Kakiemon in style, the enamel palette is Meissen. In another distinctive Baroque touch, the slender neck has an exposed white porcelain collar enhanced with a gilt foliate band. A simple gold band further decorates the foot of the bottle.

FIG. 68 Detail of underside of sake bottle

64 COVERED TUREEN

ca. 1730

Hard-paste porcelain

$7\frac{1}{2} \times 5\frac{1}{4}$ in. (19×13.3 cm);

without cover: $4\frac{1}{4} \times 5\frac{1}{8}$ in. (10.7×13 cm)

L13.62.71A–B (CAT. NO. 87)

•

The tureen form was first introduced at Meissen in a red-stoneware body; this example with an artichoke finial was first listed in the registers as "Deckel belmit Artischocken" (lid with artichoke).[37] The Gutter tureen and its lid are decorated with a vast array of Kakiemon motifs including phoenixes among prunus, chrysanthemums, banded hedges, and autumn grasses (*ominaeshi*) (see p. 158 for alternate view). Based on the Meissen archives, stands (or *présentoires*) do not appear to be obligatory for tureens.

The 1770 Japanese Palace inventory for N=17-/w notes six tureens;[38] however, by 1779 the inventory only specified five. Gutter has identified two other pieces from this N=17-/w group. One is in the Porzellansammlung, Dresden, and another in the Museum für Kunst und Gewerbe Hamburg (both unpublished). According to Julia Weber, the Japanese prototype no longer survives in the Porzellansammlung, Dresden;[39] however, a Japanese model is in the Rijksmuseum, Amsterdam.[40]

The enameled (overglaze) crossed swords, combined with the tureen's newly introduced, feldspathic paste and Kakiemon decoration, suggests that this piece may have been involved in the Hoym-Lemaire scandal, one of the nearly five thousand pieces of Meissen seized from Hoym's palace and registered into the royal collection (see pl. 61).

65 OCTAGONAL DISH WITH SCENE FROM THE OPERA *FLORA: OR, HOB IN THE WELL*

ca. 1730
Hard-paste porcelain
1¾ × 11 in. (4.5 × 28 cm)
L13.62.73 (CAT. NO. 88)

•

Japanese Kakiemon decoration rarely takes up figural scenes. However, the story of the popular Chinese figure Sima Guang, an eleventh-century statesman and historian, was widely copied in Japan (under the name of Shiba Onkō) in the late seventeenth century. The scene on this octagonal dish depicts Sima as a quick-witted child, saving his friend from drowning in a large jar by breaking the jar with a rock. Another friend is shown here helping the friend from the shattering jar.

Meissen adopted the scene circa 1730; it was then copied at the Chelsea porcelain manufactory in England circa 1755. The pattern, which came to be known as Hob in the Well, was first adopted in England after a popular farce of the traditional Chinese tale called "Flora: or, Hob in the Well."

Numerous related Japanese octagonal dishes survive in public collections (including the Ashmolean [1978.573], the Rijksmuseum [BK-1989-8], and a pair at Burghley House [cero483], as well as the Meissen copies);[41] a possible Japanese prototype can be found in the Porzellansammlung, Dresden, with the inventory number N=14-/□. Although Meissen replicated the Japanese model faithfully, it also modified the scene for a round or twelve-sided dish as well.[42] As seen on the Gutter dish, the octagonal form has a flat rim decorated with chrysanthemums and peonies interspersed with a fernlike plant and is edged in brown.

Likewise, many Meissen dishes of this scene were made for the Japanese Palace, marked with various numbers interspersed throughout the inventory including N=33–39 and N=209–211. Although many of these dishes were likely ordered directly by Augustus the Strong for the Japanese Palace, there is also a strong possibility that a good number entered into the royal collection as a result of the Hoym-Lemaire affair (see pl. 61), especially as they were entered into the inventory in such numbers over a wide period of time. Offering a possible tie to Hoym and Lemaire, the Gutter dish has an enamel (overglaze) crossed-swords mark.

The Gutter collection also includes a rare Chinese export porcelain example with this scene (at right), which has a blue-and-white diaper-patterned border.

65A DISH WITH SCENE FROM THE OPERA *FLORA: OR, HOB IN THE WELL*

ca. 1700
China
Porcelain
Diameter: 12 in. (30.5 cm)
L13.62.136 (CAT. NO. 118)

•

66 BOWL

ca. 1730
Hard-paste porcelain
2⅛ × 5¼ in. (5.3 × 13.5 cm)
L13.62.89 (CAT. NO. 89)

•

Decorated with a coiled blue phoenix with red accents, this five-lobed bowl features an inner rim lined with a border of underglaze blue regularly interrupted with medallions enhanced by alternating red and green enameled flower heads and iron-red autumn grasses; the top of the rim is outlined in brown. The outside of the bowl features three red flower heads framed by an arabesque of tangled vines (*karakusa*). The footrim is encircled by blue bands.

The marks on the underside provide interesting clues to the history of the bowl (fig. 69). The underglaze-blue swords are covered by a rare, decorative gilt Kosel mark. At least two variant Kosel marks were used by the factory during the Hoym-Lemaire swindle to obscure the Meissen crossed-swords marks beneath (see pl. 61 for more on the Hoym-Lemaire affair). Curiously, the Gutter bowl was also given an overglaze (enamel) crossed-swords mark.

Other related Meissen bowls, noted below, bear Japanese Palace inventory numbers, suggesting that these pieces were likely seized in 1731 and entered into the royal collection. The Gutter bowl, still bearing enameled crossed swords and no inventory number, somehow escaped this fate.

The bowl, termed a *Spühl Näpfe* (rinsing bowl) in the inventories, was a direct copy from a Japanese Kakiemon prototype, as noted by the palette of underglaze blue, rust red, and gold. Although this Japanese source does not survive in the Porzellansammlung, Dresden, the British Museum, London, has a well-documented model in their collection with Japanese Palace inventory number N=27-/□ (1931,0417.1).[43] Meissen copies with Japanese Palace inventory numbers N=285-/w and N=203-/w can be found in the British Museum; the Rijksmuseum, Amsterdam; and the Porzellansammlung.[44]

Gutter has noted that this bowl has a slightly blue tint to the paste. It would be interesting to see if the other Meissen copies share this characteristic, which may have been adopted by the manufactory circa 1722 to keep the underglaze blue from running.

FIG. 69 Detail of underside of bowl

67 PLATE

ca. 1730–1735
Hard-paste porcelain
1⅜ × 9¾ in. (3.4 × 24.7 cm)
L13.62.84 (CAT. NO. 90)

•

Copied from a Japanese prototype, an example of which is also in the Gutter collection (see right), this shaped plate is decorated with a profusion of Kakiemon devices including a prominent coiled dragon (*ryu*) and a flaming, or hairy, tortoise (*minogame*). The border of the dish is further decorated with two cranes and the "three friends" motif of pine, bamboo, and flowering plum (prunus) with a rim outlined in brown.

Fifteen of these flaming-tortoise plates were listed in the Japanese Palace inventories under N=49-/w. No other examples of this plate without a Japanese Palace inventory number have been identified.[45] Gutter's plate is simply marked with crossed swords in underglaze blue. It appears that many of these N=49-/w plates were also involved in the Hoym-Lemaire affair (see pl. 61). There are some visible differences in the coloration of the paste and decoration between the Meissen plate and the Japanese prototype in the Gutter collection. The Meissen example is also more heavily potted. Another Japanese example in the Hans Syz collection in Washington, DC, is markedly consistent with the Gutter Japanese plate illustrated here.[46] Kakiemon decorations spread across Europe from Meissen, notably to Chelsea in England and Chantilly in France. This flaming-tortoise pattern was also copied at Chelsea circa 1750.

67A PLATE

ca. 1690–1700
Japan
Porcelain
Diameter: 9⅞ in. (25 cm)
L13.62.142 (CAT. NO. 119)

•

68 SHELL-SHAPED DISH

ca. 1730

Hard-paste porcelain

1¾ × 9¼ in. (4.3 × 23.4 cm)

L13.62.85 (CAT. NO. 91)

•

One half of this shell-shaped dish with molded ribbon edge is decorated with a Kakiemon water and floral scene. The other half features an Imari checkerboard pattern, which displays squares of various underglaze-blue trellis motifs alternating with squares in various enameled colors and patterns. Scholar Oliver Impey suggests that this checkerboard motif was likely derived from textiles.[47] The dish is further enhanced with gilding.

Both decorative schemes, as well as the form's shell shape, were inspired by Japanese models;[48] however, the combination of the two is distinctly Meissen. Some of the Meissen dishes utilize underglaze blue in their decoration, but others do not. Variants on this asymmetrical shape are also seen in Japanese and Meissen models. Although the shape of the Gutter dish is of a clamshell, other shell or leaf shapes were adopted. Some of these dishes, such as this example, are decorated with underglaze blue in combination with overglaze enamels, and others are decorated solely in enamel.[49] Sixteen other pieces in this N=57-/w group have been identified by Gutter.[50]

The underside of the dish is further decorated with a Japanese-inspired flower head and underglaze-blue vines (*karakusa*) (fig. 70), and displays an enameled crossed-swords mark, identifying it as a Hoym-Lemaire specimen.

FIG. 70 Detail of underside of shell-shaped dish

69 DISH FROM THE *GELBER LÖWE* (YELLOW LION) SERVICE

1734
Hard-paste porcelain
2½ × 14 in. (6.4 × 35.6 cm)
L13.62.52 (CAT. NO. 92)

•

The so-called *Gelber Löwe* (or Yellow Lion) service—the "lion" is in fact a tiger—was chosen by Augustus the Strong, and later by his son Augustus III, for the Saxon-Polish royal household's exclusive use.[51] The Gelber Löwe was the earliest large service made at Meissen (ca. 1728–1730) and was added to by Augustus III through the 1730s. The Porzellansammlung, Dresden, contains many pieces dating from its inception to the twentieth century; however, the Japanese porcelain prototype for this service does not survive in the royal collection. An early seventeenth-century, two-paneled screen of tigers and bamboo, attributed to Kanō Tan'yū in the Nanzen-ji temple in Kyoto, Japan, may have been the original design source. As many pieces of Gelber Löwe were involved in the Hoym-Lemaire affair (particularly those pieces marked *N=8-/w*), one can speculate that Lemaire returned to Paris with the Japanese model (see pl. 61 for more on the Hoym-Lemaire scandal).[52]

The twenty-nine dishes engraved with *N=149-/w* do not appear in the 1770 Japanese Palace or 1769 Turmzimmer inventories, as this group, along with other Gelber Löwe pieces, were removed from the collection and delivered to the Warsaw royal pantry in 1734.[53] This practice continued through the 1730s.

Following known Japanese models, the yellow tiger twists around flowering bamboo on the left side of the composition, while a thicket of pine and flowering plum (prunus) grows on the right of this dish. The dish is trimmed in brown enamel. In imitation of the Japanese model, Meissen produced rimless examples as well as dishes with wells and tureens with this pattern. The pattern was also produced in the Jingdezhen kilns in China and at manufactories in Saint-Cloud, France, and Chelsea, England.

CHAPTER 8

MEISSEN ARMORIALS AND DIPLOMATIC GIFTS

The fame of the Meissen manufactory's achievements symbolized the great wealth and stature of Saxony and Poland under the rule of Augustus the Strong, and the king took extreme measures to protect the formula, or the arcanum, for creating hard-paste porcelain. As no other European monarch at the time could produce true porcelain—often referred to as "white gold"—in the early eighteenth century, Meissen porcelain became the ultimate status symbol.

Perpetuating a centuries-old European tradition of bestowing diplomatic gifts upon important visitors as a gesture of courtesy or political prestige, Augustus and his son Augustus III (fig. 71) presented numerous visiting foreign ambassadors and representatives of royal courts with Meissen objects.[1] Documented diplomatic gifts of red stoneware were made by Augustus the Strong as early as 1709–1710 to John Dalrymple, second Earl of Stair (1673–1747), and in 1711 to Augustus's cousin Frederick IV of Denmark (1671–1730).[2] As a testament to the desirability of Höroldt's chinoiseries, in 1728 Augustus the Strong sent six crates of Meissen porcelain with such decoration as a diplomatic gift to Elizabeth Petrova (1709–1762), later empress of Russia, in exchange for exotic animals for Augustus's menagerie.

By the 1730s, Meissen began to create great porcelain services commissioned by nobility and courts throughout Europe. Many of these services bear the heraldic arms of the families for whom they were made. Dresden ministers and diplomats such as count Heinrich von Brühl (1700–1763) and Johann Ernst Gotzkowsky (1710–1775) acquired Meissen to enhance their political position as well as their fashionable tables.

Following the death of Augustus the Strong in 1733 and a waning focus on the Japanese Palace project, Augustus III turned the manufactory's efforts away from Asian decorations to European motifs and services. Augustus III fully embraced the tradition of diplomatic gifts. Under his reign, remarkable services were produced for many European courts and grand families. Notable examples are represented in the Gutter collection.

There was a particularly vibrant Italian patronage for Meissen during the early eighteenth century, forged through close ties between Dresden, Rome, Naples, and Venice. This alliance was enhanced in part through Augustus the Strong and his son's conversion to Catholicism, as well as the marriage of Augustus III's daughter Maria Amalia of Saxony (1724–1760) to Charles III (1716–1788), king of Spain and king of Naples (as Charles VII). Furthermore, diplomatic gifts of Meissen were presented to noble Italian families who hosted the crown princes during their grand tour of Italy.[3]

Pair of candlesticks from the *Schwanenservice* (Swan service), ca. 1739 (cat. no. 110/pl. 74)

FIG. 71 (ABOVE) *Augustus III, King of Poland*, late eighteenth or nineteenth century. Hard-paste porcelain, colored enamels, and gilding, 29 × 11 in. (73.7 × 28 cm). Museum of Fine Arts, Boston, Bequest of William A. Coolidge, 1993.57

70 PLATE FROM THE *KRONUNGSSERVICE* (CORONATION SERVICE) WITH THE ARMS OF SAXONY-POLAND

ca. 1733–1734

Hard-paste porcelain

Diameter: 9 in. (22.8 cm)

L13.62.99 (CAT. NO. 105)

•

Augustus III succeeded as elector of Saxony after the death of his father in February 1733. He was bestowed the additional title of king of Poland in October of that same year. The coronation service, named for its intended display at Augustus III's opulent coronation on January 17, 1734, was likely commissioned by his father prior to his death. All seventy-seven pieces of the service were absorbed into the Japanese Palace depot and recorded in the inventory under numbers 147 and 148. In 1838 the service was moved to the *Hofwirtschaft* (court's tableware office), whereafter it was occasionally used.[4]

The plate is decorated with the large impaled, or aligned, coat of arms (*Wappen*) of Poland, Saxony, and Lithuania, framed by gilt and Böttger-luster drapery and palms and surmounted by a crown. The left side of the coat of arms displays the crossed swords adopted by Meissen as its manufactory mark. The rim of the dish is decorated with a gilt border of *Laub- und Bandelwerk*. The white porcelain field is further enhanced with scattered *indianische Blumen* and Kakiemon bundles of corn (or banded hedges).

The Japanese Palace inventory for 1770 reads: "Ein Tafel-Service, mit dem Königl. Pohlnis und ChurFürstl. Sächsi. Wappen, fein mit Golde und Zierrathen, aufm Boden mit gebundenen Korn-Aehren, und kleinen Blümgen, der Rand sehr reich mit vergoldten Zierra(80) then eingefasst, besteht in . . . , No. 147" (A table service with the royal arms of Poland and the electoral arms of Saxony, finely decorated on the inside with gold and ornaments and bound sheaves of corn and small flowers, the rims decorated with elaborate gilded scrollwork, . . . [contents listed], no. 147).[5] For a monumental 1978 exhibition at the Legion of Honor, *The Splendor of Dresden*, one small and two large dishes from this service were lent from Dresden (PE 954, PE 1829, and PE 1328b).[6]

71 BEAKER WITH THE ARMS OF NAPLES-SICILY AND SAXONY-POLAND-LITHUANIA

ca. 1737
Painting possibly by Johann Georg Heintze (b. 1707) or
Bonaventura Gottlieb Häuer (1710–1782)
Hard-paste porcelain
3⅛ × 2¾ in. (7.8 × 7 cm)
L13.62.98 (CAT. NO. 106)

•

In celebration of the marriage of Augustus III's daughter, Maria Amalia of Saxony, to Charles VII of Naples, or the Two Sicilies, Augustus III commissioned two large Meissen services. The event took place in Dresden by proxy in May 1738. On April 17, 1738, a large silver toilet service—including six porcelain teabowls, saucers, and individual chocolate beakers—had been sent to Naples.[7] This was followed in June 1739 by a table service, possibly as a gift to Charles VII's mother, Elisabeth Farnese, queen of Spain (1692–1766).

Over correspondence, Gutter and Meissen specialist Sebastian Kuhn have identified three of the six beakers and five of the six teabowls.[8] Only one is documented in a public collection, at the Museo Internazionale delle Ceramiche in Faenza, Italy.[9] None of the silver, nor the porcelain saucers from the toilet service, appears to have survived.

Prominent on this small beaker are the arms of Naples-Sicily linked with those of Saxony-Poland-Lithuania, topped by a unifying crown. The royal emblems are superimposed over a continuous *Kauffahrtei* scene. Such background scenes vary among the identified pieces of this service. The base and interior of the beaker are gilt.

72 TEA CADDY WITH THE ARMS OF GRADENIGO

ca. 1740
Painting possibly by Johann Georg Heintze or
Bonaventura Gottlieb Häuer
Hard-paste porcelain
$4 \times 2\frac{5}{8} \times 1\frac{7}{8}$ in. ($10.3 \times 6.8 \times 4.9$ cm)
L13.62.96 (CAT. NO. 107)

•

Part of a tea and coffee service, this tea caddy was presented as a diplomatic gift to a Venetian noble family. It was likely made for Girolamo Gradenigo (1708–1786) or one of his brothers, Piero or Vincenzo II.[10] As noted in the chapter introduction, a number of notable Meissen services for Italian noble families were produced in the mid-1730s to 1740s.[11]

Based on a silver shape, the tea caddy features the arms of the Gradenigo family, surrounded by an elaborate gilt and puce frame surmounted by a coronet and grounded by a mask below. The arms are laid over a landscape and river scene that continues over all four sides. The teabowls and saucers from the service also prominently display the Gradenigo arms over other landscape scenes. Probably inspired by a seventeenth-century print source, the reverse scene on the Gutter tea caddy depicts two figures loading a packhorse alongside a boat (fig. 72). A gilt band encircles the base and shoulders. The shoulders are also enhanced with gilt *Laub- und Bandelwerk*, while the top of the tea caddy is decorated with *indianische Blumen*. The highly refined decoration suggests the hand of either Johann Georg Heintze (b. 1707) or Bonaventura Gottlieb Häuer (1710–1782), two of Meissen's most accomplished landscape painters.

Gutter has identified several pieces from this service that have appeared in publications and on the market, including a sugarbowl, five teabowls and saucers, and a beaker.[12] Several pieces from the Gradenigo service, including the Gutter tea caddy and a pair of beakers and saucers, were once in the Klemperer collection.[13] In one photograph the tea caddy is shown with its original lid, which is now lost (fig. 73).

FIG. 72 Reverse view of tea caddy

FIG. 73 Tea caddy reproduced in plate 27 of Schnorr von Carolsfeld 1928

73 DISH FROM THE *SCHWANENSERVICE* (SWAN SERVICE) WITH THE ARMS OF BRÜHL AND KOLOWRAT-KRAKOWSKA

ca. 1738–1739

Hard-paste porcelain

2 × 11⅞ in. (5 × 30.2 cm)

L13.62.97 (CAT. NO. 108)

•

The iconic *Schwanenservice* (Swan service) was originally made for Count von Brühl, the prime minister of Saxony and director of the Meissen manufactory from 1733 to 1763 under Augustus III. The table service was designed by the firm's renowned sculptor Johann Joachim Kändler and contained more than two thousand pieces upon its completion in 1743.[14] The Gutter collection includes this dish and a rare pair of candlesticks (see next page) from the original Schwanenservice commission, as well as a dish from a later service with a similar molded pattern.[15]

Kändler joined Meissen in 1731 and worked under Johann Gottlieb Kirchner until 1733, when he took over the position of *Modellmeister*, or chief modeler. At this time he began to incorporate a rich vocabulary of ornaments and relief onto Meissen tablewares. One of the first services incorporating this modeling can be seen on the Sulkowski service, circa 1735–1737. Aleksander Józef Sułkowski (1695–1762) was the minister of the manufactory before Brühl was appointed by Augustus III. For the design of the Schwanenservice, Kändler was possibly inspired by engravings (Nuremberg, 1700/1707) after the Bohemian Wenceslaus Hollar (1607–1677), although a 1654 print designed by Francis Barlow (ca. 1626–1704) has now been identified as a more probable source.[16]

Two documented formers (or potters)—Johann Elias Grund the Elder (1703–1758) and Johann Martin Kittel (1706–1762)—were responsible for many of the plates in this service, which comprised dinner and soup plates, as well as five sizes of serving dishes. Plate sizes are identified by incised marks on the plates' undersides. Gutter's dish, with two lines, designates the smallest size, 11¾ inches.

The dish bears the enameled arms of Count von Brühl and his wife, Franziska von Kolowrat-Krakowska (1712–1762), with scattered flowers on the rim. The gilt, wavy-edged dish is molded to resemble a shell, with two swans and cranes cavorting amid aquatic flora in the plate's center. A play on the Brühl name ("marshy ground") may have led to the aquatic theme of this service and other art in his collection.[17] This service was used by Brühl for several royal receptions in Dresden; it was then left to his heir of the Brühl family estate, Schloss Pförten (now Brody) in Lower Lusatia, Poland. Following World War II, the estate was occupied and then overtaken by Soviet troops in early 1945. Although representative pieces are in the Porzellansammlung, Dresden, lent by the Brühl

74 PAIR OF CANDLESTICKS FROM THE *SCHWANENSERVICE* (SWAN SERVICE)

ca. 1739

Hard-paste porcelain

9⅝ × 5¾ in. (24.5 × 14.5 cm) each

L13.62.100.1–2 (CAT. NO. 110)

•

FIG. 74 Detail of Juste Aurèle Meissonnier, design for a candlestick, second view of plate 11, *Oeuvre de Juste-Aurèle Meissonnier* (Paris: Gabriel Huquier, 1748). Cooper Hewitt, Smithsonian Design Museum Collections; purchased for the Museum by the Advisory Council, 1921-6-212-7-b

family prior to World War II, much of the service was seized and destroyed following the war. Many pieces survive in public and private collections, including a 13¾-inch platter in the collection of the Fine Arts Museums of San Francisco (65.30).

Meissen produced several pieces during this period that were not enameled or gilt. These remained undecorated due to some minor or major flaws with the paste, modeling, or firing. Several examples were decorated later, accommodating the nineteenth-century taste for decorated porcelains. The candlesticks in the Gutter collection are without enamel decoration. They were modeled by Kändler and his assistant Johann Friedrich Eberlein (1696–1749) after designs by French designer and goldsmith Juste Aurèle Meissonnier (1695–1750). Meissonnier's Rococo designs, intended for silver models, were published in *Dousième livre des oeuvres de J. A. Messonnier* [*sic*] (Twelve books of works by J. A. Meissonnier, 1734–1735). Still preserved in the manufactory archive are three prints of Meissonnier's design by Louis Desplaces (1682–1739) and Gabriel Huquier (1695–1772). These designs depict two putti entwining a candlestick that stands on a shell-shaped base. The Meissonnier designs even incorporate a cartouche, ideal for the placement of the enameled Brühl coat of arms. The shell base ties the design to the Swan service water theme. Eberlein's work report of September 1739 notes: "1 Tafel-leuchter vor Ihro. Excellenz den Herrn Graf Brühl mit zweyen Kindern, zweyen Schültern und vielen Muschel wercke" (A table candlestick for his Excellency Count von Brühl with two children, two cartouches for a Coat of Arms, and much shellwork).[18]

Like the dishes for the Swan service, several candlesticks survive in public collections.[19] Nearly all known examples are enameled and gilt; however, several examples are known with later decoration. Gutter's examples may be the only known undecorated pair. There are some imperfections in the paste and visible firing cracks that may have prevented their decoration and delivery to Brühl. Ulrich Pietsch, former director of the Porzellansammlung, Dresden, displayed or documented several undecorated objects in his 2000 Swan service exhibition and catalogue,[20] including a glass cooler, three plates, and a terrine.

Although not seen on every surviving example, the former's number (or *Pressnummer*) 46 for Johann Georg Möbius is the only numeral used for candlesticks of the Swan service and of the related Saint Andrew service (see cat. no. 111/pl. 75). Eberlein modified the Swan service candlestick circa 1744–1745 for the Saint Andrew service, ten examples of which the State Hermitage Museum, Saint Petersburg, retains.[21] The same model was also used for the candlesticks of the Gotzkowsky service (ca. 1743–1744).

75 PLATE FROM THE SAINT ANDREW THE FIRST-CALLED SERVICE

ca. 1744

Hard-paste porcelain

1¼ × 9⅝ in. (3.2 × 24.5 cm)

L13.62.95 (CAT. NO. 111)

•

The Andreaskreuz (Saint Andrew) service represents an important diplomatic gift from Saxony to one of its greatest allies, Russia. The recipient, Elizabeth Petrovna, later empress of Russia (r. 1741–1761), was a dedicated and passionate Meissen client, having already commissioned other services in 1741 and 1744.[22] The purpose of this significant gift was twofold: to reinforce the Saxon-Russian treaty, renewed in January 1744, as well as to celebrate the dynastic 1745 marriage between the tsarina's nephew, Peter von Holstein-Gottorp (later Tsar Peter III, r. 1762), and Sophie Friederike Auguste von Anhalt-Zerbst-Dornburg (later Tsarina Catherine II, or Catherine the Great, r. 1762–1796), of a ruling Prussian family.[23] Commissioned by Augustus III in 1744, the gift of Meissen comprised a four-hundred-piece table service; a related coffee, tea, and chocolate service; and several figures and other works.[24] This entire shipment, packed in ten crates, was sent to Russia in 1745.

The plates of this service, featuring lobed edges enhanced with a gilt lattice pattern, were modeled by Eberlein. They are molded with the Eberlein-designed Gotzkowsky service floral relief and enameled in the well and on two sides of the rim with deutsches Holzschnittblumen (German woodcut flowers). These flowers were derived from Johann Wilhelm Weinmann (1734–1788)'s Phytanthoza Iconographia (Regensburg, 1737–1741), a botanical atlas that was available to the Meissen decorators. Pietsch suggests Gottlob Siegmund Birckner (ca. 1721–1771) as the flower painter for the Saint Andrew service based on manufactory work records.[25]

The service is decorated with the arms of Imperial Russia, a two-headed eagle bearing a coat of arms depicting Saint George, at the top of the rim. The bottom of the plate is enameled with the badge of the Order of Saint Andrew, the highest order of chivalry bestowed by the Russian empire, which depicts a cross supporting the crucified figure of Andrew that displays the letters S (Sanctus), A (Andreas), P (Patronus), and R (Russiae). Saint Andrew was credited with bringing Christianity to Russia. Tsar Peter I founded the order of Saint Andrew in 1698.

The State Hermitage Museum, St. Petersburg, retains ten plates with Pressnummer 16 and twenty-four with Pressnummer 20 from this service. Meissen supplemented the service in 1750, and the St. Petersburg Imperial Porcelain Manufactory also added to the service in the mid-nineteenth century.[26] Many pieces from the Saint Andrew service came onto the market following the 1917 Russian revolution and are now in public collections, including the Schneider collection, Schloss Lustheim (ES 2444);[27] the Arnhold collection, New York;[28] the Wark Collection, Cummer Museum of Art and Gardens (AG.1966.23.4); and the Victoria and Albert Museum, London (C.26-1988), to name a few.

MALCOLM D. GUTTER

A COLLECTOR'S MEMOIR

My answer to the now-familiar question, "Why (and how) did you start to collect?" has been, "It's in the bones." I have found that the propensity to collect starts at an early age. It certainly did with me, as a pubescent collector of postage stamps and far less worthy enjoyments. There is a mentality that fellow collectors—of anything—understand. Certain people love objects, and they love to have them around; others are totally indifferent to them.

For me, collecting porcelain and furniture broaden and deepen my understanding of art and history and hone connoisseurship—itself a great source of pleasure. I do my own research while performing other necessary steps to acquire fine objects; collecting moves from an avocation to simulated professional, curatorial work. I have found it enjoyable to tread the same paths as dealers, buy where they buy. A collector should develop his or her own connoisseurship abilities, lessening the requirement to seek outside advice and expertise. Touch, a sense essential to the connoisseurship of ceramics, may be underappreciated by collectors of European porcelain. Why do I get a different sensation from European hard- or soft-paste porcelain, or a piece of Japanese porcelain? European and Japanese porcelains for me have human skin–like qualities, making their appeal so sensual; Chinese porcelain—even the finest imperial ware—flatters the eye, but handling conveys an inanimate surface.

Collecting has thus changed my life, so many waking (and more than a few non-waking) hours devoted to thinking about and "doing" antiques, porcelain especially. Personal associations—and deep and lasting friendships—have been formed through my collecting experiences. But why antique Meissen porcelain? History has always been—along with music—the love of my intellectual life. As the nineteenth century was, arguably, the century of music in Europe, the eighteenth century was of high-fired ceramics. Hard-paste porcelain was rediscovered as a noble and princely art form in the first years of the century (by the final decade, it had metamorphosed into an industrialized, widely available product of commerce and trade). Meissen porcelain was at the forefront of this artistic and technological development, essentially compressing almost a thousand years of Asian production into its first forty-five. Few

Tureen and cover (*Oliotopf*), ca. 1723–1725, painting possibly attributed to Johann Gregorius Höroldt (cat. no. 52/pl. 58)

COLLEEN O'SHEA

A TECHNICAL ANALYSIS OF OVERGLAZE ENAMELS ON FUNCKE-ATTRIBUTED MEISSEN PORCELAIN

Malcolm Gutter's collection of Meissen porcelain strongly represents the early stages of production at the Meissen manufactory, providing an opportunity to study the techniques and colorants used by different artists at the time. One question that the collection helps address is characterizing the composition of the enamels used by goldsmith and painter Johann Georg Funcke (active 1692–1727) in the earliest days of Meissen, circa 1713–1726. Comparatively little has been published about the enamel palette and methods of Funcke, whereas the recipe book and other archival documents exist for the artist who followed him, Johann Gregorius Höroldt (1696–1775), who began enameling at Meissen in 1720. To begin to understand Funcke's methods and to address the question of what colorants he used, five objects attributed to Funcke from Gutter's collection were selected for technical study: the two-handled waste bowl with applied grapevines (ca. 1715–1720, cat. no. 23/pl. 16), small dish (ca. 1718–1720, cat. no. 30), teapot (ca. 1718–1720, cat. no. 27/pl. 20), two-handled chocolate beaker (ca. 1717, cat. no. 25/pl. 18; see opposite), and enameled incense burner (ca. 1715–1717, cat. no. 33/pl. 14). For comparative purposes, two objects decorated under Höroldt's direction were also studied: the cup and saucer with mythological scenes (ca. 1721–1722, cat. no. 59/pl. 42) and Kakiemon-style dish (ca. 1729–1730, cat. no. 103/pl. 62a).

All objects were examined under high magnification to better understand their composition. X-radiographs were taken of all objects to aid in determining their construction. To highlight differences in materials used, a series of images was taken of all objects under normal illumination, ultraviolet-induced visible fluorescence, and reflected infrared radiation. Finally, readings were taken of the colorants using a portable X-ray fluorescence (XRF) spectrometer. Due to the nature of the comparatively large spot size (8 mm) on the XRF unit and the geometry of the head of the instrument, readings could not be taken of all colors.

EXAMINATION

Visually, the enamels on the five Funcke-attributed objects do appear distinctive from that of the two objects attributed to Höroldt's studio. The enamels attributed to Funcke appear almost experimental: the colors are not very brilliant, they have

Two-handled chocolate beaker, ca. 1717, enameling and gilding by Johann Georg Funcke (cat. no. 25/pl. 18)

particulate inclusions visible to the naked eye, the application is done with a somewhat unsteady line, and the motifs themselves are much more delicate and indistinct as compared to the painterly techniques of Höroldt. These differences might be attributable to Funcke's training as a goldsmith rather than as a painter.

Other differences in appearance may in fact result from the techniques of preparing the raw materials for the colorants. Both Funcke and Höroldt painted wares with overglaze decoration, which, as the name suggests, refers to glazes applied on top of the body glaze after it has been fired. To avoid risk to the underlying glaze, overglaze enamels are fired at much lower temperatures. Overglaze enamels, like glazes, consist of metallic oxides as the colorant, silica as the frit (which makes the glaze hard and glass-like), and, in the case of all of the objects analyzed here, lead oxide as a flux (an agent that reduces the temperature required for firing into a glaze). A considerable amount of lead was used in order to bring down the firing temperature.[1] The presence of aluminum would lower the viscosity of the glaze as well as prevent crystallization during cooling. A small amount of tin may have been added as an opacifying agent.[2] All components were ground into a powder, which is the overglaze enamel. This process was repeated for every color used. The overglaze enamel was then mixed with a medium such as linseed oil and then applied to the surface of the vessel with a brush or other tool.

With regard to the differences in appearance of overglaze enamels, it is important to note that not all metallic oxides are equally easy to incorporate into a fine homogenous substance. Some oxides remain gritty unless very finely ground.[3] In the case of the greens attributed to Funcke, the oxides appear poorly incorporated. The visible particulate may be cobalt, iron, or manganese oxides (all detected as trace elements by X-ray fluorescence; see table on p. 230). It is possible that the two artists ground their raw materials to different degrees of fineness. In the one vessel attributed to Höroldt's studio that formed part of this study, dark flecks are present in some areas of green, though these are less prevalent than in the Funcke examples.

DISCUSSION OF COLORANTS

GREENS

The principal colorant in all the green areas is copper. In the three objects attributed to Funcke on which the green is accessible with the XRF instrument, traces of cobalt were also found. These cobalt oxides may be the darker particulate visible in the green matrix. No cobalt traces were found on the two later objects attributed to Höroldt's studio. Traces of tin in the green glazes suggest that bronze filings were used as a source of copper, providing incidental tin. This practice was documented in Höroldt's recipe book of 1731.[4]

BLUES

The blues are predominately made from cobalt with minor amounts of copper. Minor and trace amounts of iron, nickel, arsenic, and manganese have all been found in blue overglazes of this period, and their presence is unsurprising given the traces of arsenic and nickel found with cobalt mined from the Schneeberg district of Saxony.[5]

The turquoise-blue colorant found on several of the objects mostly consists of copper; traces of cobalt were found on only one of the objects with the turquoise colorant: the enameled incense burner (see fig. 77). Under infrared radiation, only the turquoise dots remain, while the dark blue areas disappear (see fig. 78). This suggests that their chemical composition is quite different; in fact, it may be that

FIG. 77 Rear view of enameled incense burner (cat. no. 33/pl. 14) in visible light

FIG. 78 Enameled incense burner under reflected-infrared radiation; note that the only colors visible at this wavelength are the turquoise dots

FIG. 79 Enameled incense burner with a compiled false-color infrared radiation; this compilation helps locate the turquoise dots

the difference is the relative presence of copper (significant in the turquoise, not as significant in the dark blue). The false-color infrared image was compiled to aid in showing the different placement of colors (see fig. 79).

REDS

All reds were found to be primarily composed of iron oxide (Fe_2O_3), with trace amounts of copper in two of the objects attributed to Funcke. No zinc was found, supporting the dating of these objects before circa 1755–1763.[6]

PINKS

The pink colorants examined were generally iron based with traces of copper. On the small dish, traces of gold were detected. The pink areas appear to be outlined with traces of gold. No tin was detected in any pink sampled.

YELLOWS

The colorant used in yellow areas is not entirely clear. The yellow areas are composed of iron, lead, and copper. Naples yellow ($Pb_2Sb_2O_7$) was commonly used at the time and was expected to be the yellow colorant; however, antimony (Sb) was detected on only one object—the teapot—in trace amounts unlikely to affect the overall color.[7] It may be that, rather than being the expected Naples yellow, the yellows are yellow iron oxide, or that the elevated levels of lead helped turn the iron into a yellow shade.

PURPLE

The lustrous purple color edging the floral robe of the enameled incense burner is possibly Purple of Cassius, colloidal gold precipitated by a reaction with tin salts.[8] Trace amounts of gold and tin were found. However, study of these areas using an instrument with a smaller area of detection is recommended because the areas of purple colorant are so narrow.

GOLD AND COPPER

The gilded banding on the chocolate beaker is nearly pure gold, with traces of copper, nickel, and chromium. The gilding on the cup and saucer is not quite as pure, with traces of iron, copper, arsenic, chromium, manganese, and nickel. The copper-colored striping on the chocolate beaker appears to be the result of more iron in the gold, with traces of copper. Gilding on Meissen objects from around 1715 to 1747 is expected to have high levels of gold and trace amounts of nickel due to the high quality of gold used at the Meissen factory,[9] and that is indeed the case with all of the objects studied here.

BROWNS AND BLACKS

Areas of brown and black colorants were too faint or narrow to be accessed successfully by the handheld XRF.

CONCLUSION

The analysis of the five Funcke-attributed objects in this study are helping identify his palette. The greens are copper based, with traces of cobalt and other oxides including iron and manganese. It is these minor elements that result in the occasional dark particulate in the green areas that can be seen by the naked eye or using magnification. The dark and light blues are cobalt based with traces of copper. The turquoise-blue color was unique to the Funcke-attributed objects; this color was not present on either of the two comparative objects enameled under Höroldt's direction. Though in some cases difficult to access with the XRF unit, the turquoise colorant seems to result from a major amount of copper and only a trace amount of cobalt. The reds and pinks consist of iron with trace amounts of copper. The yellow colorant is primarily

Table 1. Elements likely related to metallic oxides in colorants

	DATE	GREEN	BLUE	LIGHT BLUE	RED	PINK	DARK YELLOW	YELLOW	PURPLE	BROWN	BLACK	GOLD	COPPER
Two-handled waste bowl (cat. no. 23/pl. 16)	ca. 1715–1720	Cu, Co, As, Ni, Pb, Sn	Cu, Fe, trace Sb (Pb)	no access	Fe, Cu, trace Sb (Pb)	no access	n/a	no access	n/a	n/a	no access	n/a	n/a
Enameled incense burner (cat. no. 33/pl. 14)	ca. 1715–1717	n/a	Co, Cu, As, Pb, Ni, trace Sn	Cu, Pb, Fe; traces Co, Ni	n/a	Fe, Pb, trace Cu	n/a	Fe, Pb, As; traces Co, Ni	As, Fe, Pb, Co, Cu, Ni; minor Au, Sn	n/a	n/a	n/a	n/a
Small dish (cat. no. 30)	ca. 1718–1720	Cu, Pb, trace Co	n/a	Cu, Pb, Fe, Sn	Fe, Au, trace Cu	Fe, Au, trace Cu	n/a	Pb, Fe, Cu	n/a	n/a	n/a	n/a	n/a
Enameled teapot (cat. no. 27/pl. 20)	ca. 1718–1720	Cu, Pb; traces Co, Sb, Sn, Zn, Ni, Mn	As, Co, Cu, Ni, Pb	Cu, Pb, Fe; traces Ni, Sn	n/a	Cu, Fe, trace Ni	Fe, Pb, Cu	Fe, Pb, Cu, Mn, trace Sb	n/a	n/a	no access	n/a	n/a
Two-handled chocolate beaker (cat. no. 25/pl. 18)	ca. 1717	no access	no access	no access	n/a	Fe, Pb; trace Cu	n/a	n/a	n/a	n/a	n/a	Au; traces Cu, Cr, Ni	Au, Fe; trace Cu
Cup and saucer with mythological scenes (cat. no. 59/pl. 42)	ca. 1721–1722	Cu, Pb; traces Mn, Sn, Zn	Cu, Fe, Pb	n/a	Fe, trace Ni	no access	n/a	no access	no access	no access	n/a	Au, Fe; traces Cu, As, Cr, Mn, Zn, Ni	n/a
Kakiemon-style dish (cat. no. 103/pl. 62a)	ca. 1729–1730	Bluish green: Cu, Zn, Pb, Mn, trace Sn	Co, Pb, Ni; minor Cu, As; trace Mn	n/a	Fe, Pb	n/a	Yellowish green: Fe, Cu, Pb; traces Co, Mn, Zn, Sn	Fe, Pb, trace Mn	n/a	no access	n/a	n/a	n/a

composed of iron, lead, and copper. The purple areas contain trace amounts of gold and tin. Areas of brown or black were too small for the instrumentation used in this study to detect.

The differences between the palettes of Funcke and Höroldt lie mainly in the trace components of the colorants. Study of additional Funcke-attributed objects would be helpful, as this group of five objects is a very small sample size from which to draw conclusions. Differences in enamel preparation technique and application style between the two artists are evident with visual examination. Computational technologies that assign quantitative values to brush patterns or depth of overglaze application could be useful in assessing differences between the artists, and could be cross-referenced with the elemental data to assess the attribution.

Other suggestions for future research include employing comparative techniques to confirm these results and to answer further questions about the nature of the pigments that could not be characterized as part of this study due to size and geometry limits. Raman spectroscopy has potential for nondestructive characterization;[10] investigation at a synchrotron may be useful, and elemental mapping with a three-dimensional scanning unit is also recommended. An XRF unit with a smaller spot size used in concert with calibration standards could provide semiquantitative results.

EXPERIMENTAL APPENDIX

DIGITAL IMAGES

Photographs were taken with a modified UV-Vis-IR Nikon D7100 camera. Reference images were taken with tungsten lamps and a Peca 918 filter. Ultraviolet-induced visible fluorescence images were captured using standing UV lamps, and a Peca 918 filter plus a Kodak 2E filter. Infrared images were captured using tungsten lamps and a MaxMax X-Nite 715nm filter. False-color infrared images were made by the author using standard channel-substitution methods.[11]

X-RADIOGRAPHY

X-radiographs were taken with the following parameters: 36-inch focus-to-film distance, 55 or 65 kV, 5 mA, for 42 seconds. The digital plates were scanned using a Carestream Industrex HPX-1 unit. Select images were enhanced in Adobe Photoshop using the Unsharp Mask filter.

X-RAY FLUORESCENCE SPECTROMETRY

A Bruker Tracer handheld spectrometer with rhodium tube excitation and silicon p-type intrinsic n-type (PIN) detector was used. Operating parameters were 40 kV and 2 µA with a vacuum, 120 seconds live time. The spot size was 8 mm. When possible, readings from three distinct areas of the same color were taken. Spectral interpretation was performed using Bruker Artax Control software.

NOTES

KUHN

1 Sir Charles Hanbury-Williams, the British envoy to the Saxon court between 1747 and 1755, observed: "I was once at a Dinner where we sat down at one table two hundred and six People (twas at Count Brühl's) when the Desert [sic] was set on, I thought it was the most wonderful thing I ever beheld. I fancyd myself either in a Garden or at an Opera. But I coud [sic] not imagine that I was at a Dinner. . . . I verily believe that Count Brühl has above thirty thousand Pounds worth of China in his house." Quoted by the Earl of Ilchester in Fox-Strangways Holland 1929, 188.

2 See Cassidy-Geiger 2007.

3 An auction catalogue published in Leipzig in 1792 refers, for example, to "Böttgerisches Porzellan" (porcelain of the period of Johann Friedrich Böttger [1682–1719]).

4 In 1764 the influential art historian Johann Joachim Winckelmann (1717–1768) famously dismissed most Rococo porcelain figures as "ridiculous dolls," and the material became increasingly associated with reproduction and mass production toward the end of the eighteenth century.

5 Kunze 1982, 37–56, ills. 3–4 and 7–8.

6 The Oppenheimer collection was acquired by the Amsterdam-based collector Fritz Mannheimer (1890–1939) in 1936; after the war it became the property of the Dutch state. Most remains in the Rijksmuseum in Amsterdam, but a part was sold at auction in 1952.

7 A report on the 1920 sale (see Donath 1920) notes that there was standing room only at the auction. In the front row were seated a remarkable roll call of great museum directors and scholars, including Hans Posse, Ernst Zimmermann, Karl Berling, Otto von Falke, Ludwig Schnorr von Carolsfeld, Robert Schmidt, Max Sauerlandt, and Paul von Ostermann; behind them were many of the greatest collectors of the day, including Graf Seebach, v. Berger, Gustav von Klemperer, Hermine Feist, Wolfgang von Dallwitz, Dr. Wilhelm Dosquet, Paul Rosenbacher, and Albert Dasch, as well as dealers from all over Germany, Vienna, Amsterdam, The Hague, and London.

8 Roberts 2013, 16.

9 The firm of Jacob Rosenbaum, founded in Frankfurt in the 1860s, was forced to move from Germany when Hitler came to power. Isaac Rosenbaum moved to Amsterdam, while his nephews, Saemy Rosenberg and Hans and Eric Stiebel, established themselves in London, Paris, and New York. After World War II, the business was consolidated in New York as Rosenberg and Stiebel.

10 Bischoff 1982.

11 Ibid.

12 The Pflueger collection is now mostly in the holdings of the Museum of Fine Arts, Boston; see Morley-Fletcher 1993.

13 According to Hans Syz, Beckhardt "maintained the spirit of a collector. He very generously imparted his knowledge and experience to his customers, and I learned a great deal from him." Syz, Miller, and Rückert 1979, 9.

14 The Hans Syz Collection was mostly bequeathed to the Smithsonian Institution, while the Metropolitan Museum of Art, New York, was the beneficiary of numerous porcelain collectors, including Jack and Belle Linsky, Irwin Untermyer, and R. Thornton Wilson.

15 Roberts 2013, 23–24.

16 Prior to opening in New York, the Antique Porcelain Company had been represented in the city by the dealer J. J. Klejman; see Roberts 2013, 54.

17 Arnhold moved to New York after World War II.

18 Edward Pflueger took the opportunity to purchase the Höchst and Fürstenberg series of Italian Comedy figures from the Blohm Collection. The bulk of the collection was later sold by Sotheby's, London, in 1960 and 1961.

19 The exhibition ran from March 18 to May 15, 1949.

20 See Pietsch 2011.

21 Her collection of almost six hundred pieces was donated to the Dixon Gallery and Gardens, Memphis, in 1985; see Roberts 2013 for a fascinating and detailed history of Stout's collecting career.

22 Scott 1961.

23 The exhibition ran from October 25 to December 6, 1965.

24 Writing of the Meissen and other European porcelain bequeathed by the great Victorian collector Wilfred De Winton to the National Museum Wales; De Waal 2005, 7.

CATALOGUE INTRODUCTION

1 As seen in the 1930 American Art Association, Anderson Galleries, New York, sales catalogue featuring the contents of their French residence, Villa Baratier in Saint-Jean-Cap-Ferrat, Mr. and Mrs. Claus Spreckels, Adolph's parents, concentrated their porcelain collecting primarily on small eighteenth-century Meissen figures, including a pair of "Chinois" statuettes. Many of their German porcelains were acquired from Founès and Jacques Seligmann.

2 Swan service platter, gift of the Golden Gate Collectors, 65.30; and Madagascar hoopoe birds, purchase through the Samuel Untermyer II Purchase Fund, 1979.37.1–2. Another pair of these hoopoe birds was restituted to Henry Arnhold in 2008 (see Vignon 2016, 7).

CHAPTER 1

1 As the title of king in Poland was an elected rather than inherited one during this time, some historians refer to the position as "king in Poland" rather than "king of Poland."

2 Cassidy-Geiger 1995, 21.

3 Five surviving vases, referred to as the Dragoon vases, are now in the Porzellansammlung, Dresden (PO 9130). Another pair is in the British royal collection (RCIN 43929), and the Rijksmuseum, Amsterdam, holds one single vase.

4 Cassidy-Geiger 1995, 17–21.

5 See Cassidy-Geiger 1996b for a transcription.

6 See Boltz 1996 for a transcription of the *Japanisches Palais-Inventar 1770* and *Turmzimmer-Inventar 1769*.

7 See Cassidy-Geiger 2007, 90, for more on Plaue.

8 See Gutter 2001 for a discussion of the clay compositions and surface details apparent on these various red wares.

9 Boltz 2000, 147–148.

10 Loesch 2009, 191. A group of papers focusing on Böttger black-glazed wares in the Dresden royal collection, including analyses of their chemical composition, is compiled in Loesch, Ulbricht, and Schwarm 2013. Furthermore, the team of Gulsu Simsek, Philippe Colomban, Francesca Casadio, and others has published several scientific studies analyzing Böttger red stoneware, most recently related to glaze and gilding. See Simsek, Colomban, and Casadio 2015.

11 Gutter 2001.

12 Boltz 2000.

13 Boltz 1982, 15–36.

14 Steinbrück 1982.

15 Braun 2007, 28.

16 Boltz 2000, 147–148.

17 Boltz 1982, 23.

18 Gutter 2001, 13–14 and footnote 8.

19 Boltz 2000, 42.

20 Gutter, 1976–2015.

21 Unglazed Böttger stoneware, or "Braun Sächsisch- oder sogenanntes Böttgerisches Porcellain" (Saxon brown or so called Böttger porcelain), is listed at the end of the 1770 and 1779 Japanese Palace inventories. The *kendis*, near the end of the accounting (the last number is 244), are entered as "Neun und Fünfzig Stück hohe Thée Kannen, mit langen Hälsen, und kurzen Schnäutzgen, davon 5. Stück mit kleinen Deckeln, 7 1/2 . Zoll hoch, 4. Zoll in Diam: No. 252" (Fifty-nine high teapots with long necks and short spouts, five with small covers, No. 252). Boltz 1996, 107. By the second inventory of 1779, almost all the unglazed *kendis* had lost their stoppers.

22 Claus Boltz, letter to Malcolm Gutter, August 18, 2000. For further discussion of the Böttger Creditwesen and its relation to the inventories of the Japanese Palace, see Cassidy-Geiger 2004, 72–81.

23 The 1920 sale saw another nine: five unglazed (lots 59–63); two black-glazed, lacquered, and gilded (lots 110 and 111); and two with an *Eisenporzellan* surface (lots 84 and 85).

24 The 1927 catalogue of the Olsen collection (Schmitz 1927) mistakenly identifies the *kendi* from the first Johanneum auction (October 7 and 8, 1919) as lot 44 rather than the correct lot 36. This error (along with a mistaken height measurement) is repeated in the Winkel and Magnussen sales catalogue of February 28–March 4, 1944. For more information on the Olsen collection, see Kuhn 2008.

25 Terese Tse Bartholomew, former curator of Himalayan art and Chinese decorative art at the Asian Art Museum, San Francisco, explained in conversation with Malcolm Gutter that the mold lines on Yixing examples were carefully removed before firing.

26 For more on Irminger, see Reinheckel 1965.

27 Weinhold 2009.

28 Gutter 2001.

29 Cassidy-Geiger 2004, 74.

30 Simsek, Colomban, and Casadio 2015.

31 Cassidy-Geiger 2004, 44.

32 Gutter 2001, 2–23.

33 Syndram and Weinhold 2009, 48–50.

34 Other comparable tankards, like one in the Gardiner Museum, Toronto, bear a dated (1727) engraved coat of arms, which suggests a considerable period of time between production and engraving. Indeed, the engraving of arms on some red-stoneware pieces remains incomplete. See, for example, the teapot in the Kunstgewerbemuseum, Berlin, where the oval in the center of the arms is left blank (Bursche 1980, 48, cat. no. 12), and the Arnhold collection coffeepot and teapot (Cassidy-Geiger 2008, 336–337, cat. nos. 106 and 107).

CHAPTER 2

1 Pietsch and Banz 2010.

2 Röntgen 1984.

3 Dawson 2005, 19.

4 Honey 1946.

5 Gutter, 1976–2015.

6 Cassidy-Geiger 1998.

7 The ten N=180/R examples include four in the Porzellansammlung, Dresden, and one in each of the following collections: Metropolitan Museum of Art (45.81); Wark Collection, Cummer Museum of Art and Gardens (AG.1965.36.16); Musée national de Céramique, Sèvres; formerly Siegfried Salz collection, Berlin (sold Cassirer & Helbing, Berlin, 1929 [lot 49]); Franz Oppenheimer collection (whereabouts unknown); and Gutter collection.

8 Cassidy-Geiger 2008, cat. no. 35.

9 Boltz 1996, 420. One of these N=220/w figures is in the Rijksmuseum, Amsterdam, and comes from the Mannheimer collection (BK-17476). There were forty such figures in the Mannheimer collection alone; Den Blaauwen 2000, 420. Den Blaauwen has identified the locations of many of these models.

10 The Metropolitan Museum of Art has a related Funcke-decorated incense-burner figure in its collection, decorated predominantly in green and pink with touches of red (1977.216.35).

11 Boltz 2002, 113. "Grotesque" here refers to a fantastic and distorted representation of a human or animal.

12 Cassidy-Geiger's work on graphic sources for Meissen porcelain notes two Jacques Stella sheets owned by the Meissen manufactory in 1846 and five sheets by Jean Le Pautre. Cassidy-Geiger 1996a, 124, cat. no. 183c.

13 Boltz 2002, 113.

14 Goder 1982, 258.

15 Cassidy-Geiger 2008, 584–585, cat. no. 281.

CHAPTER 3

1 See Chilton 2009, vol. 1, 414.

2 Boltz 2000, 93.

3 Ill. Pietsch 2011, cat. no. 29, and *The Wark Collection* 1984, cat. nos. 23 and 30.

4 A suggested pair to this vase was sold at Christie's, New York, April 23, 1998, lot 20.

5 Zumbulyadis 2013, 3–4.

6 Boltz 2006 and 2000, 143.

7 Gutter has noted a red-stoneware example in the Peter Ludwig collection, Bamberg (ill. Hennig 1995, 106, cat. no. 103). White porcelain examples with similar molded decoration, but without enameling, are in the Arnhold collection, New York (Cassidy-Geiger 2008, 340, cat. no. 110), and the Porzellansammlung, Dresden (PE 2 840) (Rückert and Willsberger 1982, 92, fig. 16).

8 Boltz 2000, 143; see also cat. no. 25/pl. 18.

9 Ill. Rückert and Willsberger 1982, 94, fig. 18.

10 Sold Julius Böhler, Munich 1936, lot 771.

11 Both are illustrated in Schmidt 1953, 30–31.

12 Gutter, 1976–2015.

13 Maurice and Mayr 1980, 75–77, 228. The configuration of the numerals on the clockface is not consistent with that of a Renaissance clock. Furthermore, the small face would be positioned below, not above, the larger dial.

14 Köhler was employed by the manufactory around 1704 to 1723, where he was responsible for developing an underglaze blue (see chapter 4).

15 The stock *Fels und Vogeldekor* (rock and bird pattern) pieces were frequently enhanced by *Hausmaler* as late as 1740–1750 in the Thuringian workshop of F. J. Ferner (active 1740–1750).

CHAPTER 4

1 Rückert 1990, 50.

2 Pietsch 2011, 26.

3 In an attempt to secure his position, Ripp supplied an itemized list of blue-and-white pieces he decorated between May 1, 1722, and April 14, 1723, to the factory commission on April 30, 1723. Over twelve months he had decorated 4,806 pieces. Arnold 1989, 32–34.

4 According to Gutter's research, only the blue-and-white vase attributed to Ripp in the Porzellansammlung, Dresden, is taller, at 30½ inches (77.5 cm; PE 2194), as is one other pair, formerly of the Dresden collection. One vase from the latter pair reappeared in the Oppenheimer collection (see Schnorr von Carolsfeld 1927, cat. no. 40).

5 *Porzellan, Gemälde* 1920 and Schnorr von Carolsfeld 1927, cat. nos. 41–42. These vases are now in the Rijksmuseum collection, Amsterdam (BK-17334-A/B) (den Blaauwen 2000, 40–41, cat. no. 15).

6 See Kuhn 2008, 81–82, for more details on the Mannheimer collection.

7 Its whereabouts are unknown.

8 As suggested by Claus Boltz, in a 2001 letter with Gutter.

9 Boltz 1996, 99–102.

10 PE 596, 1376, and 2200. Ill. Pietsch 2010, 36, cat. no. 24, and Arnold 1989, 137–138 and 140–141, cat. nos. 20, 22, and 24.

11 Cassidy-Geiger 2008, 198–199, cat. nos. 19a and 19b.

12 Syndram 1997, vol. 1, 362, fig. XI 46.2.

13 Pietsch 2011, 118.

14 Zumbulyadis 2006, 78, fig. 97.

15 Arnold 1989, 33–34.

16 This piece was sold in the third duplicate sale of the Saxon royal collection in 1926.

17 1779 Inventory, vol. V.

18 Gutter, 1976–2015.

19 See Victoria and Albert Museum, London (C.133 A-1951).

20 Weber 2013, vol. 1, 10–11; vol. 2, 76, fig. 13.

CHAPTER 5

1 This may have been in part due to the Hoym-Lemaire scandal.

2 The Schulz Codex, which was named for a previous owner, is now in the collection of the Grassi Museum für Angewandte Kunst, Leipzig. See Rudi 2010.

3 One rarely sees other European porcelains directly adopt Höroldt Baroque chinoiseries. As art dealer Errol Manners notes, the English—and Chelsea in particular—favored "the lighter French Rococo version as created by François Boucher and Jean Pillement" (Manners 2015).

4 Den Blaauwen 2000, 49.

5 Walcha 1973, 462.

6 Den Blaauwen 2000, 62–63, cat. no. 52.

7 Ill. Cassidy-Geiger 2008, 368, cat. no. 135.

8 Gutter suggests that this addition may have been made to improve the stability of the piece.

9 See Gutter 2010 for a further discussion of Allard and other contemporary travel books' influence on Meissen designs. These Allard prints no longer appear to survive in the Dresden or Meissen archives (Cassidy-Geiger 2010, 54, and Pietsch and Banz 2010, 84–93).

10 For another related chinoiserie coffeepot with similar mounts, see the Arnhold collection (Cassidy-Geiger 2008, 344, cat. no. 114).

11 Scholar Diethard Lübke addresses some of these challenges in Lübke 2002.

12 An olive green–ground vase formerly in the Dresden Turmzimmer (now lost) depicts Augustus the Strong with a crown and scepter. Ingelore Menzhausen, former curator of the Staatliche Kunstsammlungen Dresden, dated that Höroldt-decorated vase to 1726/1727 (Menzhausen 1988, 23, fig. 25).

13 Gutter suggests that by 1723 *indianische Blumen* and insects began to spread beyond the handle and spout to voids on the porcelain bodies. He has also observed that the earliest services, circa 1723–1724, commonly feature sky and clouds in their enameled scenes, whereas the later works are frequently bereft of sky.

14 A teapot from this service sold at the same sale where Gutter acquired his teabowl and saucer.

15 Gutter 1988, 72.

16 For discussion on other pieces in this service, see Gutter 1988, 70–76.

17 See Victoria and Albert Museum, London, C.27:1, 2-2006.

18 Pietsch and Banz 2010, 55. For a Japanese incense-burner model, see Rijksmuseum AK-NM-6351-A.

19 Chilton 2009, 1291–1293.

20 For the Du Paquier *Oliotopf* in Budapest, see Pietsch and Banz 2010, 55, cat. no. 46; for the Meissen pair, see Bayerisches Nationalmuseum, Schneider collection, Schloss Lustheim (ill. Eikelmann 2004, 216, cat. no. 80) and Rijksmuseum (ill. den Blaauwen 2000, 216, cat. no. 133).

21 See Cassidy-Geiger 2010, 52, and Cassidy-Geiger 1996a, 100–102.

22 Ill. in Däberitz and Eberle 2011, 60–61, cat. no. 12, and Rudi 2010, 284, cat. no. R 2 b.

23 To enhance this argument, Gutter has also noted a mounted example in the Staatliches Museum Schwerin (ill. Seyffarth 1981, figs. 24–26) as well as an unmounted one from a private collection (sold at Christie's, London, December 11, 2007, lot 28; then resold at Bonhams, London, November 26, 2014, lot 140).

24 Den Blaauwen 2000, 259. See chapter 6 for more on print sources used at Meissen.

25 This source survives in the Dresden print room (Cassidy-Geiger 1996a).

26 Pietsch 2011, 24.

27 Den Blaauwen 2000, 293, cat. no. 213.

   Errol Manners has speculated that the yellow luster number 127 on the underside of the saucer was made by a nineteenth-century repairer in Bristol. A pair to this piece can be found in the A. du Boulay Collection, Dorchester. This example is inscribed with a fired red luster. This mark has been identified as that of an eighteenth-century restorer working at 31 Old Bond Street, London.

CHAPTER 6

1 Cassidy-Geiger 1996a, 100–101 and cat. no. 36.

2 Notable research on the print archives of the Staatliche Porzellan-Manufaktur Meissen has been published by Cassidy-Geiger in the Metropolitan Museum of Art journal (see Cassidy-Geiger 1996a for further study).

3 Behrends 1978, 46n88, and Cassidy-Geiger 1996a, 102n21.

4 Gutter has written extensively on this teabowl and its print sources in Gutter 2010.

5 Stokes 1915–1928, vol. 1, 142.

6 Scenes on the Meissen "Canada" bowl in the Gardiner Museum, Toronto, were also taken from Allard, plates 77 and 79. For more on this piece, see Chilton 1995. A saucer from this service, depicting the same New Yorkers on Gutter's teabowl, is in the collection of the Victoria and Albert Museum, London (C.351A-1918).

7 The Musée Ariana teabowl and saucer share the same gilding patterns, cartouche design, and unusual Buddhist symbols as the Gutter teabowl.

8 Gutter has identified only two versions in red stoneware, from the Hans Syz collection (now at the Smithsonian National Museum of American History, 1980.0024.01ab) and the Museum of Decorative Arts in Prague.

9 Gilding on both lid and teapot are an exact match and fit, leading Gutter to believe they were fired together.

10 Printed by Gaspard Duchange (Paris/Amsterdam, 1708). Thanks to professor Jeffrey Ruda, University of California, Davis, for identifying this print source.

11 Gutter has identified a teapot in the Designmuseum Danmark, Copenhagen, depicting Amymone's rescue from the satyr by Neptune, from the same service as his teabowl and saucer.

12 For red-stoneware figures, see the six players at Schlossmuseum Gotha (St 24a-f; ill. Rückert 1985, 82–85, figs. 6–7) and the Pantalone and Brighella figures at the Metropolitan Museum of Art, New York (64.101.86 and 54.147.66).

13 See Cassidy-Geiger 1996a, 105n29, and Chilton 2001, 106, 164–173.

14 Gutter has identified other pieces in this service. A teapot, marked *MPM* in the Arnhold collection; a sugar box, marked *KPF* in a private collection, London; and five teabowls and saucers (three in a London private collection; one formerly in the collection of Madame Barilla, Geneva; and one with Gutter). All the saucers noted display an unrecorded, yellow luster mark.

15 Several prints of dwarfs by an unidentified artist survive in the archives of the Staatliche Porzellan-Manufaktur Meissen (Clarke 1988, 6–57, and Cassidy-Geiger 1996a, 105–107, 117). Furthermore, Cassidy-Geiger has noted eight sheets with figures by Callot that were owned by the manufactory, based on a 1846 inventory (1996a, 123).

16 These two dancing dwarfs are taken up again in a later milk jug (ca. 1740–1745) in the Rijksmuseum (BK-17465).

17 Two other pieces in this Callot-influenced service have been identified by Gutter and include a teapot, marked *MPM*, private collection (ill. Berges 1980, 104), and a waste bowl in the Gardiner Museum.

18 Cassidy-Geiger 1996a, 108.

19 The bridge was reconstructed in 1727–1731 by Matthäus Daniel Pöppelmann, Augustus the Strong's architect. Gutter 1976–2015.

20 In a fascinating coincidence, Bach's appointment by the Leipzig town council in April 1723 roughly coincides with the approximate date of this *Olienbecher*.

21 A small *écuelle* and cover with a virtually identical scene, probably by the same hand, is in a private collection, London.

22 Boltz 2002, 69.

23 The identification of the scene and print source was made by Bernard Dragesco and Malcolm Gutter. The manufactory archives contain a sheet categorized as "Landschaften, Prospecten und Seestücke" (landscapes, perspectives and sea-scapes) (Cassidy-Geiger 1996a, 125).

24 Gutter suggests the same flower painter worked on this piece and two others in his collection, cat. nos. 45 and 47/pls. 31 and 33.

25 Other pieces from this service with the same cartouche decoration and gilder's number have been identified by Gutter; however, the quality of painting and differences in pigment quality have led him to believe that some may be later replacements.

26 When it appeared on the market in 1992, the teapot was traditionally considered part of a larger service. However, its decoration was later recognized as earlier in date from the other pieces in the service. It was therefore sold as a separate lot at a Christie's auction in 1994, where Gutter acquired it.

27 Gutter has identified several pieces from this service that were sold at Christie's, London, July 5, 1971 (lots 104–109). They all share the same gilder's mark 54 and cartouche design. The other pieces depict daytime harbor or landscape scenes. This particular teabowl and saucer were inde-pendently retained by the owner from the 1971 Christie's sale but eventually sold at Christie's by the estate in 2001.

28 Comparable pieces can be found in the Arnhold collection, New York (Cassidy-Geiger 2008, 422, cat. no. 173); the Bayerisches Nationalmuseum, Schneider collection (ES 249) (Eikelmann 2004, 214–215, cat. no. 78); a private collection, Switzerland; and a larger, 15⅜-inch version, pri-vate collection, London.

29 Sauerlandt 1926, 97.

30 Pietsch 2011, 521, cat. 636, and *The Wark Collection* 1984, 117, no. 126.

31 Ill. Palmer and Chilton 1984, 52.

CHAPTER 7

1 See Wittwer 2006, 41 and 43–49; and Löffler 1958, figs. 161–162.

2 Boltz 1996, 3–118.

3 See cat. nos. 37, 67, and 68/pls. 25, 50, and 51 for other notable examples in the Gutter collection.

4 1. pair of AR vases, collection of Henry Arnhold, New York (ill. Cassidy-Geiger 2008, 212–213, cat. no. 25); 2. covered AR baluster vase, Porzellansammlung, Dresden (ill. Pietsch 1996, 154–155, cat. no. 123); 3. covered AR baluster vase (ill. Zimmermann 1926, pl. 4); 4. covered AR vase, Rijksmuseum, Amsterdam (ill. den Blaauwen 2000, 50–51, cat. no. 22); 5. pair of vases (unmarked), Rijksmuseum, Amsterdam (ill. den Blaauwen 2000, 42–43, cat. no. 16); 6. pair of AR beaker vases, private collection, London; and 7. pendant AR beaker vases, collection of Malcolm D. Gutter, San Francisco, and private collection, London.

5 Some text from Santangelo 2014 was freely used in this entry.

6 The Lustheim vase is illustrated and cited in Rückert 1966, cat. no. 342, pl. XII; Just 1960; Eikelmann 2004, 196–197, 416, cat. no. 69; Schnorr von Carolsfeld 1956, 78, fig. 41; and Eikelmann and Weber 2013, vol. II, cat. no. 22.

  The surviving fragments derive from three distinct sections of the vase: a) the upper bulb (lacking the flaring upper section constituting the rim of the vase), continuing through the waist to a section of the larger lower bulb; b) a fragment, contiguous, but part of the lower bulb; two large contiguous fragments from the central portion of the lower bulb; and c) a small section made up of four contiguous shards from the lower bulb, including a portion of the foot. Sections b and c are "free floating," or separate from each other. The fragments have been fitted into a plaster com-pound material that conveys both the form of the original and the integrity of the extant decoration.

7 Sebastian Kuhn, in Cassidy-Geiger 2008, note 132, 116.

8 See Kuhn in Cassidy-Geiger 2008, 23–119.

9 Meissen's first experienced blue-and-white painter, Johann Caspar Ripp, was certainly influenced by his work at the faience factories in Frankfurt am Main, Hanau, and Zerbst.

10 Related Meissen pieces with lotus decora-tion can be seen in the following collections: Kunstgewerbemuseum, Berlin (AR beaker vase, ca. 1726–1730; AR trumpet vase, ca. 1726–1730; and mounted tankard, ca. 1726–1730); Henry Arnhold collection, New York (*écuelle* stand, ca. 1730; waste bowl, ca. 1726–1730; and an AR ovoid-shaped vase, ca. 1727–1730); Lustheim (pair to Arnhold AR vase, though lacking a cover, ca. 1727–1730); and the Metropolitan Museum of Art, New York (tankard, ca. 1727–1730).

11 See Boltz 1996 for a thorough discussion on the 1770 Japanese Palace inventory and 1769 Turmzimmer inventory.

12 The 1770 Japanese Palace inventory lists this group as "Fünf und Fünfzig Stück schlechten (Spühl Compen, differenter Grösse und Mahlerey, No. 502)" (Fifty-five bowls poorly potted, different sizes and decoration). Other known pieces in this 502 group, as identified by Boltz, are in the British Museum (Franks.30; Boltz 1996, 68, figs. 49–50); the Porzellansammlung, Dresden (Boltz 1996, 67, figs. 47–48); and the Hans Syz collection (Syz, Miller, and Rückert 1979, 174–175, fig. 102).

13 A similar, but slightly more refined, rendition of this butterfly grouping can be seen on a cov-ered bowl in the Schneider collection, Schloss Lustheim (inv. 350) (ill. Rückert and Willsberger 1982, 134, fig. 58).

14 Ill. Boltz 1996, 59, figs. 26–27.

15 Ill. Emerson, Chen, and Gates 2000, 32, pls. 2–4.

16 Boltz 1996, 59–60. A group of seven saucers are noted in the Japanese Palace inventory as "Sieben Stück runde Coffée Tassen mit (57b) Henckeln und Schnauzgen, auswendig mit erhabenen Nahmen AR. und kleinen Blümgen vergold-ten Rändgen um den Fuss, inwendig oben mit goldenen Zierrathen gemahlt, 2½ Zoll hoch, und 3½ Zoll in Diam.: nebst Sieben darzu gehörigen Unterschaalen mit 2. Handgriffen 1¼ Zoll hoch, 5½ Zoll in Diam: No. 421" (Seven round coffee cups each with a handle and spout, on the outside with a raised monogram AR and small flowers, the rim gilded and at the top of the foot a gilt ornamentation, 2½ inches high, and 3½ inches in diameter; together with seven saucers each with two handles, 1¼ inches high, 5½ inches in diameter).

17 Some text from Santangelo 2014 was freely used in this entry.

18 This pendant vase, from the Schneider collection, was formerly in Schloss Lustheim. For publica-tions, see Rückert 1966, 89–90, cat. no. 274, and Just 1960, 39–42, figs. 117–118.

19 This little dot appears in the same spot on the AR marks of several other vases, such as two in the Rijksmuseum (den Blaauwen 2000, 86–89); a vase in the Kunstgewerbemuseum, Berlin (Bursche 1980, 224–225, mark ill. 524); and one in Lustheim (Eikelmann 2004, 150–151 and 408). All of these vases date to circa 1725–1730.

20 Den Blaauwen 2000, fig. 127; and Loesch, Pietsch, and Reichel 1998, 4 and 6.

21 Sonntag and Karpinski 1991, 187, cat. nos. 4/5.

22 Boltz 1996, 60 and 16. Made in great number, the 1770 Japanese Palace inventories records for N=397-/w: "Sieben Dutzendt und (9) 8. Stück detto Chocolaten Becher mit (56b) belegten Blümgen, ohne Henckel, 3½. Zoll hoch, 3¼. Zoll in Diam: nebst Drey Dutzendt und 6. Stück dazu gehörigen Unterschaalen, 1¼ Zoll tief, 5½. Zoll in Diam, No. 397, einige defect" (Seven dozen and (9) eight pieces, the same [white], chocolate beakers with applied flowers and without handles, 3½ inches high, 3¼ inches in diameter, along with three dozen and six matching saucers, 1¼ inches deep, 5½ inches in diameter, No. 397, some defec-tive). 1769 Turmzimmer inventory records for no. 397: "Drey Stück detto Japanisch mit der Marque /W" (Three additional Japanese pieces marked /W).

23 Examples include the Victoria and Albert Museum, London (C.450&A-1922); the Isaacson collection, Seattle (sold Sotheby's, New York, May 22, 2001, lot 177); Cummer Museum of Art and Gardens (AG.1965.56.39; AG.1965.56.40) (*The Wark Collection* 1984, cat. nos. 28–29; and Pietsch 2011, 81, cat. nos. 27–28); Porzellansammlung, Dresden (one noted in Pietsch 1996, 23); Gutter collection, San Francisco; and private collection, London (included in the same Christie's 2002 lot as Gutter's).

24 Boltz 2002, 108–109.

25 Ill. Jedding 1982, 127–128, cat. no. 112. For another Japanese bowl with this decoration, see Jenyns 1965, fig. 67B. See Arnhold collection (Cassidy-Geiger 2008, 397, cat. no. 157) for a Meissen copy of that Japanese bowl.

26 Ill. Rückert and Willsberger 1982, 114, fig. 59; and Menzhausen 1990, pl. 59.

27 Ayers, Impey, and Mallet 1990, 170, cat. no. 150.

28 The Hoym-Lemaire subject is well documented in several publications, including Boltz 1980; Cassidy-Geiger 1994; Le Duc 1997a and 1997b; and Weber 2014.

29 Weber 2014.

30 The location of this bowl's prototype, formerly in the Porzellansammlung, Dresden, is currently unknown. The entry for number 119 in the 1721 inventory reads: "Ein 10. seiten spühl napf mit überschlagenen Kanten, auch Pferden und Blumen gemahlt von Indianischen Porzellan, 3½ Zoll hoch, 8. Zoll in Diam, No 119" (A ten-sided waste bowl of Indian porcelain with out-turned rim decorated with horses and flowers, 3½ inches high, 8 inches in diameter, No. 119). The entry for Japanese Palace inventory number N=447-/w lists: "Zehen Stück detto kleinere Spühl Näpffe in-und auswendig mit Blumen, Vögeln und Thieren gemahlt, der grösste 3½. Zoll hoch, 8. Zoll in Diam: der kleinste 3¼. Zoll hoch, 6¾. Zoll in Diam: No. 447" (Ten pieces the same [ten-sided waste bowls with out-turned brown rims], but smaller, painted inside and outside with flowers, birds, and animals, the biggest 3½ inches high, 8 inches diameter, the smallest 3¼ inches high, 6¾ inches diameter, No. 447). Boltz 1996, 61.

31 The Japanese Palace 1770 and 1779 inventories for N=66-/w read: "Zwölf Stück detto Schüsseln, inwendig mit Vögeln, Blumen und Korn gemahlt, mitüberschlagenen Rand, 2½. Zoll teif, 10. Zoll in Diam: No. 66" (Twelve similar [as No. 65] deep dishes inside of which are painted birds, flowers, and grain, with everted rims, 2½ inches deep, 10 inches in diameter, No. 66). Ibid., 74. Other N=66-/w dishes are found in the Porzellansammlung, Dresden (unpublished, but identified by Julia Weber to Malcolm Gutter) and the Hetjens-Museum, Düsseldorf (2008-157) (ill. *Frühes Meissener Porzellan* 1997, 174, cat. no. 140).

32 See Ayers, Impey, and Mallet 1990 for a Japanese example, 151, cat. no. 121.

33 Weber 2012, 43, fig. 3.

34 Cassidy-Geiger 1996b, 120f.

35 Boltz 1996, 31.

36 The Schneider collection includes a quadrangu-lar example (ES 26) and an octagonal one (ES 3), both with Japanese Palace inventory number N=291-/w (Eikelmann 2004, 176–177, fig. 57).

37 Boltz 2002, 96.

38 The 1770 Japanese Palace inventory for N=17-/w reads: "Sechs Stück detto, mit einem blätterichten Knopf, 8. Zoll hoch, 9 3/4. Zoll in Diam: No. 17" (Six same pieces ["white tureen decorated with birds and small flowers"], each with a leafy finial, 8 inches high, 9¾ inches in diameter, No. 17). Boltz 1996, 72.

39 Weber 2013, 251–252.

40 Shono 1973, fig. 55.

41 The 1770 and 1779 Japanese Palace inventories for N=36-/w read: "Drey Stück detto 8. eckichte, mit überschlagenen braunen Rande, inwendig Pagoden gemahlt, 1¾. Zoll tief, 11¾. Zoll in Diam: No. 36" (Three pieces the same [a *Schaale*, or a dish] 8-sided with everted brown rims, in which is painted Orientals, 1¾ inches deep, 11¾ inches in diameter, No. 36).

42 For examples of eight- and twelve-sided dishes, see Porzellansammlung, Dresden (PE5222); Copenhagen (P.M.116.117); Rijksmuseum (BK-17343, BK-17344, BK-17345, BK-1968-155-A/B, and BK-NM-12181); British Museum, London (Franks.28); Museum of Fine Arts, Boston (65.2055); Arnhold collection, New York (2002.415; Cassidy-Geiger 2008, 513, cat. no. 241); Smithsonian (Syz.976); Schloss Lustheim, Munich (ES 341); and Victoria and Albert Museum, London (30-1908).

43 Ill. Jenyns 1965, pl. 74A.

44 British Museum (Franks.32), N=285-/w (ill. Jenyns 1965, pl. 74B); Rijksmuseum (BK-1968-114), N=285-/w (ill. den Blaauwen 2000, 218–219, cat. no. 157); and Porzellansammlung, which has two copies marked *N=285-/w* (one ill. Boltz 1996, 54–55, figs. 24–25, and Seyffarth 1981, figs. 75/76) and another marked *N=203-/w* (unpublished).

45 They are described as "Fünfzehn Stück 10.eckigte gemuschelte Assietten mit etwas überschlagenen braunen Rande worein grüne Drachen, Vögel und Blumen gemahlt, ... No. 49" (Fifteen ten-sided molded plates with everted brown rims wherein is painted a green dragon, birds, and flowers, ... No. 49). One known AR-marked plate was sold at Lempertz, Cologne, in 2016.

46 A Japanese plate belonging to the Ashmolean (1978.548) is illustrated in Ayers, Impey, and Mallet 1990, 153, cat. no. 124.

47 Impey 2002, 188, cat. no. 299.

48 See Shono 1973, no. 4.

49 The Japanese Palace 1770 inventory for N=57-/w reads: "Siebenzehn Stück detto, in Form einer Muschel, mit Drachen, No. 57" (Seventeen pieces the same [oyster dishes] in the form of a shell, with dragons, No. 57). Boltz 1996, 73. The water-like decorations were evidently identified as dragons.

50 Six examples are identified in the Porzellansammlung, Dresden (including PE 5204, 5206, 5207, and 5208), one published in Walcha 1981, fig. 58; and five others confirmed by Gutter with Otto Walcha. Three dishes were sold at the Meissen 1919 duplicates sale, one (lot 162) now in the Stout collection, Dixon Gallery and Gardens, Memphis, Tennessee (85.DA.130). A related dish, marked *N=52-/w*, is in the Arnhold collection. Ill. Cassidy-Geiger 2008, 506, cat. no. 235.

51 Another Kakiemon-inspired service, known as the Red Dragon (see cat. no. 102), was chosen by Augustus III for exclusive royal use in November 1733. The Red Dragon service was adopted into the Dresden royal pantry.

52 A related Japanese model can be seen in Jenyns 1965, fig. 76A, and Shono 1973, fig. 17. Japanese models can be found in the following public collections: British Museum, London (1911,0706.1, Franks.483A); Seattle Art Museum (56.122) (ill. Emerson, Chen, and Gates 2000, 170, pl. 12.16); and the Idemitsu Museum of Arts, Tokyo (Weber 2013, 125 and 246, fig. 41).

53 Boltz 1996, 100. Other identified dishes from this N=149-/w group include those in the Metropolitan Museum of Art, New York (42.205.125); Museum Angewandtekunst, Frankfurt am Main (Bauer 1983, 66, cat. no. 53); and Schneider collection at Schloss Lustheim, Bayerisches Nationalmuseum, Munich (Weber 2013, 279, no. 257). They range in size from 11⅛ to 19½ inches in diameter.

CHAPTER 8

1 Maureen Cassidy-Geiger thoroughly discusses the diplomatic role of Meissen and the European courts in Cassidy-Geiger 2007 and its related exhibition at the Bard Graduate Center for Studies in the Decorative Arts, New York.

2 Manners 2015, 29.

3 Maureen Cassidy-Geiger's essay "Princes and Porcelain on the Grand Tour of Italy" specifically addresses the close relationship between the royal courts and families of Dresden and Italy. Cassidy-Geiger 2007, 209–255.

4 Boltz 1996, 91, and Boltz 2000, letter of correspondence with Gutter.

5 Boltz 1996, 76. The majority of this service survives in the royal collection, but several examples from the N=147-/w group can be found in public and private collections. These include the Bayerisches Nationalmuseum, Ernst Schneider collection, Schloss Lustheim (inv. no. 562); the Metropolitan Museum of Art, New York (54.147.72); the Stout collection, Dixon Gallery and Gardens, Memphis (85.DA.144); the Wark Collection, Cummer Gallery of Art and Gardens, Jacksonville, Florida (AG.1966.23.7); Seattle Art Museum (69.201); Hans Syz collection, Smithsonian (Syz, Miller, and Rückert 1979, 286–287, cat. no. 180); Wawel Royal Castle, Krakow; and the Arnhold collection (Cassidy-Geiger 2008, 438, cat. no. 186).

6 *Splendor of Dresden* 1978, 195, cat. nos. 502–504.

7 Meissen specifications for this service notes: "6 Schaelgen und Coppgen inwendig gantz verguld, mit dem Koenigl. Pohl. Saechs. und Sicilianischen Wappen 6 Choclate Becer bedies in die grosse Toilett gehoerig [...] annoch in Arbeit und zu liefern" (6 saucers and bowls completely gilt on the inside, with the Royal Polish Saxon and Sicilian arms 6 chocolate beakers both belonging to the large toilet [...] still in production and to be delivered). Quoted by Boltz 1978, 5; see also Cassidy-Geiger 2007, 218 and note 50.

8 Boltz 1978; Cassidy-Geiger 2007, 218; and Kuhn 2012, 130–132, lot 41.

9 Ill. Boltz 1978, fig. 1.

10 Cassidy-Geiger 2007, 228.

11 Sebastian Kuhn has also noted a small group of armorials, possibly for Venetian patrons, dating circa 1725.

12 Those examples with known locations are three teabowls and saucers in Ca' Rezzonico, Venice (ill. Pedrocco 2005, 67), erroneously ascribed to the Cozzi factory; one teabowl and saucer, Landesmuseum Württemberg, Stuttgart (ill. Pazaurek 1929, 43, fig. 23); and one teabowl and saucer, private collection, London.

13 Ill. in Schnorr von Carolsfeld 1928, pl. 27.

14 For a thorough study of this service, see Pietsch 2000. The corresponding exhibition, held at the Dresden castle, featured a vast table laden with pieces from this tremendous service.

15 The manufactory produced numerous replacement dishes during the late eighteenth century. The Swan service is still produced today by the manufactory.

16 Cassidy-Geiger 1988, 65–68.

17 The collection of the Fine Arts Museums of San Francisco contains the Giovanni Battista Tiepolo painting *The Empire of Flora* (ca. 1743; 61.44.19), commissioned by Count Francesco Algarotti, envoy of Augustus III, and presented to Count von Brühl circa 1743. The garden fountain in the background of this painting re-creates a Neptune group on the grounds of Schloss Pförten.

18 Pietsch 2000, 167, cat. no. 41.

19 Some surviving examples can be found in the Porzellansammlung, Dresden (see Pietsch 2000); Ernst Schneider collection, Schloss Lustheim (ES 416 and 417); Detroit Institute of Arts (58.166.A–B); Metropolitan Museum of Art (50.211.234); Arnhold collection (Cassidy-Geiger 2008, 453–454, cat. nos. 200 and 201); and National Museum in Warsaw.

20 Pietsch 2000.

21 See Liackhova 2004, 81.

22 Two notable exhibitions and catalogues address the subject of Meissen services for Russia: Pietsch 2004 and Cassidy-Geiger 2007.

23 Liackhova 2004, 66.

24 See Pietsch 2004, 67 and 69, for the transcription of the Meissen packing list and the corresponding Russian inventories.

25 Pietsch 2011, 478–479, cat. no. 568.

26 For more on the Hermitage's holdings of this service, see Liackhova 2004, 74, Reinheckel 1965, and Kasakievitsch 1995.

27 Ill. Weber 2013, 326–327, cat. no. 128.

28 Cassidy-Geiger 2008, 466, cat. no. 207.

O'SHEA

1 Robin Hopper, *Making Marks: Discovering the Ceramic Surface* (Iola, WI: Krause Publications Craft, 2004).

2 K. Domoney, A. J. Shortland, and S. Kuhn, "Characterization of 18th-Century Meissen Porcelain using SEM-EDS," *Archaeometry* 54, no. 3 (June 2012): 454–474.

3 Daniel Rhoads, *Clay and Glazes for the Potter*, rev. ed. (Radnor, PA: Chilton Book Company, 1973).

4 Richard Seyffarth, "Johann Gregor Höroldt als Chemiker und Techniker," *Keramik-Freunde der Schweiz* 39 (1957): 22–25.

5 Francesca Casadio, Anikó Bezur, Kelly Domoney, Katherine Eremin, Lynn Lee, Jennifer L. Mass, Andrew Shortland, and Nicholas Zumbulyadis, "X-ray Fluorescence Applied to Overglaze Enamel Decoration on Eighteenth- and Nineteenth-Century Porcelain from Central Europe," in *Contributions to the Vienna Congress: 10–14 September 2012; The Decorative: Conservation and the Applied Arts* (Leeds, UK: Maney Publishing; and London: International Institute for Conservation of Historic and Artistic Works, 2012), S61–S72.

6 Domoney, Shortland, and Kuhn, "Characterization of 18th-Century Meissen Porcelain."

7 Anikó Bezur and Francesca Casadio, "The Analysis of Porcelain Using Handheld and Portable X-ray Fluorescence Spectrometers," in *Handheld XRF for Art and Archaeology*, ed. A. N. Shugar and J. L. Mass (Leuven, Belgium: Leuven University Press, 2012), 249–311.

8 Casadio, Bezur, et al., "X-ray Fluorescence"; and L. B. Hunt, "The True Story of Purple of Cassius," *Gold Bulletin* 9, no. 4 (December 1976): 134–139.

9 Casadio, Bezur, et al., "X-ray Fluorescence."

10 Casadio, "Decoration of Meissen Porcelain: Raman Microscopy as an Aid for Authentication and Dating," *Proceedings of the Sixth Infrared and Raman Users Group Conference (IRUG6)*, ed. Marcello Picollo (Padua, Italy: Il Prato, 2005), 178–184.

11 Jeffrey Warda, ed., *The AIC Guide to Digital Photography and Conservation Documentation*, 2nd ed. (Washington, DC: American Institute for Conservation, 2011).

Checklist of the Malcolm D. Gutter Collection

All objects in the Malcolm D. Gutter Collection have been promised to the Fine Arts Museums of San Francisco, unless otherwise noted. Dimensions are listed height by width by depth.

The provenance lists known previous owners or purveyors; when available, dates of the acquisition of the object are listed. The final entry lists the source of an object upon entering the Gutter collection.

I. BÖTTGER AND RED STONEWARE

1. Pair of teabowls, ca. 1709–1711
Red stoneware with black glaze
2 ¼ × 3 ⅝ in. (5.6 × 9.1 cm) and 2 ¼ × 3 ¾ in. (5.6 × 9.4 cm)
L13.62.2.1–2
Plate 1
Provenance
L13.62.2.1: Continental Art Shop, San Francisco; Richard W. Hanna, San Francisco, November 5, 1955. Butterfield & Butterfield, San Francisco, June 17, 1975, lot 830 (purchased with saucer [L13.62.3; cat. no. 2])
L13.62.2.2: Sotheby's, New York, October 19, 1994, lot 200
Publication history
Kopplin 2003, supplement volume, 48
Exhibition history
California Palace of the Legion of Honor, San Francisco, 1980 (L13.62.2.2 only); Legion of Honor, San Francisco, 2014–2016

2. Saucer, ca. 1709–1711
Red stoneware with black glaze
1 × 5 ⅞ in. (2.5 × 12.5 cm)
L13.62.3
Plate 2
Provenance
Continental Art Shop, San Francisco; Richard W. Hanna, San Francisco, November 5, 1955. Butterfield & Butterfield, San Francisco, June 17, 1975, lot 830 (purchased with teabowl [L13.62.2.1; cat. no. 1])
Exhibition history
California Palace of the Legion of Honor, San Francisco, 1980; San Francisco Airport Museum, 2010; Legion of Honor, San Francisco, 2014–2016

3. Saucer, ca. 1709–1711
Red stoneware with matte and slip decoration
1 ⅜ × 5 ⅜ in. (3.4 × 13.7 cm)
L13.62.4
Plate 3
Provenance
Continental Art Shop, San Francisco; Richard W. Hanna, San Francisco, November 5, 1955; Jerry Durham, San Francisco, 1975; Christie's, New York, October 27, 1986, lot 137 (unsold); consigned by Durham's estate to Richard Gould Antiques, Los Angeles. Richard Gould Antiques, Los Angeles, 1994 (with bowl [L13.62.5; cat. no. 4])
Publication history
Boltz 2001, 6, figs. 1 and 2; Gutter 2001, table 5, figs. 7 and 8
Exhibition history
San Francisco Airport Museum, 2010; Legion of Honor, San Francisco, 2014–2016

4. *Eisenporzellan* teabowl, ca. 1710–1712
Red stoneware with slip decoration
2 ½ × 4 in. (6.2 × 10.1 cm)
L13.62.5
Plate 4
Provenance
Continental Art Shop, San Francisco; Richard W. Hanna, San Francisco, November 5, 1955; Jerry Durham, San Francisco, 1975; Christie's, New York, October 27, 1986, lot 137 (unsold). Richard Gould Antiques, Los Angeles, 1994 (with saucer [L13.62.4; cat. no. 3])
Exhibition history
San Francisco Airport Museum, 2010; Legion of Honor, San Francisco, 2014–2016

5. Two-handled chocolate beaker and saucer, ca. 1710–1713
Red stoneware with black glaze
Beaker: 3 ⅛ × 3 ⅜ in. (8 × 8.5 cm); saucer: 1 ⅛ × 5 ⅞ in. (3 × 14.8 cm)
Marks: inventory numbers *AAI 69.28a* and *AAI 69.28B* (AAI for Akron Art Institute) in red enamel
L13.62.11a–b
Plate 5
Provenance
Hans Backer, Rome (probable), through Newman & Newman, London; Charles S. Reed II, Cleveland, Ohio; gifted by Reed to the Akron Art Institute, 1969; deaccessioned by the museum, 2004. Leslie Hindman, Chicago, May 23–25, 2004, lot 395
Publication history
Newman 1977, 4, fig. 2
Exhibition history
Loaned to the Cleveland Museum of Art, ca. 1960s; San Francisco Airport Museum, 2010; Legion of Honor, San Francisco, 2014–2016

6. Ewer (*kendi*), ca. 1710–1712
Red stoneware
6 ⅞ × 4 ½ in. (17.6 × 11.5 cm)
Mark: Japanese Palace inventory number *232 / R* in black enamel
L13.62.8
Plate 6
Provenance
Augustus II, elector of Saxony and king of Poland, Japanese Palace, Dresden; *Dubletten sale, Porzellane und Waffen aus den Kgl. Sächsischen Sammlungen in Dresden*, Rudolph Lepke's Kunst-Auctions-Haus, Berlin, October 7–8, 1919, lot 36; Ole Olsen, Copenhagen; Winkel & Magnussens Kunstauktioner, Copenhagen, March 1, 1944, lot 266. Christie's, London, May 18, 1999, lot 155
Publication history
Evolution of a Royal Vision 2010, 4–5; Schmitz 1927, cat. no. 1345, pl. XXIV, and 26 (text)
Exhibition history
San Francisco Airport Museum, 2010; Legion of Honor, San Francisco, 2014–2016

7. Coffeepot, ca. 1710–1713
Red stoneware
5 ⅞ × 2 ½ in. (15 × 6.4 cm)
L13.62.6a–b
Plate 7
Provenance
Russell, Baldwin & Bright, Leominster, England, February 22 or 23, 1995; "The Cambridge Family," United Kingdom. E & H Manners, London, 1995
Publication history
Gutter 2001, 11, pls. 2 and 3, figs. 3 and 4; Santangelo 2014, 16 (illus.)
Exhibition history
San Francisco Airport Museum, 2010; Legion of Honor, San Francisco, 2014–2016

8. Eagle-spout teapot, ca. 1710–1713
Red stoneware with black glaze
4 ⅜ × 4 ⅜ in. (11 × 11 cm)
L13.62.7a–b
Plate 8
Provenance
Christie's, London, November 3, 1997, lot 238
Exhibition history
San Francisco Airport Museum, 2010; Legion of Honor, San Francisco, 2014–2016

9. Teapot, ca. 1710–1713
Red stoneware with black glaze, lacquer, and gilding
3 ¾ × 3 in. (9.5 × 7.5 cm)
L13.62.9a–b
Plate 9
Provenance
Baron Edmond van Zuylen (d. 1899); Sotheby's, London, July 8, 1969, lot 11; Joseph Jackson, United Kingdom. Law Fine Art, Brimpton, England, April 24, 2001, lot 94
Publication history
Kopplin 2003, supplement volume, 44
Exhibition history
San Francisco Airport Museum, 2010; Legion of Honor, San Francisco, 2014–2016

10. Mounted tankard (Walzenkrug), ca. 1710–1713
Polished red stoneware with gilding and pewter mounts
9 ⅞ × 5 ⅛ in. (25 × 13 cm); height without cover: 7 ⅝ in. (19.5 cm)
Marks: tankard unmarked; *55* inscribed in script on interior of pewter cover
L13.62.12
Plate 10
Provenance
Dr. Georg Adolf Remé, Hamburg; Hans W. Lange, Berlin, April 7–9, 1938, lot 632; HannoVerum (Auktions & Handelshaus), Hanover, April 14, 2012, lot 378; sold to Antiquitäten Metz GmbH-Kunstauktionen, Heidelberg. Antiquitäten Metz GmbH-Kunstauktionen, Heidelberg, December 1, 2012, lot 272
Publication history
Gibson Stoodley 2015, 50 (illus.); Santangelo 2014, 4 (illus.)
Exhibition history
Legion of Honor, San Francisco, 2014–2016

11. Bowl and cover, ca. 1710–1713
Polished red stoneware
2 ¾ × 5 in. (7 × 12.6 cm)
L13.62.1a–b
Provenance
The Continental Art Shop, San Francisco; Richard W. Hanna, San Francisco, November 5, 1955. Butterfield & Butterfield, San Francisco, June 17, 1975, lot 829
Publication history
Gutter 2001, table 4, figs. 5 and 6
Exhibition history
San Francisco Airport Museum, 2010; Legion of Honor, San Francisco, 2014–2016

12. Jasper knife handle and associated blade, eighteenth century (acquired as Meissen red stoneware)
Germany
Jasper (stone) and steel
Handle length: 3 ½ in. (8.8 cm)
L13.62.10

Provenance
William Lautz, New York (reputed); Martha Isaacson, Seattle. Sotheby's, New York, May 22, 2001, lot 146
Exhibition history
San Francisco Airport Museum, 2010

13. Incense burner, ca. 1710–1713
Red stoneware
Height: 3 ⅞ in. (9.7 cm)
Mark: Japanese Palace inventory number *180* inscribed in black
L17.46.1
Plate 12
Provenance
Augustus the Strong, elector of Saxony and king of Poland, Japanese Palace, Dresden; *Dubletten* sale, *Porzellane und Waffen aus den Kgl. Sächsischen Sammlungen in Dresden*, Rudolph Lepke's Kunst-Auctions-Haus, Berlin, October 7 and 8, 1919, lot 500; Ole Olsen; private Danish collection; Christie's, London, December 6, 2004, lot 394; private collection, London. Acquired privately, 2016
Publication history
Schmitz 1927, vol. II, pl. XXIV, no. 1349

14. Scent flask, ca. 1710–1713
Red stoneware with slip decoration and silver-gilt mount
Height: 3 ½ in. (8.9 cm)
L17.94.1
Provenance
Anonymous sale; Christie's, London, March 30, 1987, lot 76; Robert Williams, England, April 1, 1987; Marjorie West, Atlanta. Christie's, New York, October 18, 2017, lot 715

15. Teapot, ca. 1710
Red stoneware with slip decoration
Height: 3 ⅜ in. (8.6 cm)
L17.94.2

Provenance
Anonymous sale; Bonhams, London, November 1, 1995, lot 181; Marjorie West, Atlanta. Christie's, New York, October 18, 2017, lot 717
Publication history
Antiques Trade Gazette 1995, 22; Tharp 1995, 9

II. BÖTTGER EARLY WHITE PORCELAIN

16. Pair of single-handled beakers, ca. 1709–1713
Decoration by Johann Georg Funcke, ca. 1718–1720
Hard-paste porcelain
3 × 2 ½ in. (7.5 × 6.2 cm) and 2 ¾ × 2 ⅜ in. (7.1 × 6.1 cm)
L13.62.24.1–2
Plate 11
Provenance
Hugo Helbing, Munich, 1911, lot 130; Dr. Mario Leproni, Lugano, Switzerland; Sotheby's, London, November 18, 2009, lot 448. E & H Manners, London, 2010
Exhibition history
Legion of Honor, San Francisco, 2014–2016

17. Incense burner, ca. 1718–1720
Hard-paste porcelain
4 ⅛ × 2 ⅞ × 2 ⅝ in. (10.4 × 7.4 × 6.6 cm)
L13.62.13
Plate 13
Provenance
George W. Ware, Berlin and Alexandria, Virginia; Sotheby's, London, May 5, 1970, lot 160; Robert Williams. Winifred Williams, London, 1975
Publication history
Exhibition of Eighteenth-Century European White Porcelain 1975, cat. no. 42; Ware 1963, fig. 4
Exhibition history
Winifred Williams, London, 1975; California Palace of the Legion of Honor, San Francisco, 1980; San Francisco Airport Museum, 2010; Legion of Honor, San Francisco, 2014–2016

18. Wassermann teapot, ca. 1719–1720
Hard-paste porcelain
6 ¼ × 6 ¾ in. (16 × 17.3 cm)
L13.62.18a–b
Plate 15
Provenance
Kate Foster Ltd., Rye, England, 1991
Publication history
Evolution of a Royal Vision 2010, 2–3 and 35
Exhibition history
San Francisco Airport Museum, 2010; Legion of Honor, San Francisco, 2014–2016

19. Two-handled chocolate beaker and saucer with applied rose sprays, ca. 1718–1721
Hard-paste porcelain
Beaker: 3 × 2 ¾ in. (7.7 × 6.9 cm); saucer: 1 × 5 ¼ in. (2.5 × 13.3 cm)
Marks: beaker unmarked; former's mark ╱ incised on inner footrim of saucer
L13.62.15a–b
Provenance
Beaker: Phillips, London, June 11, 1986, lot 410a
Saucer: Dr. Andreina Torre, Zürich, Switzerland. Sotheby's, London, November 18, 1996, lot 1
Exhibition history
San Francisco Airport Museum, 2010; Legion of Honor, San Francisco, 2014–2016

20. Coffeepot and cover with applied rose sprays, ca. 1718–1720
Hard-paste porcelain
6 ⅜ × 2 ½ in. (16.3 × 6.4 cm)
L13.62.16a–b
Provenance
Pamela Rowan, Blockley, England, 1988
Publication history
D'Albis 2000, 177, fig. 1
Exhibition history
San Francisco Airport Museum, 2010; Legion of Honor, San Francisco, 2014–2016

21. Waste bowl with applied prunus,
ca. 1718–1720
Hard-paste porcelain
3 ¼ × 7 ⅜ in. (8.4 × 18.8 cm)
L13.62.17
Provenance
Pat Ellington Antiques, Berkeley, California,
May 2, 1991
Exhibition history
Legion of Honor, San Francisco, 2014–2016

22. Leaf-shaped cup, ca. 1720–1725
Hard-paste porcelain
1 ¼ × 3 ¾ × 3 ⅛ in. (3.2 × 9.4 × 7.8 cm)
L13.62.19
Provenance
Richard Gould Antiques, Los Angeles,
October 25, 1994
Exhibition history
San Francisco Airport Museum, 2010; Legion
of Honor, San Francisco, 2014–2016

III. *HAUSMALER*- AND FUNKE-DECORATED MEISSEN PORCELAIN

**23. Two-handled waste bowl (*Spülkumme*)
with applied grapevines**, ca. 1715–1720
Enameling by Johann Georg Funcke
Hard-paste porcelain
4 × 8 ¾ in. (10.2 × 22.4 cm)
L13.62.14
Plate 16
Provenance
The Art Exchange, New York, 1976
Publication history
Boltz 2000, 88–89, figs. 112–112D
Exhibition history
California Palace of the Legion of Honor,
San Francisco, 1980; San Francisco Airport
Museum, 2010; Legion of Honor, San
Francisco, 2014–2016

24. Beaker vase, ca. 1715–1720
Gilding by Johann Georg Funcke or the
Augsburg workshop of Bartholomäus Seuter
Hard-paste porcelain
5 ¼ × 4 in. (13.4 × 10.3 cm)
Mark: .. impressed on the inner footrim under
the glaze
L13.62.48
Plate 17
Provenance
The Art Exchange, New York; Dr. Joseph M.
Kler. Christie's, New York, April 27, 1984, lot 5
Exhibition history
Legion of Honor, San Francisco, 2014–2016

25. Two-handled chocolate beaker, ca. 1717
Enameling and gilding by Johann Georg
Funcke
Hard-paste porcelain
3 ⅛ × 3 in. (7.8 × 7.5 cm)
L13.62.22
Plate 18
Provenance
Joseph Horne, Pittsburgh (reputed). Klaber &
Klaber, London
Publication history
Zumbulyadis 2013, fig. 6
Exhibition history
Legion of Honor, San Francisco, 2014–2016

26. Two-handled chocolate beaker,
ca. 1718–1720
Gilding by Johann Georg Funcke
Hard-paste porcelain
3 × 2 ½ in. (7.3 × 6.5 cm)
L13.62.23
Plate 19
Provenance
Private New York collection. Antiquitäten
Metz GmbH-Kunstauktionen, Heidelberg,
October 24, 2009, lot 565
Publication history
Evolution of a Royal Vision 2010, 2
Exhibition history
San Francisco Airport Museum, 2010; Legion
of Honor, San Francisco, 2014–2016

27. Teapot, ca. 1718–1720
Enameling by Johann Georg Funcke
Hard-paste porcelain
4 ⅞ × 4 ⅜ in. (12.5 × 11 cm)
Mark: none; labels: *1315* (Otto Blohm
Collection number) and *341*
L13.62.21a-b
Plate 20
Provenance
Otto and Magdalena Blohm; Sotheby's,
London, July 5, 1960, lot 135; Beatrice Blohm
von Rumohr. Christie's, London, June 27,
2005, lot 2
Publication history
Schmidt 1953, 30 and 32, cat. no. 16
Exhibition history
San Francisco Airport Museum, 2010;
Legion of Honor, San Francisco, 2014–2016

28. Eagle teapot (*Adlerkanne*), ca. 1720–1725
Gilding probably by Augsburg workshop of
Bartholomäus Seuter
Hard-paste porcelain
5 ¼ × 5 ⅛ in. (13.3 × 13 cm)
L13.62.50a-b
Plate 21
Provenance
A Cambridge antiques dealer. Phillips,
London, June 3, 1998, lot 214
Publication history
Cochran 2004, 94–95, 95 (illus.); *Evolution of
a Royal Vision* 2010, 24–25
Exhibition history
Chinese Culture Center, San Francisco, 2002;
San Francisco Airport Museum, 2010; Legion
of Honor, San Francisco, 2014–2016

29. Teapot, ca. 1725–1730; gilt decoration
slightly later
Gilding probably by Augsburg workshop of
Bartholomäus Seuter
Hard-paste porcelain
5 ⅜ × 4 ½ in. (13.8 × 11.3 cm)
Marks: crossed swords in underglaze blue;
Schnittmarke × incised beside the inner
footrim (turner and former's mark for Johann
Christoph Pietsch [1705–1778] or Johann

Daniel Rehschuh [1688–1752]); unidentified
initials or cipher in luster on the base
L13.62.47a-b
Plate 22
Provenance
Grosvenor Antiques Ltd. at the Chelsea Fair,
London, 1974
Exhibition history
San Francisco Airport Museum, 2010; Legion
of Honor, San Francisco, 2014–2016

30. Small dish, ca. 1718–1720
Enameling by Johann Georg Funcke
Hard-paste porcelain
1 × 4 ⅞ in. (2.4 × 12.3 cm)
Mark: large 4 in luster
L13.62.20
Provenance
E & H Manners, London, 2003
Exhibition history
San Francisco Airport Museum, 2010; Legion
of Honor, San Francisco, 2014–2016

31. Teabowl and saucer, ca. 1715–1720
Hard-paste porcelain
Teabowl: 1 ½ × 2 ¾ in. (3.9 × 7 cm);
saucer: ¾ × 4 ⅝ in. (1.9 × 11.7 cm)
Marks: *Schnittmarke* / incised on inner
footrim of each
L13.62.49a-b
Provenance
Christie's, London, June 30, 1986, part of
lots 95 (saucer) and 96 (teabowl); Robert
Williams, London. Sotheby's, New York,
October 16, 1987, lot 32
Exhibition history
San Francisco Airport Museum, 2010; Legion
of Honor, San Francisco, 2014–2016

32. Silvered cup and saucer, porcelain
1713–1715, silvered decoration 1715
Silvered decoration by Johann Georg Funcke
Hard-paste porcelain
Cup: 2 × 2 ⅞ in. (5.1 × 7.3 cm); saucer:
⅞ × 4 ⅜ in. (2.2 × 11.1 cm)
L14.98.4a-b

Provenance
Galerie Almas Maria Dietrich, Munich, 1957;
Cleo M. and G. Ryland Scott, Jr., Atlanta;
bequeathed to grandson Ryland Scott,
Atlanta. E & H Manners, London, 2013
Publication history
Scott 1961, 192, pl. 86, fig. 305
Exhibition history
Scott-Allen Collection at the High Museum
of Art, Atlanta, 1976–1996

33. Incense burner, ca. 1715–1717
Enameling by Johann Georg Funcke
Hard-paste porcelain
Height: 3 ⅞ in. (9.7 cm)
L17.46.3
Plate 14
Provenance
Private European collection. Röbbig, Munich,
2016
Publication history
Andres-Acevedo and Ottomeyer 2016, 62–65,
cat. no. 14

34. Teabowl and saucer, ca. 1715
Enameling and gilding by Johann Georg
Funcke, ca. 1718–1720
Hard-paste porcelain
Teabowl: 2 × 3 ⅛ in. (5.1 × 7.7 cm); saucer:
1 ⅝ × 4 ⅝ in. (3 × 11.6 cm)
L17.94.3
Provenance
Rudolf Just Collection; Sotheby's, London,
December 11, 2001, lot 234; Marjorie West,
Atlanta. Christie's, New York, October 18,
2017, lot 725

IV. KÖHLER AND RIPP: UNDERGLAZE-BLUE DECORATION

35. Baluster vase, ca. 1720–1721
Painting by Johann Caspar Ripp
Hard-paste porcelain
21 ⅝ × 9 in. (54.8 × 23 cm)

Mark: Oppenheimer collection mark *39* in
black enamel, partially obliterated
L13.62.26
Plate 23
Provenance
Margarete and Franz Oppenheimer, Berlin;
Dr. Fritz Mannheimer, Amsterdam; Frederik
Muller & Cie., Amsterdam, October 14–21,
1952, lot 285; Hans Backer, London (reputed);
Frederick J. and Antoinette H. Van Slyke,
Baltimore. Sotheby's, New York, September
26, 1989, lot 4
Publication history
Falke 1936; Schnorr von Carolsfeld 1927, 11,
cat. no. 39; *Evolution of a Royal Vision* 2010, 39
Exhibition history
Filoli, Woodside, California, ca. 1995; Asian
Art Museum, San Francisco, 2006; San
Francisco Airport Museum, 2010; Legion of
Honor, San Francisco, 2014–2016

36. Narrow-necked vase (Enghalsvase),
ca. 1720–1721
Painting by Johann Caspar Ripp
Hard-paste porcelain
16 ½ × 6 ½ in. (42 × 16.5 cm)
L13.62.29
Plate 24
Provenance
Possibly one of seven blue-and-white vases
given by Augustus the Strong to Vittorio
Amedeo II, king of Sardinia, 1725; a Roman
noble family (reputed); a Roman dealer;
dealer Dario Mottola, Milan. E & H Manners,
London, January 30, 2001
Publication history
McGill 2006, 29 (illus.)
Exhibition history
Asian Art Museum, San Francisco, 2006;
Legion of Honor, San Francisco, 2014–2016

37. Baluster vase and cover, ca. 1725–1730
Hard-paste porcelain
16 ¼ × 8 ½ in. (41.3 × 21.5 cm); height without
cover: 13 ¼ in. (33.5 cm)
Marks: *AR* (for "Augustus Rex") in underglaze
blue; irregular *T* (unidentified painter's mark)
in underglaze blue inside the footrim
Gift of Malcolm D. Gutter, 2015.66a–b
Plate 25
Provenance
Radziwiłł collection, Nieborów Palace,
Nieborów, Poland (probable). Sotheby's,
London, June 14, 1988, lot 127

Exhibition history
Legion of Honor, San Francisco, 2014–2016

38. Saucer, ca. 1722–1724
Painting by Johann Caspar Ripp
Hard-paste porcelain
1 × 4 ¾ in. (2.5 × 12 cm)
Marks: caduceus (*Peitschenmarke*) and large
A in underglaze blue
L13.62.31
Plate 26
Provenance
Sotheby's, Billingshurst, England, 1993;
Robert Williams and E & H Manners, London;
Dr. Roy M. Byrnes, San Juan Capistrano,
California, 1993. Purchased from Dr. Roy M.
Byrnes, 2009
Exhibition history
San Francisco Airport Museum, 2010; Legion
of Honor, 2014–2016

39. Covered fish tureen, ca. 1722–1723
Painting by Johann Caspar Ripp
Hard-paste porcelain
9 × 12 ⅜ in. (23 × 31.5 cm); height without
cover: 4 ⅜ in. (11.2 cm)
Marks: caduceus (*Peitschenmarke*) marks in
underglaze blue inside base of tureen and
inside cover
L13.62.30a–b
Plate 27
Provenance
Collector and dealer Louis Woodford, 2005.
E & H Manners, London, 2005
Publication history
Evolution of a Royal Vision 2010, 10–11; Weber
2013, 76, fig. 13
Exhibition history
San Francisco Airport Museum, 2010; Legion
of Honor, San Francisco, 2014–2016

40. Dish in Blue Onion (Zwiebelmuster)
pattern, ca. 1750
Hard-paste porcelain
2 × 11 ¾ in. (5 × 30 cm)

Marks: crossed swords, with an *o* between
the blades, in underglaze blue; *Pressnummer
14*; and *Schnittmarke* (*Ritzzeichen*) // near the
footrim
L13.62.27
Provenance
Golden Griffin, Richard Dee, and Cliff
Porazynski, Hillsborough Antiques Show,
San Mateo, California, 1992

41. Teacup and saucer, ca. 1740
Hard-paste porcelain
Teacup: 2 × 3 ⅛ in. (5.1 × 7.8 cm); saucer:
1 ⅛ × 5 ⅛ in. (3 × 13.1 cm)
Marks: crossed swords and *K* (for decorator
Peter Kolmberger [1704–1779]) in underglaze
blue on each; *o* impressed or *Ritzzeichen* on
teacup; *Pressnummer 65* on saucer
L13.62.28a–b
Provenance
Tony Greaves, Portobello Road Market,
London, 1998

V. HÖROLDT AND CHINOISERIE

42. Mounted tankard, ca. 1722–1723
Painting attributed to Johann Gregorius
Höroldt
Hard-paste porcelain and silver-gilt mount
6 ½ × 3 ½ in. (16.5 × 8.8 cm); height without
cover: 5 ⅞ in. (15 cm)
L13.62.44
Plate 28
Provenance
Ilse Bischoff, New York; private collection,
New York. Michele Beiny, Inc., New York,
2001
Publication history
McGill 2006, 19; *Evolution of a Royal Vision*
2010, 9; Scott 1961, 84, fig. 301A
Exhibition history
Asian Art Museum, San Francisco, 2006;
San Francisco Airport Museum, 2010; San
Francisco Fall Antiques Show, 2012; Legion of
Honor, San Francisco, 2014–2016

43. Waste bowl with chinoiseries,
ca. 1722–1724
Painting possibly by Johann Christoph Horn
or Johann Gregorius Höroldt
Hard-paste porcelain
3 ⅛ × 7 ⅛ in. (8 × 18 cm)
Mark: caduceus mark (*Peitschenmarke*) in
underglaze blue in a double ring
L13.62.36
Plate 29
Provenance
Sotheby's, New York, October 16, 1987, lot
14; Lempertz, Cologne, June 22, 1990, lot
1815 (unsold). Purchased by private treaty,
September 12, 1990
Exhibition history
Legion of Honor, San Francisco, 2014–2016

44. Tea caddy with chinoiserie figures,
ca. 1723
Painting attributed to Johann Gregorius
Höroldt
Hard-paste porcelain and gilt-bronze mount
3 ¾ × 1 ¾ in. (9.6 × 4.5 cm) (porcelain only)
L13.62.46
Plate 30
Provenance
Sotheby's, New York, October 12, 1973, lot
285; Antique Porcelain Company; Jarrold
M. Kunz, San Francisco; Dr. Roy M. Byrnes,
San Juan Capistrano, California. Christie's,
London, May 12, 2010, lot 18
Exhibition history
San Francisco Fall Antiques Show, 2010;
Legion of Honor, San Francisco, 2014–2016

**45. Teabowl and saucer with scenes of
porcelain production,** ca. 1723–1724
Hard-paste porcelain
Teabowl: 1 ¾ × 3 in. (4.5 × 7.5 cm); saucer:
3 × 5 in. (2.5 × 12.8 cm)
Marks: former's mark (*Schnittmarke* or
Ritzzeichen or *Formerzeichen*) / incised on
inner footrim of each
L13.62.32a–b
Plate 31

Provenance
Christie's, London, June 28, 1976, lot 125
Exhibition history
California Palace of the Legion of Honor,
San Francisco, 1988; San Francisco Airport
Museum, 2010; San Francisco Fall Antiques
Show, 2010; Legion of Honor, San Francisco,
2014–2016

46. Mounted coffeepot, ca. 1723–1724
Painting attributed to Johann Gregorius
Höroldt (mounting probably Augsburg)
Hard-paste porcelain and silver-gilt mounts
8 ½ × 4 ⅝ in. (21.5 × 11.8 cm)
L13.62.43a–b
Plate 32
Provenance
Sotheby's, London, March 5, 1985, lot 206;
Sotheby's, London, April 15, 1997, lot 34;
Sotheby's, London, November 25, 1997, lot 65.
Sotheby's, Zürich, June 8, 2000, lot 562
Publication history
Gibson Stoodley 2015, 50 (illus.)
Exhibition history
San Francisco Airport Museum, 2010; San
Francisco Fall Antiques Show, 2010; Legion of
Honor, San Francisco, 2014–2016

47. Teabowl and saucer, ca. 1723–1724
Painting attributed to Johann Gregorius
Höroldt
Hard-paste porcelain
Teabowl: 2 × 2 ⅞ in. (5 × 7.3 cm); saucer: 1 × 5
in. (2.5 × 12.6 cm)
Marks: former's mark (*Schnittmarke* or
Ritzzeichen) / incised on inner footrim of
teabowl; saucer unmarked
L13.62.33a–b
Plate 33
Provenance
Christie's, London, June 28, 1976, lot 129
(two pairs of teabowls and saucers; one pair
remains in Gutter collection)
Exhibition history
California Palace of the Legion of Honor,
San Francisco, 1980; Palace of the Legion of
Honor, San Francisco, 1988; Legion of Honor,
San Francisco, 2014–2016

48. Tea caddy and cover, ca. 1723–1725
Hard-paste porcelain
4 × 3 ⅛ in. (10 × 8 cm)
L13.62.39a–b
Plate 34
Provenance
Christie's, London, June 3, 1996, lot 458
Exhibition history
Legion of Honor, San Francisco, 2014–2016

**49. Saucer with chinoiserie and harbor
scene,** ca. 1724–1725
Painting possibly attributed to Christian
Friedrich Herold
Hard-paste porcelain
1 × 5 in. (2.6 × 12.7 cm)
Mark: former's mark (*Schnittmarke* or
Ritzzeichen or *Formerzeichen*) / incised on
inner footrim
L13.62.34
Plate 35
Provenance
Christie's, London, June 28, 1976, lot 126.
Heinz Reichert, Kunsthandel, Freiburg-im-
Breisgau, 1976
Publication history
Gutter 1988, 76–77 (illus.)
Exhibition history
California Palace of the Legion of Honor,
San Francisco, 1980; Palace of the Legion of
Honor, San Francisco, 1988; Legion of Honor,
San Francisco, 2014–2016

**50. Teabowl with chinoiserie and harbor
scene,** ca. 1726–1728
Painting possibly attributed to Christian
Friedrich Herold
Hard-paste porcelain
1 ¾ × 3 in. (4.5 × 7.5 cm)
Marks: crossed swords in underglaze blue
to one side; former's mark (*Schnittmarke* or
Ritzzeichen or *Formerzeichen*) / incised on
inner footrim
L13.62.35
Plate 36

Provenance
The Antique Porcelain Company,
New York, 1978
Publication history
Gutter 1988, 74–75 (illus.)
Exhibition history
California Palace of the Legion of Honor,
San Francisco, 1985; Palace of the Legion of
Honor, San Francisco, 1988; Legion of Honor,
San Francisco, 2014–2016

**51. Sugar box and cover with chinoiseries
and harbor scene,** ca. 1726–1728
Painting possibly attributed to Christian
Friedrich Herold
Hard-paste porcelain
3 ⅛ × 4 ½ × 3 ⅜ in. (8 × 11.3 × 8.5 cm)
Marks: *K.P.M.* (for Königliche Porzellan-
Manufaktur) and crossed swords in under-
glaze blue on the box; cover unmarked
L13.62.42a–b
Plate 37
Provenance
Christie's, London, November 8, 1999, lot 223
Exhibition history
Legion of Honor, San Francisco, 2014–2016

52. Tureen and cover (*Oliotopf*),
ca. 1723–1725
Painting possibly attributed to Johann
Gregorius Höroldt
Hard-paste porcelain
5 ⅜ × 6 ⅝ in. (13.8 × 16.7 cm)
L16.30a–b
Plate 38
Provenance
Princess Luise Dorothea of Saxe-Meiningen
(1710–1767) (possible); Schloss Friedenstein,
Gotha (which retains the pair to this
Oliotopf); Lempertz, Cologne, May 12, 2010,
lot 9; Röbbig, Munich. Koller Auktionen,
Zürich, March 17, 2016, lot 1775
Publication history
Selected Works 2011, 64, 263–264, cat. no. 26

53. Cup and saucer with Löwenfinck-contour chinoiserie, ca. 1740
Hard-paste porcelain
Cup: 2 ¾ × 3 ¾ in. (7 × 9.5 cm);
saucer: 1 ⅝ × 5 ¾ in. (4 × 14.5 cm)
Marks: crossed swords in underglaze blue on cup; saucer without manufactory mark but *127* painted in luster
L13.62.41a–b
Plate 39
Provenance
Melbury House, Evershot, Dorset, England; Christie's, October 14, 1996, lot 127. E & H Manners, London, 1997
Exhibition history
San Francisco Airport Museum, 2010; Legion of Honor, San Francisco, 2014–2016

54. Sugar box and cover, ca. 1724–1725
Hard-paste porcelain
4 ⅜ × 7 ⅛ × 3 ⅜ in. (18 × 11 × 8.5 cm)
Marks: *K.P.M.* (for Königliche Porzellan-Manufaktur) and crossed swords in underglaze blue, gilder's numeral *44* on each
L13.62.37a–b
Provenance
Theobald von Bethmann-Hollweg (1856–1921), German *Reichskanzler* (1909–1917) (reputed); John Pierpont Morgan (possible); Sotheby's, London, July 16, 1946, lot 132; The Art Exchange, New York. Sotheby's, New York, October 9, 1990, lot 242

55. Teabowl and saucer, ca. 1723–1724
Hard-paste porcelain
Teabowl: 1 ¾ × 2 ⅞ in. (4.5 × 7.2 cm); saucer: 1 × 4 ⅞ in. (2.4 × 12.3 cm)
Marks: gilder's numeral *2.* on each; former's marks (*Schnittmarke* or *Ritzzeichen* or *Formerzeichen*) × (for Johann Christoph Pietsch or Johann Daniel Rehschuh) incised on inner footrim of the teabowl and ⁄ on the inner footrim of the saucer
L13.62.38a–b
Provenance
Private collection, Glen Ellen, California. Simon Spero, London, 1991

56. Patch box, ca. 1727
Hard-paste porcelain and gilded copper
⅝ × 2 × 1 ⅜ in. (1.5 × 5 × 3.6 cm)
L13.62.40
Provenance
Dr. Andreina Torre, Zürich; Finarte, Milan, December 16, 1992, lot 309. Lukacs & Donath, Rome, 1999
Exhibition history
Legion of Honor, San Francisco, 2014–2016

VI. HÖROLDT AND EUROPEAN DECORATION

57. Teabowl, ca. 1721–1722
Hard-paste porcelain
1 ⅞ × 3 in. (4.8 × 7.5 cm)
L13.62.45
Plate 40
Provenance
Dr. Mario Leproni, Lugano, Switzerland; Sotheby's, London, May 28, 2009, lot 302. E & H Manners, London, June 8, 2009
Publication history
D'Agliano and Melegati 2001, 92, cat. no. 3, color plate 1; *Evolution of a Royal Vision* 2010, 41, back cover (illus.)
Exhibition history
Fondazione Accorsi, Turin, 2000–2001; San Francisco Airport Museum, 2010; Legion of Honor, San Francisco, 2014–2016

58. Teapot with mythological scenes, ca. 1721–1722
Hard-paste porcelain
4 ⅞ × 4 in. (12.3 × 10 cm)
L13.62.58a–b
Plate 41
Provenance
The Burbridge Foundation Collection (Robert Oscar Burbridge). Sotheby's, New York, September 11, 1996, lot 7
Publication history
Evolution of a Royal Vision 2010, 37
Exhibition history
San Francisco Airport Museum, 2010; Legion of Honor, San Francisco, 2014–2016

59. Cup and saucer with mythological scenes, ca. 1721–1722
Hard-paste porcelain
Cup: 1 ¾ × 3 in. (4.5 × 7.8 cm); saucer: 1 × 4 ⅞ in. (2.5 × 12.5 cm)
Mark: *4* in luster on the saucer
L13.62.153a–b
Plate 42
Provenance
Mrs. Anderegg, Solothurn, Switzerland. Galerie Stuker, Bern, May 22, 2014, lot 3077
Exhibition history
Legion of Honor, San Francisco, 2014–2016

60. Teabowl and saucer, ca. 1722–1723
Painting probably by Johann Gregorius Höroldt
Hard-paste porcelain
Teabowl: 2 × 3 ⅛ in. (5 × 7.9 cm); saucer: 1 × 5 in. (2.4 × 12.7 cm)
Marks: teabowl unmarked; two parallel lightning bolts (unrecorded) in luster on saucer
L13.62.60a–b
Plate 43
Provenance
A private German (Rhineland) collection. Lempertz, Cologne, May 22, 1997, lot 51
Publication history
Evolution of a Royal Vision 2010, 6; Wildtraut and Buchen 1997, figs. 8 and 14
Exhibition history
San Francisco Airport Museum, 2010; Legion of Honor, San Francisco, 2014–2016

61. Saucer, ca. 1722–1723
Painting probably by Johann Gregorius Höroldt
Hard-paste porcelain
1 × 5 in. (2.6 × 12.7 cm)
Mark: *a //.* in luster
L13.62.66
Plate 44
Provenance
Private English collection. Bonhams, London, May 17, 2006, lot 82
Publication history
Evolution of a Royal Vision 2010, 6–7

Exhibition history
San Francisco Airport Museum, 2010; Legion of Honor, San Francisco, 2014–2016

62. Covered bowl and stand (*Olienbecher*), ca. 1723–1725
Hard-paste porcelain
Bowl: 3 × 3 ¾ in. (7.5 × 9.4 cm) without cover, height with cover 4 ¼ in. (10.8 cm); stand: 1 ⅛ × 6 ¾ in. (2.9 × 17 cm)
Marks: *11* in gilt on each
L13.62.65a–c
Plate 45
Provenance
Private collection near Bath, England. Bonhams, London, November 16, 2005, lot 21
Publication history
Evolution of a Royal Vision 2010, 40
Exhibition history
San Francisco Airport Museum, 2010; Legion of Honor, San Francisco, 2014–2016

63. Teabowl, ca. 1723–1724
Hard-paste porcelain
1 ¾ × 2 ⅞ in. (4.5 × 7.4 cm)
Mark: former's mark (*Schnittmarke*) ⁄ incised on inner footrim
L13.62.63
Plate 46
Provenance
Bamfords Auctioneers, Matlock, England, May 26, 2005 (unsold). E & H Manners, London, 2005
Exhibition history
San Francisco Airport Museum, 2010; Legion of Honor, San Francisco, 2014–2016

64. Teapot, ca. 1725–1728
Hard-paste porcelain
4 ¼ × 4 ¼ in. (11 × 11 cm)
Marks: *K.P.M.* (Königliche Porzellan-Manufaktur) and crossed swords in underglaze blue; gilder's numeral *29* in gilt
L13.62.57a–b
Plate 47

Provenance
Korthaus Collection; Christie's, London, September 21, 1992, lot 47 (as a composite partial tea service; unsold). Christie's, London, December 5, 1994, lot 184
Exhibition history
San Francisco Airport Museum, 2010; Legion of Honor, San Francisco, 2014–2016

65. Teabowl, ca. 1722–1723
Hard-paste porcelain
1 ¾ × 2 ¾ in. (4.6 × 7 cm)
Mark: trace of a luster mark
L13.62.62
Plate 48
Provenance
Mrs. Charlotte Wiederkehr, Switzerland. Christie's, London, February 21, 2005, lot 19
Exhibition history
San Francisco Airport Museum, 2010; Legion of Honor, San Francisco, 2014–2016

66. Teabowl and saucer, ca. 1726–1727
Hard-paste porcelain
Teabowl: 1 ¾ × 3 in. (4.3 × 7.5 cm); saucer: ⅝ × 4 ⅞ in. (1.7 × 12.5 cm)
Mark: gilder's numeral 54 in luster on each; former's mark (Schnittmarke) / incised on inner footrim of teabowl
L13.62.61a–b
Plate 49
Provenance
Private collection, London. Christie's, London, July 9, 2001, lot 76
Exhibition history
San Francisco Airport Museum, 2010; Legion of Honor, San Francisco, 2014–2016

67. Plate, ca. 1725–1727
Hard-paste porcelain
⅞ × 8 ⅝ in. (2.3 × 21.9 cm)
Mark: large crossed swords in underglaze blue
L13.62.64
Plate 50

Provenance
Sotheby's, New York, October 22, 2005, lot 8
Publication history
Evolution of a Royal Vision 2010, 28–29
Exhibition history
San Francisco Airport Museum, 2010; Legion of Honor, San Francisco, 2014–2016

68. Saucer, ca. 1727–1730
Hard-paste porcelain
⅞ × 4 ¾ in. (2.2 × 11.9 cm)
Mark: crossed swords in underglaze blue
L13.62.59
Plate 51
Provenance
Paolo Lukacs, Rome. E & H Manners, London, 1997
Exhibition history
San Francisco Airport Museum, 2010; Legion of Honor, San Francisco, 2014–2016

69. Coffee cup and saucer, ca. 1740–1750
Painting possibly attributed to Christian Friedrich Herold
Hard-paste porcelain
Cup: 2 ¾ × 2 ¾ in. (7 × 7.1 cm); saucer: 1 ⅛ × 5 ⅛ in. (2.9 × 13 cm)
Marks: crossed swords in underglaze blue and gilder's S. on each; Pressnummer 6. impressed on cup and 52 impressed on saucer
L13.62.55a–b
Plate 52
Provenance
Ole Olsen, Copenhagen; Winkel & Magnussens Kunstauktioner, Copenhagen, May 4–8, 1953, lot 810; Ludwig Neugass, New York; William Doyle Galleries, New York, January 25, 1984, lot 292. Röbbig, Munich, March 9, 1984
Publication history
Gutter 1989, 35 (illus.); Schmitz 1927, 55, pl. LXXII, cat. no. 1754
Exhibition history
California Palace of the Legion of Honor, San Francisco, 1988; San Francisco Airport Museum, 2010; Legion of Honor, San Francisco, 2014–2016

70. Teacup and saucer, ca. 1750–1760
Hard-paste porcelain
Cup: 2 ⅜ × 3 ⅛ in. (5.9 × 7.9 cm); saucer: 1 ⅛ × 5 ¼ in. (3 × 13.2 cm)
Marks: crossed swords in underglaze blue and gilder's numeral 55 in luster on each; former's mark (Schnittmarke or Ritzzeichen) // incised inside the footrim of cup; Pressnummer 64 impressed on saucer
Gift of Malcolm D. Gutter, 2014.96.4
Provenance
Leon Snyder, Los Angeles, 1983

71. Coffee cup and saucer, ca. 1745
Hard-paste porcelain
Cup: 2 ⅝ × 2 ¾ in. (6.7 × 7 cm); saucer: 1 ⅛ × 5 ¼ in. (2.9 × 13.2 cm)
Marks: crossed swords in underglaze blue on each; Pressnummer 64 impressed on saucer
L13.62.53a–b
Provenance
Christie's, London, February 2, 1976, lot 16. Phillips, London, September 14, 1977, lot 257
Exhibition history
California Palace of the Legion of Honor, San Francisco, 1980

72. Saucer, with a bird-catcher, ca. 1722–1723
Hard-paste porcelain
1 × 5 in. (2.5 × 12.7 cm)
Mark: 6. in luster
L13.62.56
Provenance
Phillips, London (probable). Jose Polar, San Francisco, mid-1980s
Exhibition history
Legion of Honor, San Francisco, 2014–2016

73. Teabowl and saucer, ca. 1722–1723
Painting possibly by Johann Gregorius Höroldt
Hard-paste porcelain
Teabowl: 1 ¾ × 3 in. (4.4 × 7.5 cm); saucer: 1 × 4 ⅞ in. (2.5 × 12.4 cm)
L13.62.67a–b
Provenance
Hans Ringier, Zürich, Switzerland, purchased before 1971; Christie's, London, December 11, 2007, lot 88. E & H Manners, London, 2007
Publication history
Ducret 1972, 121, fig. 118, and 42 (text)
Exhibition history
Legion of Honor, San Francisco, 2014–2016

74. Saucer, ca. 1722–1723
Hard-paste porcelain
1 × 5 in. (2.5 × 12.7 cm)
L13.62.68
Provenance
Dr. Andreina Torre, Zürich, Switzerland; Sotheby's, London, November 18, 1996, lot 215; Dr. Mario Leproni, Lugano, Switzerland; Sotheby's, London, May 28, 2009, lots 302–314. E & H Manners, London, 2009

75. Teapot, ca. 1722–1723
Painting possibly by Johann Gregorius Höroldt
Hard-paste porcelain
Height: 5 ½ in. (14 cm)
L17.94.4
Provenance
Christie's, London, December 3, 1984, lot 292; Robert Williams, England, June 26, 1985; Marjorie West, Atlanta. Christie's, New York, October 18, 2017, lot 734

VII. HÖROLDT AND FAR EASTERN DECORATION

76. Beaker vase, ca. 1725
Painting attributed to Johann Ehrenfried
Stadler
Hard-paste porcelain and nineteenth-century
French gilt-bronze mount
15 ¾ × 8 in. (40 × 20.3 cm)
Mark: *AR* (for "Augustus Rex") in
underglaze blue
L13.62.90
Plate 53
Provenance
Private collection, Paris; Christie's, Paris, June
24, 2009, lot 83. E & H Manners, London
Publication history
Evolution of a Royal Vision 2010, 30–31
Exhibition history
San Francisco Airport Museum, 2010; Legion
of Honor, San Francisco, 2014–2016

77. Fragments of a bottle-gourd vase,
ca. 1726–1730
Painting attributed to Johann Ehrenfried
Stadler
Hard-paste porcelain
Reconstructed vase: height 14 ⅛ in. (36 cm),
base diameter 4 ½ in. (11.5 cm)
Mark: likely *AR* (for "Augustus Rex") in
underglaze blue (base containing mark
now missing)
L13.62.91
Plate 54
Provenance
Augustus II, elector of Saxony and king of
Poland, Japanese Palace, Dresden (probable);
Gustav and Charlotte von Klemperer,
Dresden, until 1938; German government,
1938; the State of Saxony, after 1942;
Staatliche Kunstsammlungen Dresden-
Porzellansammlung im Zwinger; restituted to
the Klemperer family, 1991. Bonhams, London,
December 8, 2010, lot 37
Publication history
De Waal 2010, 20–21 (illus.); Gibson Stoodley
2015, 52 (illus.); Santangelo 2015, 5 (illus.);
Santangelo 2014, 16 (illus.); Schnorr von
Carolsfeld 1928, 59, cat. no. 105, pl. 14
Exhibition history
Legion of Honor, San Francisco, 2014–2016

78. Waste bowl, ca. 1726
Hard-paste porcelain
3 ⅜ × 7 ¼ in. (8.5 × 18.5 cm)
Marks: crossed swords over / /. (a painter's
mark?), all in blue enamel; Japanese Palace
inventory number *N=502-/w* engraved and
blackened with pigment
L13.62.82
Plate 55
Provenance
Augustus II, elector of Saxony and king of
Poland, Japanese Palace, Dresden. Christie's,
London, May 18, 1999, lot 167
Exhibition history
San Francisco Airport Museum, 2010; Legion
of Honor, San Francisco, 2014–2016

79. Saucer, ca. 1727–1730
Hard-paste porcelain
1 ⅛ × 7 ½ in. (2.8 × 19 cm)
Mark: crossed swords in underglaze blue
L13.62.92
Plate 56
Provenance
Sotheby's, New York, October 19 and 20,
1994, lot 390; Dr. Roy M. Byrnes, San Juan
Capistrano, California. Christie's South
Kensington, London, April 19, 2011, lot 165
Exhibition history
Legion of Honor, San Francisco, 2014–2016

80. Beaker vase, ca. 1726–1730
Painting attributed to Johann Ehrenfried
Stadler
Hard-paste porcelain
15 ¾ × 9 ½ in. (40 × 24.1 cm)
Mark: *AR* (for "Augustus Rex") in underglaze
blue
L13.62.93
Plate 57

Provenance
Augustus II, elector of Saxony and king
of Poland, Turmzimmer, Residenzschloss,
Dresden (reputed); Hans W. Lange, Berlin,
January 25–27, 1940, lot 543; private collec-
tion, Switzerland. Koller Auktionen, Zürich,
September 19, 2011, lot 1641
Publication history
Santangelo 2015, 4 (illus.); Santangelo
2014, 16 (illus.); Santangelo 2015; *Weltkunst*,
January 21, 1940 (illus.)
Exhibition history
Legion of Honor, San Francisco, 2014–2016

81. Beaker and saucer, ca. 1726–1727
Hard-paste porcelain
Beaker: 3 ¼ × 3 ⅛ in. (8.3 × 7.9 cm); saucer:
1 ⅜ × 5 ½ in. (3.5 × 14 cm)
Marks: Japanese Palace inventory number
N=397-/w engraved and blackened with
pigment on each; mark (*Schnittmarke* or
Ritzzeichen or *Formerzeichen*) / incised on the
inner footrim of each
L13.62.83a–b
Plate 58
Provenance
Augustus II, elector of Saxony and king of
Poland, Japanese Palace, Dresden; Evelyn T.
Ledyard; Sotheby's, New York, January 27,
1988, lot 176; a Midwest collector. Christie's,
New York, May 24, 2000, lot 64
Exhibition history
San Francisco Airport Museum, 2010; Legion
of Honor, San Francisco, 2014–2016

82. Teapot, ca. 1724–1730
Hard-paste porcelain
4 ⅛ × 4 ⅜ in. (10.5 × 11.2 cm)
L13.62.76a–b
Plate 59
Provenance
J. J. Klejman Gallery, New York, sold 1954;
Frederick J. and Antoinette H. Van Slyke,
Baltimore. Sotheby's, New York, September
26, 1989, lot 8
Exhibition history
The Baltimore Museum of Art, March 20,
1964–October 2, 1969; San Francisco Airport
Museum, 2010; San Francisco Fall Antiques
Show, 2010; Legion of Honor, San Francisco,
2014–2016

83. Mounted tankard, ca. 1727–1728
Painting attributed to Johann Ehrenfried
Stadler
Hard-paste porcelain with silver-gilt mount
6 ⅞ × 3 ¾ in. (17.5 × 9.4 cm); height without
cover: 6 ⅜ in. (16.2 cm)
Marks: tankard unmarked; Dresden silver-gilt
mount with *IP*
L13.62.81
Plate 60
Provenance
Eduard Wallach, New York. Christie's, New
York, April 23, 1998, lot 50
Publication history
Cochran 2004, 94–95, 95 (illus.); *Evolution
of a Royal Vision* 2010, cover and inside cover
(illus.)
Exhibition history
San Francisco Airport Museum, 2010; Legion
of Honor, San Francisco, 2014–2016

84. Ten-sided bowl, ca. 1729–1730
Hard-paste porcelain
3 ⅜ × 7 ¾ in. (8.6 × 19.7 cm)
Marks: Japanese Palace inventory number
N=447-/w engraved and blackened with
pigment; crossed swords in blue enamel;
number (*Schnittmarke* or *Ritzzeichen*) *119*
impressed inside the footrim and number
(probably *N=119*) in black enamel (partially
obliterated)
L13.62.77
Plate 61
Provenance
Augustus II, elector of Saxony and king of
Poland, Japanese Palace, Dresden. Christie's,
London, June 28, 1993, lot 144
Publication history
Cassidy-Geiger 1994, fig. 1; Le Duc 1997a,
fig. 10; Le Duc 1997b, fig. 10
Exhibition history
San Francisco Airport Museum, 2010; Legion
of Honor, San Francisco, 2014–2016

85. Dish, ca. 1729–1731
Hard-paste porcelain
2 ⅛ × 9 ½ in. (5.4 × 24 cm)
Marks: crossed swords in blue enamel;
Japanese Palace inventory number *N=66-/w*
engraved and blackened with pigment
L13.62.88
Plate 62
Provenance
Augustus II, elector of Saxony and king of
Poland, Japanese Palace, Dresden; private
collection, Germany. E & H Manners, London,
2004
Publication history
Evolution of a Royal Vision 2010, 22
Exhibition history
San Francisco Airport Museum, 2010; Legion
of Honor, San Francisco, 2014–2016

86. Sake bottle, ca. 1730
Hard-paste porcelain
Height: 7 ⅝ in. (19.5 cm)
Marks: Japanese Palace inventory number
N=291-/w engraved and blackened with
pigment; mark (*Schnittmarke* or *Ritzzeichen* or
Formerzeichen) / incised on inner footrim
L13.62.79
Plate 63
Provenance
Augustus II, elector of Saxony and king
of Poland, Japanese Palace, Dresden;
J. J. Klejman Gallery, New York, sold 1956;
Frederick J. and Antoinette H. Van Slyke,
Baltimore; Sotheby's, New York, September
26, 1989, lot 54; Armin Allen, London and
New York. Sotheby's, New York, October 11,
1995, lot 175
Publication history
Battie 1990, 89 (illus.); *Evolution of a Royal
Vision* 2010, 17
Exhibition history
The Baltimore Museum of Art, March
20, 1964–October 2, 1969 (possible); San
Francisco Airport Museum, 2010; Legion of
Honor, San Francisco, 2014–2016

87. Covered tureen, ca. 1730
Hard-paste porcelain
7 ½ × 5 ¼ in. (19 × 13.3 cm); without cover:
4 ¼ × 5 ⅛ in. (10.7 × 13 cm)
Marks: crossed swords in blue enamel on the
tureen; Japanese Palace inventory number
N=17-/w engraved and blackened with
pigment
L13.62.71a–b
Plate 64
Provenance
Augustus II, elector of Saxony and king of
Poland, Japanese Palace, Dresden; Mrs.
Maria Luescher, Zürich. Sotheby's, Zürich,
May 22, 1981, lot 108
Publication history
Triptych 1988
Exhibition history
California Palace of the Legion of Honor,
San Francisco, 1988; San Francisco Airport
Museum, 2010; Legion of Honor, San
Francisco, 2014–2016

**88. Octagonal dish with scene from the
opera *Flora: or, Hob in the Well***, ca. 1730
Hard-paste porcelain
1 ¾ × 11 in. (4.5 × 28 cm)
Marks: crossed swords in blue enamel;
Japanese Palace inventory number *N=36-/w*
engraved and blackened with pigment
L13.62.73
Plate 65
Provenance
Augustus II, elector of Saxony and king of
Poland, Japanese Palace, Dresden; Hugo
Helbing, Frankfurt am Main, May 31–June 2,
1934, lot 420 (possible sale). Christie's, New
York, April 27, 1984, lot 158
Exhibition history
California Palace of the Legion of Honor,
San Francisco, 1988; San Francisco Airport
Museum, 2010; Legion of Honor, San
Francisco, 2014–2016

89. Bowl, ca. 1730
Hard-paste porcelain
2 ⅛ × 5 ¼ in. (5.3 × 13.5 cm)

Marks: two sets of crossed swords in under-
glaze blue, one covered by Kosel mark in gold;
H painted in underglaze blue and former's
(*Dreher's*) mark // incised inside footrim
L13.62.89
Plate 66
Provenance
A German noble collection (reputed).
Sotheby's, Olympia, London, October 6,
2005, lot 22
Publication history
Weber 2013, vol. 1, 39, fig. 17 (underside illus.)
Exhibition history
San Francisco Airport Museum, 2010; Legion
of Honor, San Francisco, 2014–2016

90. Plate, ca. 1730–1735
Hard-paste porcelain
1 ⅜ × 9 ¾ in. (3.4 × 24.7 cm)
Mark: crossed swords in underglaze blue
L13.62.84
Plate 67
Provenance
Michael Weisbrod, New York. Sotheby's,
New York, May 22, 2001, lot 161
Publication history
McGill 2006, 27
Exhibition history
Asian Art Museum, San Francisco, 2006; San
Francisco Airport Museum, 2010; Legion of
Honor, San Francisco, 2014–2016

91. Shell-shaped dish, ca. 1730
Hard-paste porcelain
1 ¾ × 9 ¼ in. (4.3 × 23.4 cm)
Marks: crossed swords in blue enamel;
Japanese Palace inventory number *N=57-/w*
engraved and blackened with pigment
L13.62.85
Plate 68
Provenance
Augustus II, elector of Saxony and king of
Poland, Japanese Palace, Dresden. Sotheby's,
London, April 2, 2003, lot 25
Publication history
Evolution of a Royal Vision 2010, 18–19
Exhibition history
San Francisco Airport Museum, 2010; Legion
of Honor, San Francisco, 2014–2016

**92. Dish from the *Gelber Löwe* (Yellow Lion)
service**, 1734
Hard-paste porcelain
2 ½ × 14 in. (6.4 × 35.6 cm)
Marks: crossed swords in underglaze
blue; former's mark (*Ritzzeichen* or
Formerzeichen) × for either Johann Christoph
Pietsch or Johann Daniel Rehschuh incised on
the inner footrim; Japanese Palace inventory
number *N=149-/w* engraved and blackened
with pigment
L13.62.52
Plate 69
Provenance
Augustus III, elector of Saxony and king of
Poland, Japanese Palace, Dresden; trans-
ferred to the *Hofconditerei* (royal pantry),
Warsaw, 1734; the Royal Collections of
Saxony; Lee Bizzell, Trophy Room Antiques,
Gloucester, Virginia; Charles and Margot
Nesbitt, Oklahoma City, Oklahoma; *Christie's
Interiors*, New York, December 11, 2013, lot 277.
Freeman's, Philadelphia, May 20, 2014, lot 236
Exhibition history
Legion of Honor, San Francisco, 2014–2016

93. Pair of Fliegender Hund plates, ca. 1735
Hard-paste porcelain
1 ⅜ × 9 ⅛ in. (3.5 × 23.3 cm) each
Marks: crossed swords in underglaze blue
on each
Gift of Malcolm D. Gutter, 2011.47 and
2012.62.1
Provenance
Jean Sewell Antiques Ltd., London, 1974

94. Kakiemon cup and saucer, ca. 1735–1740
Hard-paste porcelain
Cup: 2 ¾ × 2 ½ in. (7 × 6.4 cm); saucer: 1 × 4 ⅝
in. (2.4 × 11.8 cm)
Marks: crossed swords in underglaze blue;
Pressnummer 2 on saucer
Gift of Malcolm D. Gutter, 2014.96.3
Provenance
Cup: Mercury Antiques, London, 1983;
saucer: Stockspring Antiques, London, 2003
Exhibition history
Legion of Honor, San Francisco, 2014–2016

95. Teabowl and saucer, ca. 1730–1735
Hard-paste porcelain
Teabowl: 1 ¾ × 2 ⅞ in. (4.4 × 7.3 cm); saucer:
1 × 4 ¾ in. (2.5 × 12.2 cm)
Marks: crossed swords in underglaze blue on
each; unidentified painter's mark *E1* in under-
glaze blue on teabowl; former's mark *oo* for
Johann Gottlieb Kühnel, senior (1702?–1774),
inside the footrim of saucer
L13.62.69a–b
Provenance
Gump's, San Francisco, sold 1940. Gale
Blosser, Millbrae, California, 1976–1977

96. Teabowl and saucer, 1729–1731
Hard-paste porcelain
Teabowl: 1 ¾ × 2 ¾ in. (4.3 × 7 cm);
saucer: ⅞ × 4 ⅞ in. (2.2 × 12.5 cm)
Marks: crossed swords in overglaze blue
enamel on teabowl; Japanese Palace
inventory number *N=243-/w* engraved and
blackened with pigment on each; mark
(*Schnittmarke, Ritzzeichen,* or *Formerzeichen*) /
incised on saucer
L13.62.70a–b
Provenance
Augustus II, elector of Saxony and king of
Poland, Japanese Palace, Dresden. Andrew
Dando, Bath, England, 1983
Exhibition history
Legion of Honor, San Francisco, 2014–2016

97. Fork handle, ca. 1730
Hard-paste porcelain
Length: 8 in. (20.3 cm) overall; handle
length: 3 ¼ in. (8.3 cm)
L13.62.74
Provenance
Kilgour Antiques, Glasgow, Scotland, 1984

98. Pentafoil saucer-dish, ca. 1729–1731
Hard-paste porcelain
1 ⅝ × 5 ¼ in. (4 × 13.2 cm)
Marks: crossed swords in blue enamel;
former's mark (*Schnittmarke, Ritzzeichen,* or
Formerzeichen) × for Johann Christoph Pietsch
or Johann Daniel Rehschuh incised on the
inner footrim; Japanese Palace inventory
number *N=338-/w* engraved and blackened
with pigment
L13.62.75
Provenance
Augustus II, elector of Saxony and king of
Poland, Japanese Palace, Dresden. Davis-
Holdship (William E. Davis), 1987

99. Two-handled coffee cup and saucer,
ca. 1729–1731
Hard-paste porcelain
Cup: 2 ⅜ × 2 ⅞ in. (6 × 7.3 cm); saucer:
1 ⅛ × 5 ¼ in. (3 × 13.3 cm)
Marks: crossed swords in underglaze blue
on each; mark (*Schnittmarke, Ritzzeichen,* or
Formerzeichen for Johann Gottlieb Geithner
[1701–1761]) // incised on cup; Japanese
Palace inventory number *N=344-/w*
engraved and blackened with pigment on
saucer
L13.62.78a–b
Provenance
Cup: Jose Polar, San Francisco, mid-1980s
Saucer: Augustus II, elector of Saxony and
king of Poland, Japanese Palace, Dresden.
Guest & Gray, London, 1994

100. Plate, ca. 1740–1745
Hard-paste porcelain
1 ⅜ × 9 ⅜ in. (3.5 × 23.8 cm)
Marks: crossed swords in underglaze blue;
Pressnummer 16 impressed
L13.62.80
Provenance
Estate of Don Ritchie. Butterfield &
Butterfield, San Francisco, December 15, 1996,
lot 7526

101. Teabowl and saucer, ca. 1723–1725
Hard-paste porcelain
Teabowl: 1 ¾ × 2 ⅞ in. (4.4 × 7.3 cm); saucer:
1 × 4 ¾ in. (2.5 × 12.1 cm)
Marks: *8* in iron-red luster on each; *Dreher's/*
former's mark × (for Johann Christoph
Pietsch or Johann Daniel Rehschuh) incised
on teabowl
L13.62.86a–b
Provenance
Teabowl: Phillips, London, September 26,
1984, lot 313; Jose Polar, San Francisco;
Dr. Roy M. Byrnes, San Juan Capistrano,
California. Acquired by exchange from Dr.
Roy M. Byrnes, 2004
Saucer: Christie's, Paris, May 15, 2003, lot 363
Exhibition history
Legion of Honor, San Francisco, 2014–2016

**102. Two-handled beaker and saucer, Red
Dragon pattern**, ca. 1740
Hard-paste porcelain
Beaker: 2 ¾ × 2 ½ in. (7 × 6.2 cm); saucer:
1 × 5 ⅛ in. (2.5 × 13 cm)
Marks: crossed swords in underglaze blue;
Pressnummer 2 impressed on inner footrim
of saucer
L13.62.87a–b
Provenance
Woolley & Wallis, Salisbury, England, May
25, 2004, lot 460
Exhibition history
Legion of Honor, San Francisco, 2014–2016

103. Dish, ca. 1729–1730
Hard-paste porcelain
1 ⅜ × 9 ⅞ in. (3.6 × 25 cm)
Marks: caduceus mark in underglaze blue;
Japanese Palace inventory number *N=65-/w*
engraved and blackened with pigment
L17.46.4
Plate 62a
Provenance
Augustus II, elector of Saxony and king of
Poland, Japanese Palace, Dresden. Christie's,
London, May 17, 2017, lot 164

104. Pentafoil saucer-dish, ca. 1728
Hard-paste porcelain
Diameter: 5 ¾ in. (14.6 cm)
Marks: crossed swords in blue enamel,
Japanese Palace inventory number *N=108/w*
incised and enriched in green pigment
L17.94.5
Provenance
Augustus II, elector of Saxony and king of
Poland, Japanese Palace, Dresden; *Dubletten*
sale, *Porzellane und Waffen aus den Kgl.
Sächsischen Sammlungen in Dresden,* Rudolph
Lepke's Kunst-Auctions-Haus, Berlin,
October 7–8, 1919, lots 117–122 (probable);
Anna-Maria and Stephen Kellen Foundation,
New York. Christie's, New York, October 18,
2017, lot 807

VIII. MEISSEN ARMORIALS AND DIPLOMATIC GIFTS

105. Plate from the *Kronungsservice*
(Coronation service) with the arms of
Saxony-Poland, ca. 1733–1734
Hard-paste porcelain
Diameter: 9 in. (22.8 cm)
Marks: crossed swords in underglaze blue;
former's four triangles arranged in a square
in the sunken base, possibly for Johann Elias
Grund the Elder; Japanese Palace inventory
number *N=147-/w* engraved and blackened
with pigment
L13.62.99
Plate 70
Provenance
Augustus II and III, electors of Saxony and
kings of Poland, Japanese Palace, Dresden.
Georg Monheim, Lempertz, Cologne,
February 5, 2000, lot 29
Exhibition history
San Francisco Airport Museum, 2010; Legion
of Honor, San Francisco, 2014–2016

106. Beaker with the arms of Naples-Sicily
and Saxony-Poland-Lithuania, ca. 1737
Painting possibly by Johann Georg Heintze
(b. 1707) or Bonaventura Gottlieb Häuer

(1710–1782)
Hard-paste porcelain
3 ⅛ × 2 ¾ in. (7.8 × 7 cm)
Mark: crossed swords in underglaze blue
within double underglaze-blue rings around
the inner footrim
L13.62.98
Plate 71
Provenance
Princess Maria Amalia of Saxony and Charles
VII, king of Naples; Christie's, London,
December 2, 1974, lot 139; Kate Foster Ltd.,
London; Reverend Harry Gallup, Milwaukee.
Butterfield & Butterfield, San Francisco,
November 3, 1993, lot 429
Publication history
Cassidy-Geiger 2007, 219, fig. 10-20; *Evolution
of a Royal Vision* 2010, 22–23
Exhibition history
Bard Graduate Center, New York, 2007–2008;
San Francisco Airport Museum, 2010; Legion
of Honor, San Francisco, 2014–2016

107. Tea caddy with the arms of Gradenigo,
ca. 1740
Painting possibly by Johann Georg Heintze or
Bonaventura Gottlieb Häuer
Hard-paste porcelain
4 × 2 ⅝ × 1 ⅞ in. (10.3 × 6.8 × 4.9 cm)
Mark: gilder's four-dots mark
L13.62.96
Plate 72
Provenance
Girolamo, Piero, or Vincenzo II Gradenigo,
Venice (probable); Gustav von Klemperer;
The Antique Porcelain Company, New York;
private collector, New York; Sotheby's, New
York, October 13, 1983, lot 98 (unsold).
Sotheby's, New York, October 16, 1987, lot 43
Publication history
Cassidy-Geiger 2007, 229, fig. 10-42; Gibson
Stoodley 2015, 52 (illus.); Schnorr von
Carolsfeld 1928, pl. 27, no. 258, 98 (text)
Exhibition history
Bard Graduate Center, New York, 2007–2008;
San Francisco Airport Museum, 2010; Legion
of Honor, San Francisco, 2014–2016

**108. Dish from the *Schwanenservice*
(Swan service) with the arms of Brühl and
Kolowrat-Krakowska**, ca. 1738–1739
Hard-paste porcelain
2 × 11 ⅞ in. (5 × 30.2 cm)
Marks: crossed swords in underglaze blue;
former's four points for Johann Elias Grund

the Elder and *Grossennummer (Ritzzeichen)*
// incised
L13.62.97
Plate 73
Provenance
Heinrich Graf von Brühl, Schloss Pförten,
Saxony; Ailsa Mellon Bruce (possibly
purchased from The Antique Porcelain
Company, New York); unknown consignor
to Sotheby's, New York, May 5, 1977, lot
273; Reverend Harry Gallup, Milwaukee.
Butterfield & Butterfield, San Francisco, June
2, 1992, lot 420
Publication history
Pietsch 2000, 157; *Evolution of a Royal Vision*
2010, 20–21
Exhibition history
San Francisco Airport Museum, 2010; Legion
of Honor, San Francisco, 2014–2016

109. Plate from a Dutch service, ca. 1774–1813
Hard-paste porcelain
1 ⅜ × 9 in. (3.5 × 22.9 cm)
L13.62.94
Provenance
A late eighteenth-century Dutch collector
(possible), Dr. William P. Harbeson; Parke-
Bernet Galleries, New York, December 10,
1971, lot 152. N. Sakiel & Son, late December
1971
Exhibition history
San Francisco Airport Museum, 2010

**110. Pair of candlesticks from the
Schwanenservice (Swan service)**, ca. 1739
Hard-paste porcelain
9 ⅝ × 5 ¾ in. (24.5 × 14.5 cm) each
Marks: crossed swords in underglaze blue
on each; *Formernummer 46* for Johann Georg
Möbius (1710–1759) impressed on one
L13.62.100.1-2
Plate 74
Provenance
Heinrich Graf von Brühl, Schloss Pförten,
Saxony; Christie's, Geneva, May 9, 1988, lot
57; Christie's, London, December 9, 2004, lot
170. E & H Manners, London, 2005
Publication history
Antiques Trade Gazette 2005, 11 (illus.); Gibson
Stoodley 2015, 48 (illus.); *Evolution of a Royal
Vision* 2010, 20–21
Exhibition history
San Francisco Airport Museum, 2010; Legion
of Honor, San Francisco, 2014–2016

**111. Plate from the Saint Andrew the First-
Called service**, ca. 1744
Hard-paste porcelain
1 ¼ × 9 ⅝ in. (3.2 × 24.5 cm)
Marks: crossed swords in underglaze blue;
Pressnummer 20 impressed
L13.62.95
Plate 75
Provenance
Empress Elizabeth I of Russia; Imperial
Collection at the Hermitage, St. Petersburg
(Leningrad). Ed Hardy, San Francisco, April
18, 1978
Exhibition history
California Palace of the Legion of Honor,
San Francisco, 1980; San Francisco Airport
Museum, 2010; Legion of Honor, San
Francisco, 2014–2016

IX. MEISSEN FIGURES

**112. Absinthe seller from the *Cris de Paris*
series**, ca. 1753–1757
Modeling by Peter Reinicke (1711–1768) after
design of Christophe Huet
Hard-paste porcelain
Height: 5 ¾ in. (14.6 cm)
Marks: crossed swords in underglaze blue;
Pressnummer 17 impressed
Gift of Malcolm D. Gutter, 2014.96.1
Provenance
Phillips, London, May 12, 1976, lot 175

**113. Vegetable salesman from the *Cris de
Paris* series**, ca. 1745
Modeling by Johann Friederich Eberlein
Hard-paste porcelain
Height: 7 in. (17.9 cm)
Gift of Malcolm D. Gutter, 2014.96.2
Provenance
Phillips, London, July 25, 1979, lot 188

**114. Avvocato (lawyer) from the Venetian
Carnival series**, ca. 1745–1750
Modeling by Johann Joachim Kändler
Hard-paste porcelain
Height: 6 ⅛ in. (15.6 cm)
L13.62.103
Provenance
Dr. Joseph Kler, New Jersey. Christie's, New
York, April 27, 1984, lot 87

**115. Scaramouche and Columbine from the
Commedia dell'Arte series**, ca. 1740
Modeling by Johann Joachim Kändler
Hard-paste porcelain
Height: 7 in. (17.8 cm)
L13.62.104
Provenance
Phillips, London, June 11, 1986, lot 424

X. CHINESE AND JAPANESE
PORCELAINS

116. Ewer (*kendi*), ca. 1700–1710
China
Red stoneware
8 × 4 ½ in. (20.3 × 11.4 cm)
L13.62.147
Plate 6a
Provenance
Christophe Perlès, Paris; Antiquitäten Metz
GmbH-Kunstauktionen, Heidelberg, April
2006, lot 574. E & H Manners, London, 2006
Publication history
Evolution of a Royal Vision 2010, 4–5
Exhibition history
San Francisco Airport Museum, 2010; Legion
of Honor, San Francisco, 2014–2016

117. Bowl, ca. 1700–1720
China, Jingdezhen
Porcelain
2 ⅝ × 6 in. (6.7 × 15.2 cm)
Mark: Japanese Palace inventory number
N=531-/☐ engraved and blackened with
pigment
L13.62.105
Plate 26a
Provenance
Augustus II, elector of Saxony and king of
Poland, Japanese Palace, Dresden; Paul
Cassirer und Hugo Helbing, Berlin, March
23–24, 1926, lot 266; Antiquitäten Metz
GmbH-Kunstauktionen, Heidelberg, April 25,
2009, lot 147. Elfriede Langeloh, Weinheim
Publication history
Evolution of a Royal Vision 2010, 14–15
Exhibition history
San Francisco Airport Museum, 2010; San
Francisco, Legion of Honor, 2014–2016

Francisco Airport Museum, 2010; Legion of
Honor, San Francisco, 2014–2016

120. Dish, ca. 1690–1700
Japan
Porcelain
1 ⅝ × 11 in. (4.1 × 27.9 cm)
Mark: Japanese Palace inventory number
N=122-/☐ engraved and blackened with
pigment
L13.62.106
Provenance
Augustus II, elector of Saxony and king of
Poland, Japanese Palace, Dresden. Geoffrey
Godden, West Sussex, England, 1988
Exhibition history
San Francisco Airport Museum, 2010; Legion
of Honor, San Francisco, 2014–2016

**118. Dish with scene from the opera *Flora:
or, Hob in the Well***, ca. 1700
China
Porcelain
Diameter: 12 in. (30.5 cm)
L13.62.136
Plate 65a
Provenance
J. B. Garrard, London, 2002
Exhibition history
San Francisco Airport Museum, 2010; Legion
of Honor, San Francisco, 2014–2016

121. Dish, ca. 1700–1720
China
Porcelain
Diameter: 8 ⅝ in. (21.9 cm)
Mark: Japanese Palace inventory number
N=330-/+ engraved and blackened with
pigment
L13.62.107
Provenance
Augustus II, elector of Saxony and king
of Poland, Japanese Palace, Dresden. Erik
Thomsen Gallery, New York, 2002
Exhibition history
San Francisco Airport Museum, 2010

119. Plate, ca. 1690–1700
Japan
Porcelain
Diameter: 9 ⅞ in. (25 cm)
L13.62.142
Plate 67a
Provenance
Phillips, London, June 13, 2001, lot 418
Publication history
McGill 2006, 26–27; Scott 1961, 84, fig. 301A
Exhibition history
Asian Art Museum, San Francisco, 2006; San

122. Dish, ca. 1690–1720
China
Porcelain
1 × 11 in. (2.5 × 27.9 cm)
Mark: Japanese Palace inventory number
N=218-/☐ engraved and blackened with
pigment
L13.62.108
Provenance
Augustus II, elector of Saxony and king of
Poland, Japanese Palace, Dresden. Portobello
Road, London, mid-1970s

Exhibition history
San Francisco Airport Museum, 2010; Legion
of Honor, San Francisco, 2014–2016

123. Plate, ca. 1700–1720
China
Dutch-decorated porcelain
Diameter: 8 ¾ in. (22.2 cm)
Mark: Japanese Palace inventory number
N=78-/ˆ engraved and blackened with
pigment
L13.62.109
Provenance
Augustus II, elector of Saxony and king of
Poland, Japanese Palace, Dresden. Bluett &
Sons, London, 1989
Exhibition history
San Francisco Airport Museum, 2010; Legion
of Honor, San Francisco, 2014–2016

124. Pair of bowls, ca. 1700
China
Porcelain
3 ½ × 7 ¼ in. (8.9 × 18.4 cm) each
Mark: Japanese Palace inventory number
N=80-/ˆ engraved and blackened with
pigment
L13.62.110.1–2
Provenance
Augustus II, elector of Saxony and king of
Poland, Japanese Palace, Dresden; Paul
Cassirer und Hugo Helbing, Berlin, March
23–24, 1926, lot 88
Exhibition history
San Francisco Airport Museum, 2010

125. Teabowl and saucer, ca. 1700
China
Porcelain
Teabowl: 1 ⅝ × 3 ⅛ in. (4.1 × 7.9 cm); saucer:
diameter 5 in. (12.7 cm)
Mark: Japanese Palace inventory number
N=152-/l, engraved and blackened with
pigment
L13.62.111a–b
Provenance

Augustus II, elector of Saxony and king of
Poland, Japanese Palace, Dresden; Sotheby's,
New York. Ralph Chait, New York
Exhibition history
San Francisco Airport Museum, 2010

126. Bowl, ca. 1700
China
Porcelain
2 ½ × 6 ½ in. (6.2 × 16.5 cm)
Mark: Japanese Palace inventory number
N=148-/l engraved and blackened with
pigment
L13.62.112
Provenance
Augustus II, elector of Saxony and king of
Poland, Japanese Palace, Dresden. Henry
Moog, Atlanta, 1996
Exhibition history
San Francisco Airport Museum, 2010

127. Bowl, ca. 1700
China
Porcelain
2 ¼ × 6 in. (5.7 × 15.2 cm)
Mark: Japanese Palace inventory number
N=18-/l engraved and blackened with
pigment
L13.62.113
Provenance
Augustus II, elector of Saxony and king of
Poland, Japanese Palace, Dresden. Henry
Moog, Atlanta, 1996
Exhibition history
San Francisco Airport Museum, 2010

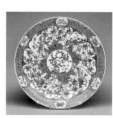

128. *Famille verte* dish/charger, ca. 1690
China
Porcelain
Diameter: approximately 20 in. (50.8 cm)
Mark: Japanese Palace inventory number
N=6-/l engraved and blackened with pigment
L13.62.114
Provenance
Augustus II, elector of Saxony and king of
Poland, Japanese Palace, Dresden. Sotheby's,

London, May 3, 1996, lot 33
Exhibition history
San Francisco Airport Museum, 2010

129. Dish, ca. 1700
Japan, Arita
Porcelain
1 ⅛ × 6 in. (2.9 × 15.2 cm)
Mark: Japanese Palace inventory number
N=193-/☐ engraved and blackened with
pigment
L13.62.115
Provenance
Augustus II, elector of Saxony and king of
Poland, Japanese Palace, Dresden. Jeremy
Mason, London, 1983
Exhibition history
San Francisco Airport Museum, 2010; Legion
of Honor, San Francisco, 2014–2016

130. Dish, late 1600s
Japan, Arita
Porcelain
Diameter: 7 in. (17.8 cm)
Mark: Japanese Palace inventory number
N=378-/☐ engraved and blackened with
pigment
L13.62.116
Provenance
Augustus II, elector of Saxony and king of
Poland, Japanese Palace, Dresden; Dr. Carew-
Shaw. S. Marchant & Son, London, 1984
Exhibition history
San Francisco Airport Museum, 2010; Legion
of Honor, San Francisco, 2014–2016

131. Bowl, early nineteenth century
Japan
Porcelain
3 ¼ × 7 in. (8.3 × 17.9 cm)
L13.62.117
Provenance
Gabor Cossa Antiques, Cambridge,
England, 1976

132. Plate with fisherman scene, ca. 1640
Japan
Porcelain
Diameter: 7 ½ in. (19 cm)
L13.62.118
Provenance
Yamanaka, Kyoto, Japan, 1986
Exhibition history
San Francisco Airport Museum, 2010

133. Vinegar bottle, pewter spout, ca. 1700
Japan
Porcelain
Height: 3 ½ in. (9 cm)
L13.62.119

134. Dish, ca. 1700
Japan
Porcelain
Diameter: 9 ⅝ in. (24.5 cm)
L13.62.120
Provenance
Michael Willcox, London, 1983

135. Dish depicting a gourd vase, ca. 1690
Japan
Porcelain
Diameter: 8 ½ in. (21.5 cm)
L13.62.121
Provenance
Sotheby's, London, June 12–13, 1986, lot 624

**136. Dish with chrysanthemums and
peonies**, ca. 1690
Japan
Porcelain
Diameter: 7 ⅞ in. (20 cm)
L13.62.122

137. Octagonal bowl, late seventeenth–early
eighteenth century
Japan
Porcelain
2 ¾ × 4 ¾ in. (7 × 12 cm)
L13.62.123
Provenance
Richard de la Mare; Sotheby's, London, June
2, 1976, lot 21. Bluett & Sons, London, 1984
Exhibition history
San Francisco Airport Museum, 2010

138. Bowl, ca. 1680
Japan
Porcelain
1 ¾ × 4 ⅞ in. (4.5 × 12.5 cm)
L13.62.124
Provenance
Bluett & Sons, London, 1984

139. Teabowl and saucer, ca. 1700
Japan
Porcelain
Teabowl: 1 ⅝ × 2 ½ in. (4 × 6.5 cm); saucer:
diameter 4 ⅜ in. (11 cm)
L13.62.125a–b
Provenance
C. Anthony Gray, London, 1988

**140. Dish with mons (emblem or heraldic
symbol) decoration**, ca. 1700
Japan
Porcelain
Diameter: 7 ½ in. (19 cm)
L13.62.126

141. Ten-sided white plate, ca. 1700
Japan
Porcelain
Diameter: 7 ½ in. (19 cm)
L13.62.127
Provenance
Joseph Handley, Carmel, California, mid-1990s

142. Pair of Imari dishes, ca. 1700
Japan
Porcelain
Diameter: 10 in. (25.4 cm) each
L13.62.128.1–2

143. Lidded vase with lion finial, ca. 1700
Japan
Porcelain
Height: 16 in. (40.6 cm)
L13.62.129a–b
Provenance
Bonhams & Butterfields, San Francisco, July
21–22, 1981, lot 895

144. Imari dish/charger, ca. 1700
Japan
Porcelain
Diameter: approximately 14 in. (35.6 cm)
L13.62.130
Provenance
Butterfield & Butterfield, San Francisco, 1990s

145. Imari barber's bowl, ca. 1700
Japan
Porcelain
Diameter: 10 ½ in. (26.7 cm)
L13.62.131

146. Ewer with strap handle, ca. 1680
Japan
Porcelain
Height: 7 ¼ in. (18.5 cm)
L13.62.132
Provenance
C. Anthony Gray, London, 1984

147. Lidded vase with black registers,
ca. 1700
Japan
Porcelain
Height: 7 ⅝ in. (19.5 cm)
L13.62.133a–b

**148. Pair of lidded teabowls and saucers
with Imari decoration featuring dragon
medallion**, ca. 1700
Japan
Porcelain
Teabowls: 2 ¾ × 3 ⅛ in. (7 × 8 cm) each;
saucers: diameter 5 ½ in. (14 cm) each
L13.62.134.1a–c and .2a–c
Provenance
Kunst- en Antiekgalerie "Het Loo,"
Apeldoorn, The Netherlands, 1997

149. Dish with Pompadour pattern, ca. 1740
China
Porcelain
Diameter: 9 ⅞ in. (25 cm)
L13.62.135

**150. Teabowl and saucer with Imari decora-
tion featuring butterflies**, ca. 1700
Japan
Porcelain
Teabowl: 1 ¾ × 2 ¾ in. (4.5 × 7 cm); saucer:
diameter 4 ¾ in. (12 cm)
L13.62.137a–b

**151. Pair of chinoiserie teabowls and
saucers**, ca. 1735–1750
China
Porcelain
Teabowls: 1 ⅝ × 3 in. (4 × 7.5 cm) and
1 ⅝ × 2 ¾ in. (4 × 7 cm); saucers: diameter
4 ¾ in. (12 cm) and 4 ½ in. (11.5 cm)
L13.62.138.1a–b and .2a–b
Exhibition history
San Francisco Airport Museum, 2010; Legion
of Honor, San Francisco, 2014–2016

152. Yixing teapot, pierced body and lid,
ca. 1750
China
Red stoneware
4 ⅛ × 6 ⅛ in. (10.5 × 15.5 cm)
L13.62.139
Provenance
Asian Art Museum, San Francisco. Moy Ying
Ming, Chicago, 1981

153. Imari saucer, ca. 1700
Japan
Porcelain
Diameter: 5 ½ in. (14 cm)
L13.62.140
Provenance
Justin Garrard, London

**154. Pair of teabowls and saucers with Imari
decoration**, ca. 1700
Japan
Porcelain
Teabowls: 1 ¾ × 3 in. (4.5 × 7.5 cm) each;
saucers: diameter 5 ⅛ in. (13 cm) each
L13.62.141.1a–b and .2a–b
Provenance
Kunst- en Antiekgalerie "Het Loo,"
Apeldoorn, The Netherlands, 1997

**155. Bowl with Imari diaper pattern and
figures**, ca. 1700
Japan
Porcelain
4 ½ × 9 ⅝ in. (11.4 × 24.4 cm)
L13.62.143
Provenance
Gregg Baker, London, 1986

156. Group of twenty saucers, late
seventeenth–eighteenth century
China and Japan
Porcelain
Diameter: 3 ⅛–5 ½ in. (8–14 cm) each
L13.62.144.1–20

157. Double-bodied cruet, ca. 1700
China
Porcelain
Approximately 7 ¾ × 4 in. (19.7 × 10.2 cm)
L13.62.145
Provenance
Tony Greaves, London

**158. Blue-and-white porcelain bowl with
molded base and diaper pattern**, ca. 1700
China
Porcelain
4 ⅛ × 8 in. (10.5 × 20.3 cm)
L13.62.146
Provenance
Tony Greaves, London, 2000s

159. Tripod coffeepot with handle, ca. 1700
Japan
Porcelain
12 ¾ × 6 ⅛ in. (32.4 × 15.6 cm)
L13.62.148

160. Porcelain saucer with Kakiemon decoration, ca. 1700
Japan, Arita
Porcelain
Diameter: approximately 4 in. (10.2 cm)
L13.62.149
Exhibition history
San Francisco Airport Museum, 2010

161. Teapot with Imari decoration, ca. 1750
China
Porcelain
Height: 4 ¼ in. (10.8 cm)
L13.62.150
Provenance
Law Fine Art, Brimpton, England, 2001
Exhibition history
San Francisco Airport Museum, 2010

162. Small bowl with Kakiemon decoration, ca. 1700
Japan
Porcelain
1 ⅜ × 4 ½ in. (3.5 × 11.5 cm)
L13.62.151
Provenance
Justin Garrard, London

163. Teabowl and saucer with engraved brown glaze, ca. 1700
China
Porcelain
Teabowl: 1 ⅜ × 2 ⅜ in. (3.5 × 6 cm); saucer: diameter 4 ⅛ in. (10.5 cm)
L13.62.152a–b

164. *Famille verte* dish/charger, ca. 1700
China
Porcelain
Diameter 16 in. (40.6 cm)
Mark: Japanese Palace inventory number *N=498-/-* engraved and blackened with pigment
L.18.10
Provenance
Augustus II, elector of Saxony and king of Poland, Japanese Palace, Dresden; *Dubletten* sale, Bernheimer, Munich; Porzellan/ Gemälde Elfenbeinskulpturen Waffen aus den Sächsischen Staatsammlungen in Dresden, Rudolph Lepke's Kunst-Auktions-Haus, Berlin, October 12–14, 1920, lot 728; S. Marchant & Son, London. Christie's, New York, January 18, 2018, lot 61

XI. MISCELLANEOUS

165. Georg Friedrich Dinglinger (1668–1720) Miniature of Augustus "the Strong", ca. 1710
Copper with enamel
2 ¼ × 1 ¾ in. (5.7 × 4.4 cm)
L13.62.154
Provenance
Augustus II, elector of Saxony and king of Poland (probable); Gustav and Charlotte von Klemperer, Dresden. Sotheby's, London, December 16, 1998, lot 22
Publication history
Schnorr von Carolsfeld 1928, cat. no. 62, pl. 3
Exhibition history
Legion of Honor, San Francisco, 2014–2016

166. Bernardo Bellotto (Italian, 1720–1780) *Perspective de la galerie, et du Jardin de son Excellence Mgr. Le Compte de Brühl*, ca. 1747
Etching
21 ½ × 33 ¼ in. (54.6 × 84.5 cm)
L13.62.155
Provenance
Galerie Gerda Bassenge, Berlin, December 3, 2003, lot 5397

SELECTED EXHIBITION HISTORY FEATURING OBJECTS IN THE MALCOLM D. GUTTER COLLECTION

Winifred Williams, London, 1975
Exhibition of Eighteenth-Century European White Porcelain, Winifred Williams, London, June 10–27

California Palace of the Legion of Honor, San Francisco, 1980
English & Continental Porcelain from Public & Private Collections, California Palace of the Legion of Honor, San Francisco, March–October

Chinese Culture Center, San Francisco, 2002
China and Beyond: Artistic Influences Into and Out of China, Chinese Culture Center, San Francisco, May 16–August 20

Asian Art Museum, San Francisco, 2006
A Curious Affair: The Fascination between East and West, Asian Art Museum, San Francisco, June 17–September 3

Bard Graduate Center for Studies in the Decorative Arts, Design, and Culture, New York, 2007–2008
Fragile Diplomacy: Meissen Porcelain for European Courts, ca. 1710–1763, Bard Graduate Center for Studies in the Decorative Arts, Design, and Culture, New York, November 15, 2007–February 10, 2008

San Francisco Airport Museum, 2010
Evolution of a Royal Vision: The Birth of Meissen Porcelain from the Collection of Malcolm D. Gutter, San Francisco Airport Museum, March 29–September 13. Exh. cat.

San Francisco Fall Antiques Show, 2010
Chinoiserie: Rococo to Eco, San Francisco Fall Antiques Show, Fort Mason, October 27–31

San Francisco Fall Antiques Show, 2012
Sea Worthy: The Best of Nautical Art and Antiques, San Francisco Fall Antiques Show, Fort Mason, October 25–28

Legion of Honor, San Francisco, 2014–2016
A Princely Pursuit: The Malcolm D. Gutter Collection of Early Meissen Porcelain, Legion of Honor, San Francisco, December 13–March 13. Exh. brochure

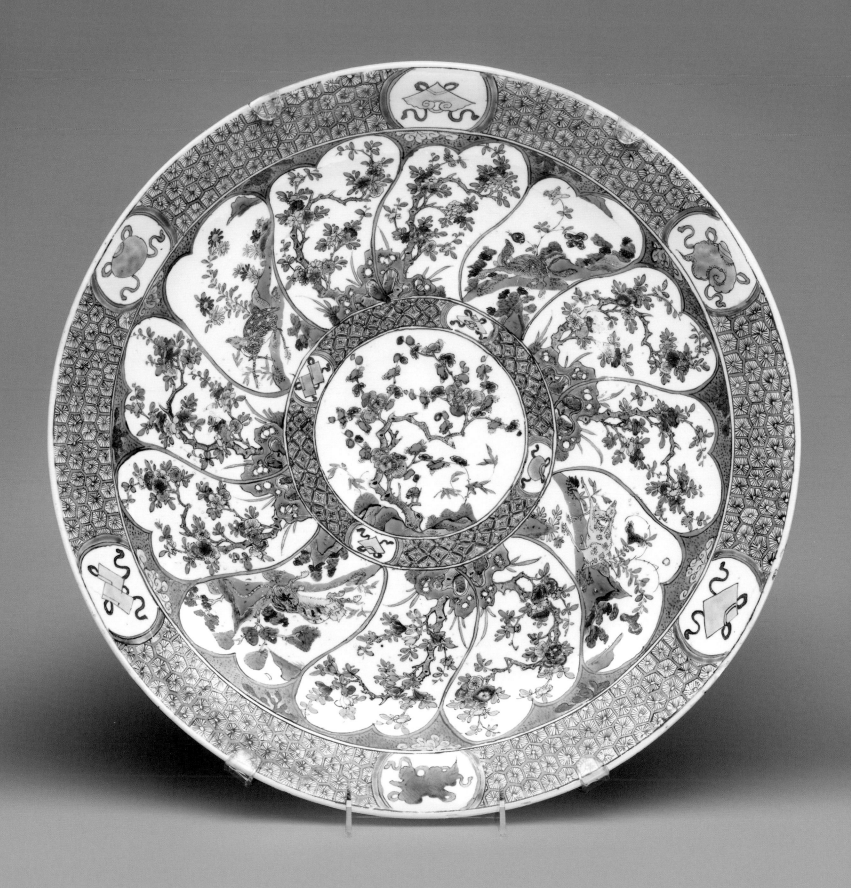

OBJECTS BEARING JAPANESE PALACE INVENTORY NUMBERS OR AR MONOGRAMS IN THE MALCOLM D. GUTTER COLLECTION

Böttger and Red Stoneware

Ewer (*kendi*), ca. 1710–1712, cat. no. and pl. 6 (Japanese Palace inventory number 232/R)

Incense burner, ca. 1710–1713, cat. no. 13/pl. 12 (Japanese Palace inventory number 180)

Underglaze-Blue Decoration

Baluster vase and cover, ca. 1725–1730, cat. no. 37/pl. 25 (AR monogram in underglaze blue)

Höroldt and Far Eastern Decoration

Beaker vase, ca. 1725, cat. no. 76/pl. 53 (AR monogram in underglaze blue)

Fragments of a bottle-gourd vase, ca. 1726–1730, cat. no. 77/pl. 54 (likely AR monogram in underglaze blue [base containing mark now missing])

Waste bowl, ca. 1726, cat. no. 78/pl. 55 (Japanese Palace inventory number N=502-/w)

Beaker vase, ca. 1726–1730, cat. no. 80/pl. 57 (AR monogram in underglaze blue)

Beaker and saucer, ca. 1726–1727, cat. no. 81/pl. 58 (Japanese Palace inventory number N=597-/w on both)

Ten-sided bowl, ca. 1729–1730, cat. no. 84/pl. 61 (Japanese Palace inventory number N=447-/w and partially obliterated black enamel number N=119)

Dish, ca. 1729–1731, cat. no. 85/pl. 62 (Japanese Palace inventory number N=66-/w)

Sake bottle, ca. 1730, cat. no. 86/pl. 63 (Japanese Palace inventory number N=291-/w)

Covered tureen, ca. 1730, cat. no. 87/pl. 64 (Japanese Palace inventory number N=17-/w)

Octagonal dish with scene from the opera *Flora: or, Hob in the Well*, ca. 1730, cat. no. 88/pl. 65 (Japanese Palace inventory number N=56-/w)

Shell-shaped dish, ca. 1730, cat. no. 91/pl. 68 (Japanese Palace inventory number N=57-/w)

Dish from the *Gelber Löwe* (Yellow Lion) service, 1734, cat. no. 92/pl. 69 (Japanese Palace inventory number N=149-/w)

Teabowl and saucer, 1729–1731, cat. no. 96 (Japanese Palace inventory number N=243-/w)

Pentafoil saucer-dish, ca. 1729–1731, cat. no. 98 (Japanese Palace inventory number N=338-/w)

Two-handled coffee cup and saucer, ca. 1729–1731, cat. no. 99 (Japanese Palace inventory number N=344-/w)

Dish, ca. 1729–1730, cat. no. 103/pl. 62a (Japanese Palace inventory number N=65-/w)

Pentafoil saucer-dish, ca. 1728, cat. no. 104 (Japanese Palace inventory number N=108/w)

Meissen Armorials and Diplomatic Gifts

Plate from the *Kronungsservice* (Coronation service), with the arms of Saxony-Poland ca. 1733–1734, cat. no. 105/pl. 70 (Japanese Palace inventory number N=147-/w)

Chinese and Japanese Porcelains

Chinese bowl, ca. 1700–1720, cat. no. 117/pl. 26a (Japanese Palace inventory number N=531-/□)

Japanese dish, ca. 1690–1700, cat. no. 120 (Japanese Palace inventory number N=122-/□)

Chinese dish, ca. 1700–1720, cat. no. 121 (Japanese Palace inventory number N=330-/+)

Chinese dish, ca. 1690–1720, cat. no. 122 (Japanese Palace inventory number N=218-/□)

Chinese plate, ca. 1700–1720, cat. no. 123 (Japanese Palace inventory number N=78-/^)

Pair of Chinese bowls, ca. 1700, cat. no. 124 (Japanese Palace inventory number N=80-/^)

Chinese teabowl and saucer, ca. 1700, cat. no. 125 (Japanese Palace inventory number N=152-/I)

Chinese bowl, ca. 1700, cat. no. 126 (Japanese Palace inventory number N=148-/I)

Chinese bowl, ca. 1700, cat. no. 127 (Japanese Palace inventory number N=18-/I)

Chinese *famille verte* dish/charger, ca. 1690, cat. no. 128 (Japanese Palace inventory number N=6-/I)

Japanese dish, ca. 1700, cat. no. 129 (Japanese Palace inventory number N=195-/□)

Japanese dish, late 1600s, cat. no. 130 (Japanese Palace inventory number N=378-/□)

Chinese famille verte dish/charger, 1700, cat. no. 164 (Japanese Palace inventory number N=498-/-)

Chinese *famille verte* dish/charger, ca. 1690 (cat. no. 128)

SELECTED BIBLIOGRAPHY

Andres-Acevedo, Sarah-Katharina, and Hans Ottomeyer, eds. 2016. *From Invention to Perfection: Masterpieces of Eighteenth-Century Decorative Art.* Munich: Röbbig; and Stuttgart: Arnoldsche Art Publishers.

Antiques Trade Gazette. 1995. "Other Runners in Böttger Stakes." November 18, 22.

Antiques Trade Gazette. 2005. "2005 Ceramics Fair." July 16, 11.

Arnold, Klaus-Peter. 1989. *Meissener Blaumalerei aus drei Jahrhunderten.* Exh. cat. Hamburg: Museum für Kunst und Gewerbe.

Ayers, John, Oliver Impey, and J. V. G. Mallet, eds. 1990. *Porcelain for Palaces: The Fashion for Japan in Europe 1650–1750.* Exh. cat. London: British Museum and Oriental Ceramic Society.

Battie, David. 1990. *Sotheby's Concise Encyclopedia of Porcelain.* Boston: Little Brown & Co.

Bauer, Margrit. 1983. *Deutsches Porzellan des 18. Jahrhunderts: Geschirr und Ziergeräte.* Frankfurt am Main: Museum für Kunsthandwerk.

Behrends, Rainer. 1978. *Das Meissener Musterbuch für Höroldt-Chinoiserien: Musterblätter aus der Malstube der Meissener Porzellanmanufaktur (Schulz Codex).* Leipzig: Edition Leipzig.

Berges, Ruth. 1980. *The Collector's Cabinet.* New York: A. S. Barnes.

Berling, Karl. 1925. *Das Brühlsche Schwanenservice.* Vienna: Belvedere.

Bischoff, Ilse. 1982. Interview by Robert Brown, January 27, for the Archives of American Art, Smithsonian Institution, transcript available at https://www.aaa.si.edu/download_pdf_transcript/ajax?record_id=edanmdm-AAADCD_oh_212528.

Boltz, Claus. 1978. "Ein Beitrag zum grünen Watteau-Service für Neapel." *Keramos,* no. 79: 5–24.

———. 1980. "Hoym, Lemaire und Meissen: Ein Beitrag zur Geschichte der Dresdner Porzellansammlung." *Keramos,* no. 88: 3–101.

———. 1982. "Formen des Böttgersteinzeugs im Jahre 1711." *Keramikfreunde der Schweiz, Mitteilungsblatt,* no. 96 (March): 15–56.

———. 1996. "Japanisches Palais-Inventar 1770 und Turmzimmer-Inventar 1769." *Keramos,* no. 153 (July): 5–118.

———. 2000. "Steinzeug und Porzellan der Böttgerperiode: Die Inventare und die Ostermesse des Jahres 1719." *Keramos,* no. 167/168 (April): 3–156.

———. 2001. "Meissen Porcelain in the Rijksmuseum." *Keramos,* no. 172: 5–11. Review of Abraham L. den Blaauwen's 2000 publication *Meissen Porcelain in the Rijksmuseum.*

———. 2002. "Die wöchentlichen Berichte über die Tätigkeit der Meissner Dreher und Former vom 6. Juni 1722 bis 31. Dezember 1728." *Keramos,* no. 178: 3–147.

———. 2006. "Technical and Artistic Problems in the Production of Hard-Paste Porcelain at Meissen until about 1730." Paper presented at the International Ceramics Fair and Seminar, London, June 15–18.

Braun, Peter. 2007. *Böttgersteinzeug: Eine Meissener Faszination.* Meissen: Staatliche Porzellan-Manufaktur; and Dresden: Sandstein Verlag.

Bursche, Stefan. 1980. *Meissen: Steinzeug und Porzellan des 18. Jahrhunderts Kunstgewerbemuseum Berlin.* Berlin: Staatliche Museen Preussischer Kulturbesitz.

Cassidy-Geiger, Maureen. 1988. "Von Barlow zu Buggel: Eine neuentdeckte Vorlage für das Schwanenservice/From Barlow to Buggel: A New Source for the Swan Service." *Keramos,* no. 119: 63–68.

———. 1994. "Zurück zu 'Hoym, Lemaire und Meißen'/Returning to 'Hoym, Lemaire, and Meissen.'" *Keramos,* no. 146 (October): 3–8.

———. 1995. "The Japanese Palace Collections and Their Impact at Meissen," 14–24. *The International Fine Art and Antique Dealers Show, New York.* London: International Fine Art and Antique Dealers Show.

———. 1996a. "Graphic Sources for Meissen Porcelain: Origins of the Print Collection in the Meissen Archives." *Metropolitan Museum Journal* 31: 99–126.

———. 1996b. "Meissen Porcelain Ordered for the Japanese Palace: A Transcription of the *Specification von Porcilan* of 1736." *Keramos,* no. 153 (July): 119–130.

———. 1998. "Gestochene Quellen für frühe Höroldt-Malereien/Engraved Sources for Early Höroldt Decoration." *Keramos,* no. 161 (July): 3–38.

———. 2004. "Lacquer-Style Production at the Meissen Manufactory." In Kopplin 2004, 72–81.

———, ed. 2007. *Fragile Diplomacy: Meissen Porcelain for European Courts ca. 1710–63.* Exh. cat. New York: Bard Graduate Center for Studies in the Decorative Arts, Design and Culture; and New Haven: Yale University Press.

———. 2008. *The Arnhold Collection of Meissen Porcelain, 1710–1750.* New York: Frick Collection; and London: D. Giles Limited.

———. 2010. "'Verknüpfungen herstellen': Zusammenhänge zwischen der Druckgraphik, dem Schulz-Codex und der frühen narrativen Malerei in Meissen." In Rudi 2010, 50–55.

Chilton, Meredith. 1995. "The Canada Bowl: A Rare Small Porcelain Bowl in the Gardiner Museum Reveals an 18th-Century Fascination with Canada." *Rotunda* (Royal Ontario Museum) 28, no. 1 (Summer): 26–33.

———. 2001. *Harlequin Unmasked: The Commedia Dell'Arte and Porcelain Sculpture.* Exh. cat. Toronto: Gardiner Museum of Ceramic Art; and New Haven: Yale University Press.

Chinese plate, ca. 1700–1720 (cat. no. 123)

———, ed. 2009. *Fired by Passion: Vienna Baroque Porcelain of Claudius Innocentius Du Paquier.* 3 vols. Stuttgart: Arnoldsche Art Publishers.

Clarke, T. H. 1988. "Equestrian and Other Dwarfs on Early Meissen Porcelain/Reitende und andere Zwerge auf frühem Meißen-Porzellan." *Keramos*, no. 119: 6–57.

Cochran, Rebecca Dimling. 2004. "100 Top Collectors." *Art & Antiques* 27, no. 3 (March): 94–95.

Continental Table Porcelains of the Eighteenth Century. 1965. Exh. cat. San Francisco: M. H. de Young Museum.

Däberitz, Ute, and Martin Eberle. 2011. *Das weisse Gold: Die Sammlung Meissener Porzellan des 18. Jahrhunderts auf Schloss Friedenstein Gotha.* Gotha: Stiftung Schloss Friedenstein.

D'Agliano, Andreina, and Luca Melegati. 2001. *I fragili lussi: Porcellane di Meissen da musei e collezioni italiane.* Exh. cat. Turin: Fondazione Pietro Accorsi and Omega Art.

D'Albis, Antoine. 2000. "Herstellungsverfahren von Porzellan in Frankreich im späten 17. und beginnenden 18. Jahrhundert/Methods of Manufacturing Porcelain in France in the Late Seventeenth and Early Eighteenth Centuries." *Keramos*, no. 167/168 (April): 175–195.

Dawson, Aileen. 2005. "The Glory of Saxony: Meissen Porcelain in the British Museum," 18–26. In *The International Ceramics Fair & Seminar Handbook.* London: International Ceramics Fair and Seminar.

De Waal, Edmund. 2005. *Arcanum: Mapping Eighteenth-Century Porcelain.* Exh. cat. Cardiff: National Museum and Gallery of Wales.

———. 2010. "From the Ashes: The von Klemperer Collection of Meissen Was the Finest in Private Hands," 20–21. In *Bonhams Fine European Ceramics Including Porcelain from the von Klemperer Collection.* Sales cat. London: Bonhams.

Den Blaauwen, Abraham L. 2000. *Meissen Porcelain in the Rijksmuseum.* Amsterdam: Rijksmuseum.

Donath, Adolph. 1920. "Die Dresdner Porzellan-Auktion." *Der Kunstwanderer: Zeitschrift für alte und neue Kunst, für Kunstmarkt und Sammelwesen,* 2. Oktoberheft: 69–72.

Ducret, Siegfried. 1964. *Meissen Porcelain.* Bern, Switzerland: Hallwag.

———. 1972. *Bunte Augsburger Hausmalereien.* Vol. 2 of *Meissner Porzellan bemalt in Augsburg, 1718 bis 1750.* Braunschweig: Verlag Klinkhardt & Biermann.

Eikelmann, Renate. 2004. *Meissener Porzellan des 18. Jahrhunderts in Schloss Lustheim.* Munich: Verlag C. H. Beck.

———, and Julia Weber. 2013. *Meissener Porzellane mit Dekoren nach ostasiatischen Vorbildern.* Munich: Hirmer.

Emerson, Julie, Jennifer Chen, and Mimi Gardner Gates. 2000. *Porcelain Stories: From China to Europe.* Exh. cat. Seattle: Seattle Art Museum.

Evolution of a Royal Vision: The Birth of Meissen Porcelain from the Collection of Malcolm D. Gutter. 2010. Exh. cat. San Francisco: SFO Museum, San Francisco Airport Commission.

Exhibition of Eighteenth-Century European White Porcelain. 1975. Exh. cat. London: Winifred Williams.

Falke, Otto von. 1936. *Katalog der Sammlung F[ritz] M[annheimer].* Amsterdam: Fritz Mannheimer.

Fox-Strangways Holland, Giles Stephen. 1929. "A Notable Service of Meissen Porcelain." *Burlington Magazine* 55, no. 319 (October): 188.

Frühes Meissener Porzellan: Kostbarkeiten aus deutschen Privatsammlungen. 1997. Exh. cat. Munich: Hirmer.

"Gallery Dedications." 1988. *Triptych* (Fine Arts Museums of San Francisco), no. 42 (June–August), 19, fig. 3.

Gibson Stoodley, Sheila. 2015. "Meissen Men." *Art & Antiques* 38, no. 4 (April): 46–52.

Gillmeister, Kathy. 1985. *Meissen Porcelain: The Kathy Gillmeister Collection.* Exh. cat. Aptos, CA: Karon Enterprises.

Goder, Willi, ed. 1982. *Johann Friedrich Böttger: Die Erfindung des europäischen Porzellans.* Frankfurt: Büchergilde Gutenberg.

Goss, Holland. 2010. "Chinoiserie: Rococo to Eco." *San Francisco Fall Antiques Show,* 32–37.

Gutter, Malcolm D. 1976–2015. Collection catalogue manuscript.

———. 1988. "Meissen Chinoiserie & Harbour Scenes." *Antique Collector,* May, 70–76.

———. 1989. "Meissen Red Ground Wares." *Antique Collector,* February, 30–39.

———. 2001. "Through the Looking Glass: Viewing Böttger and Other Red Stoneware/Unter die Lupe genommen: Betrachtung von Böttger- und anderem rotem Steinzeug." *Keramik-Freunde der Schweiz, Mitteilungsblatt,* no. 114 (December): 5–23.

———. 2010. "Eine bemerkenswerte Entdeckung: Die früheste Darstellung von Amerikanern auf europäischem Porzellan/A Notable Discovery: The Earliest Depiction of Americans on European Porcelain." *Keramos,* no. 207 (January): 49–60.

Hennig, Lothar, ed. 1995. *Glanz des Barock: Sammlung Ludwig in Bamberg, Fayence und Porzellan.* Exh. cat. Bamberg: Fränkischer Tag.

Honey, W. B. 1946. *Dresden China: An Introduction to the Study of Meissen Porcelain.* Troy, NY: David Rosenfeld.

Impey, Oliver. 2002. *Japanese Export Porcelain: Catalogue of the Collection of the Ashmolean Museum, Oxford.* Amsterdam: Hotei Publishing; and Oxford: Ashmolean Museum.

Jedding, Hermann. 1982. *Meissener Porzellan des 18. Jahrhunderts in Hamburger Privatbesitz*. Exh. cat. Hamburg: Museum für Kunst und Gewerbe.

Jenyns, Soame. 1965. *Japanese Porcelain*. New York: Frederick A. Praeger.

Johann Friedrich Böttger zu Ehren. 1982. Exh. cat. Dresden: Staatliche Kunstsammlungen.

Just, R. 1960. "Die Sammlung Dr. Ernst Schneider." In *250 Jahre Meissner Porzellan: Die Sammlung Ernst Schneider in Schloss Jägerhof*. Basel: Keramikfreunde der Schweiz.

Kasakievitsch, Natalia. 1995. "Entstehung und Geschichte des Andreas-Services." *Keramos*, no. 149: 47–52.

Kopplin, Monika, ed. 2003. *Schwartz Porcelain: Die Leidenschaft für Lack und ihre Wirkung auf das europäische Porzellan*. Munich: Hirmer Verlag.

———, ed. 2004. *Schwartz Porcelain: The Lacquer Craze and its Impact on European Porcelain*. Munich: Hirmer Verlag.

———, 2005. "Lacquer Painting on Böttger Stoneware: Three *Walzenkruge* and the Problem of Attribution to Martin Schnell," 27–37. In *The International Ceramics Fair and Seminar*. London: Haughton International.

Kuhn, Sebastian. 2008. "Collecting Culture: The Taste for Eighteenth-Century German Porcelain." In Cassidy-Geiger 2008, 25–119.

———, ed. 2012. *The Marouf Collection, Part I: Highly Important 18th-Century Meissen Porcelain*. London: Bonhams.

Kunze, Joachim. 1982. "Die Bedeutung des 'Englischen Handels' mit Porzellanen im 'Altfranzösischen Geschmack' der Meißner Manufaktur in der ersten Hälfte des 19. Jahrhunderts." *Keramos*, no. 95 (January): 37–56.

Le Duc, Geneviève. 1997a. "Rodolphe Lemaire et la manufacture de porcelaine de Meissen: Style extrême-oriental ou goût français?" *Revue de l'art*, no. 116: 54–60.

———. 1997b. "Rodolphe Lemaire und das Meissner Porzellan: Fernöstlicher Stil oder französischer Geschmack?" *Keramos*, no. 158 (October): 37–52.

Liackhova, Lydia. 2004. "The Saint Andrew Service: Making and Form." In Pietsch 2004, 66–69.

Loesch, Anette. 2009. "Black-Glazed Böttger Stoneware in the Porcelain Collection at Dresden." In Syndram and Weinhold 2009.

———, Heike Ulbricht, and Elisabeth Schwarm. 2015. *"Sächsisch schwarz lacquirtes Porcelain": Das schwarz glasierte Böttgersteinzeug im Bestand der Dresdner Porzellansammlung*. Dresden: Sandstein Verlag and Staatliche Kunstsammlungen.

———, Ulrich Pietsch, and Friedrich Reichel. 1998. *Porzellansammlung Dresden: Führer durch die ständige Ausstellung im Dresdner Zwinger*. Dresden: Staatliche Kunstsammlungen.

Löffler, Fritz. 1958. *Das alte Dresden: Geschichte seiner Bauten*. Dresden: Sachsenverlag.

Lübke, Diethard. 2002. "Höroldts Farbpalette: Die Verwendung der Aufglasurfarben bei frühen Meissner Porzellanen." *Keramos*, no. 177 (July): 19–40.

———. 2008. "Schindler? Horn?—oder doch Dietze? Zuschreibungen von Malereien auf frühen Meißner Porzellanen." *Keramos*, no. 200: 5–20.

The Magnificent Spreckels Collection. 1930. Sales cat. New York: American Art Association, Anderson Galleries, Inc.

Manners, Errol. 2015. "The Rococo Porcelain of Europe and its Influence on English Ceramics." In *Scrolls of Fantasy: The Rococo and Ceramics in England, c. 1735–c. 1775*. Papers given at a seminar at the Victoria and Albert Museum, 2013. London: English Ceramic Circle.

Maurice, Klaus, and Otto Mayr, eds. 1980. *The Clockwork Universe: German Clocks and Automata, 1550–1650*. Exh. cat. Washington, DC: Smithsonian Institution Press.

McGill, Forrest. 2006. *A Curious Affair: The Fascination between East and West*. Exh. cat. San Francisco: Asian Art Museum.

Menzhausen, Ingelore. 1988. "Höroldt und sein 'Seminarium'-Meissen, 1720 bis 1750." *Keramos*, no. 120: 5–38.

———. 1990. *Early Meissen Porcelain in Dresden*. London: Thames & Hudson.

Miedtank, Lutz. 2014. "Johann Caspar Ripp—vom Wandermaler in der Fayence zum Blaumaler in Meissen und zum 'Hoffabrikant' in Zerbst." *Keramos*, no. 224 (February): 5–22.

———. 2016. "Zur Einführung und nament-lichen Zuordnung von Zahlen als Dreher- und Formerzeichen auf Meissener Porzellan ab September 1739." *Keramos*, no. 232: 5–20.

Morley-Fletcher, Hugo. 1993. *Early European Porcelain and Faience as Collected by Kiyi and Edward Pflueger*. 2 vols. London: Christie, Manson and Woods.

Newman, Michael. 1977. *Die deutschen Porzellan-Manufakturen*. 2 vols. Braunschweig: Klinkhardt & Biermann.

Owsley, David T. 1972. "The Ailsa Mellon Bruce Collection of Continental Porcelain." *The Magazine Antiques* (May), 856–843.

Palmer, J. P., and Meredith Chilton. 1984. *Treasures of the George R. Gardiner Museum of Ceramic Art*. Toronto: George R. Gardiner Museum of Ceramic Art.

Pazaurek, Gustav E. 1929. *Meissner Porzellanmalerei des 18. Jahrhunderts*. Stuttgart: Matthaes.

Pedrocco, Filippo. 2003. *Ca' Rezzonico: Museum of 18th-Century Venice*. Venice: Marsilio and Musei civici veneziani.

COLLECTOR'S ACKNOWLEDGMENTS

The publication of this catalogue has fulfilled a major chapter in my life as a collector of antique Meissen porcelain. An ongoing labor of love for the past fifteen years, its genesis lies with my dear friend, Jody Wilkie, international specialist head of Christie's department of European ceramics and glass. After purchasing a piece in 2002, I broached the idea of getting someone to start a catalogue of my collection. In her inimitable and disarming manner, she planted a flea in my ear: "Why don't you write your own catalogue?" Within days I had conceived a two-pronged entry for each of my pieces, first covering its connoisseurship (the piece in its context as an art object) and the second its provenance (its history as far as I could discern, as well as the whys and wherefores of my acquisition).

The catalogue has now been brought to fruition by the Fine Arts Museums of San Francisco through the noble and perceptive efforts of Maria L. Santangelo, former associate curator of European decorative arts and sculpture. In addition, I owe a great debt of thanks to Julian Cox, former founding curator of photography and chief curator, for his support, encouragement, and reassurance; never have I left a lunch or coffee with Julian without a song in my heart. Likewise, both curator in charge of European decorative arts and sculpture Martin Chapman and former chief conservator Lesley Bone have been invaluable sources of support over many years. I cannot underestimate the support and encouragement I have received from Max Hollein, director and CEO, and Colin B. Bailey, former director of the Fine Arts Museums. Sebastian Kuhn, departmental director of European ceramics, Bonhams, London, has been especially generous and supportive over many years.

A very special recognition and thanks to long-time Meissen hunters and close friends Errol and Henriette Manners and Sir Jeffrey Tate and Klaus Kuhlemann. In addition, the following fellow collectors, museum curators, and porcelain dealers have over the years of my collecting provided much insight, invaluable support, and most of all, friendship: Tracey Albainey, Henry Arnhold, Klaus-Peter Arnold, Thomas Baxter, Claus Boltz, Anthony du Boulay, Meredith Chilton, Michael Conforti, Jan Daniël van Dam, Lady Kate Davson, Bernard Dragesco and Didier Cramoisan, Julie Emerson, Katharina Hantschmann, Michele Beiny Harkins, Chris Jussel, Daniela Kumpf, Johanna Lessmann, J. V. G. Mallet, Nette Megens, Richard Mellott, Ingelore Menzhausen, Joachim Menzhausen, Thomas Michie, Dan Mingledorff, Jeffrey Munger, Christina H. Nelson, Friedrich Reichel, Alfredo Reyes, Letitia Roberts, Pamela Klaber Roditi, Jeffrey Ruda, Dominic Simpson, Richard Sutherland and Duane Wakeham, Angela Gräfin von Wallwitz, Jeffrey Weaver, Julia Weber, John Whitehead, Hilary Young, and Alfred Ziffer. Many other individuals, whose names over the years can now only tax and defeat an elderly collector's power to recollect, provided much input and wisdom to me, proving that successful collecting is a cooperative endeavor.

I dedicate this book to my partner, Timothy Thornburn, and to my late brother Robert Gutter, who spent his entire life with and for music, porcelain's great sister art.

—MALCOLM GUTTER

PHOTOGRAPHY CREDITS

Published by the Fine Arts Museums of San Francisco in association with Hirmer Publishers.

This book is published with the assistance of the Andrew W. Mellon Foundation Endowment for Publications.

Library of Congress Cataloging-in-Publication Data
Names: Santangelo, Maria L., 1972– author. | Legion of Honor (San Francisco, Calif.), organizer, host institution.
Title: A princely pursuit: the Malcolm D. Gutter collection of early Meissen porcelain / Maria L. Santangelo; with Malcolm Gutter and Sebastian Kuhn.
Description: San Francisco: Fine Arts Museums of San Francisco—Legion of Honor, and Hirmer, 2018. | Includes bibliographical references and index.
Identifiers: LCCN 2017040004 | ISBN 9783777429847 (hardcover)
Subjects: LCSH: Meissen porcelain—Private collections—United States—Exhibitions. | Gutter, Malcolm D.—Art collections—Exhibitions.
Classification: LCC NK4380.S27 2018 | DDC 738.2075--dc23 LC record available at https://lccn.loc.gov/2017040004

ISBN: 978-3-7774-2984-7

Published by the
Fine Arts Museums of San Francisco
de Young, Golden Gate Park
50 Hagiwara Tea Garden Drive
San Francisco, CA 94118
www.famsf.org

Leslie Dutcher, Director of Publications
Danica Michels Hodge, Managing Editor
Jane Hyun and Victoria Gannon, Editors
Trina Enriquez, Associate Editor
Diana K. Murphy and Adrienn Mendonça-Jones, Editorial Assistants

Project management and editing by Jane Hyun
Picture research by Diana K. Murphy
Proofread by Susan Richmond, with Trina Enriquez and Victoria Gannon
Indexed by Jane Friedman
Designed and typeset by Bob Aufuldish, Aufuldish & Warinner
Separations by Reproline Mediateam, Munich
Printing and binding by Printer Trento
Printed in Italy

Published in association with
Hirmer Verlag GmbH
Nymphenburger Strasse 84
80636 Munich
Germany
www.hirmerpublishers.com